DECOLONIAL CONVERSATIONS IN POSTHUMAN AND NEW MATERIAL RHETORICS

NEW DIRECTIONS IN RHETORIC AND MATERIALITY
Wendy S. Hesford, Christa Teston, and Shui-Yin Sharon Yam, Series Editors

DECOLONIAL CONVERSATIONS IN POSTHUMAN AND NEW MATERIAL RHETORICS

Edited by Jennifer Clary-Lemon
and David M. Grant

THE OHIO STATE UNIVERSITY PRESS
COLUMBUS

Library of Congress Cataloging-in-Publication Data

Names: Clary-Lemon, Jennifer, editor. | Grant, David M., 1969– editor.

Title: Decolonial conversations in posthuman and new material rhetorics / edited by Jennifer Clary-Lemon and David M. Grant.

Other titles: New directions in rhetoric and materiality.

Description: Columbus : The Ohio State University Press, [2022] | Series: New directions in rhetoric and materiality | Includes bibliographical references and index. | Summary: "Brings together new materialist and decolonial rhetorics to respond to frustrations of erasure, otherness, and marginalization in the fields of rhetoric, writing, and communication"—Provided by publisher.

Identifiers: LCCN 2022018753 | ISBN 9780814214923 (cloth) | ISBN 0814214924 (cloth) | ISBN 9780814282335 (ebook) | ISBN 0814282334 (ebook)

Subjects: LCSH: Rhetoric—Social aspects. | Decolonization. | Indigenous peoples. | Posthumanism. | Materialism.

Classification: LCC P301.5.S63 D43 2022 | DDC 808—dc23/eng/20220615

LC record available at https://lccn.loc.gov/2022018753

Other identifiers: ISBN 9780814258446 (paper) | ISBN 0814258441 (paper)

Cover design by Susan Zucker
Text composition by Stuart Rodriguez
Type set in Minion Pro

CONTENTS

ACKNOWLEDGMENTS

We acknowledge here that it takes more than the usual village to coedit a book during a pandemic. We appreciate the patience and dedication of those who have devoted their time and energy into making this volume as strong as it could be. First and foremost, we thank every contributing author who appears here for putting their trust in this collaboration, working not only with incommensurable subjects, but also working during a time of great duress. We also thank the anonymous reviewers and editorial team at The Ohio State University Press, who were a vital part of seeing this manuscript through to being its best possible self.

We thank the locations and traditional lands upon which each piece in this collaborative project was written, which fall across North America and are distributed with every writer who has written a chapter for inclusion, from the American desert southwest to the Great Lakes to those writing from each ocean coast. This volume could not have been written without the support of the University of Waterloo and the territory on which it sits, land borrowed from the Neutral, Anishinaabe, and Haudenosaunee people. The support of the land of Ioway, Dakota, and Meskwaki people, on which the University of Northern Iowa sits, is also honored and thanked. We thank the faculty and students of the Department of Writing, Rhetoric, and American Cultures at Michigan State University as well as those members of the scholarly community who have shared with us their thoughts and ideas, without whom we would not have gotten to know one another, nor would we have been challenged in ways that have led to this book. We see this volume as a gift, to both have been able to write, to be able to listen to, and to be able to share.

Lastly, we'd like to take a small space for personal acknowledgments. David would like to thank Jen as coeditor and collaborator. Without her continual leadership, knowledge, and dedication, David would have been lost in making some tough decisions on how to braid these diverse strands together. David's thinking comes, too, from two special Rhetoric Society of America workshops, one led by Ellen Cushman and another co-led by Diane Davis and Thomas Rickert. These scholars and the amazing workshop participants are all influential in their own way. The College of Humanities, Arts, and Sciences at the University of Northern Iowa helped fund part of this project. Lastly, this collection would not have been possible without the patience of David's wife, Rhianon, his children, many crazy animal companions, and all the untamed places from which we gather so much.

Jen would like to thank David, as coeditor and collaborator, for his near-boundless energy for this project. In so many moments it seemed like seeing this project through to print might be impossible, and it should be known that in every case, David was the person to relight the fire, to allow breathing room, and to take on what seemed like impossible tasks. She thanks the University of Waterloo SSHRC Institutional Grant for indexing support of this manuscript. For other supports, large and small, Jen thanks those in her pandemic bubble that kept her safe and sane: her daughter, her mother, her partner, and her little dog.

FOREWORD

To Listen You Must Silence Yourself

JOYCE RAIN ANDERSON

Writing this foreword from Wampanoag territory in 2020 has been nothing short of ironic. The year was to be the one that celebrated the 1620 landing of the Pilgrims and all the mythology that accompanies that act of settler colonialism, but a pandemic has swept in and cleared the area of the expected tourism and events that were planned.[1] Meanwhile, the Mashpee Wampanoag had still been fighting for their sovereignty as the land in trust (321 acres); in June 2020 a federal judge had remanded to the secretary of the interior to reevaluate the evidence and make a new decision on rescinding the land in trust. Absurdly, the history of America's beginnings—which includes Wampanoag people—attempts to still divorce them from land in contemporary times. As Robert Lestón points out in this collection, "Decoloniality is the struggle" (22). With all this in mind, *Decolonial Conversations in Posthuman and New Material Rhetorics* arrives and situates itself in this time and place, giving us a means to further challenge the status quo as we build toward a more just future.

As a Native woman and scholar, I live by and act through Indigenous principles of respect, relationality, responsibility, and reciprocity. The time of COVID and our witnessing climate change phenomena has us recognizing

1. The Indigenous History Conference, a signature event of Plymouth 400, became the first event to take place in 2020 at Bridgewater State University. This conference offered the (hi)stories and continuous presence of New England Natives mostly in their voices.

how our devastation of the Earth has given cause for her striking back at humans. Likewise, these turbulent and divisive times have brought renewed attention to the deep-seated inequalities that exist in the world, our country, and our own spaces—academic and otherwise. These ideologies stem from settler colonialism and its aftermath. It is long past time to hear the stories and, as Christina Cedillo argues in this volume, to hold up Tezcatlipoca's smoking mirror to "see all," including ourselves, so we can critically examine how we have been complicit in perpetuating these inequalities. It is time to re-right the world through embracing Indigenous knowledge, not to just extract from, but to critically imagine ourselves and our institutions enacting the kind of systemic changes that Indigenous scholars and knowledges urge. It is time to move forward with decolonial practices that are grounded in relationality, beginning with our relationships with land. It is time to reframe our practices and "de-link" (Mignolo) from the colonial-imbedded mindset that is rooted in our disciplines. When we think about relationships and reciprocity as practices, we are beginning to *think otherwise.* Posthumanist moves to decenter humans provide space for all our relations to be heard, understood, centered, and therefore a site for learning how to delink and work for decolonial changes.

At my university, many faculty ask about decolonial practices, and I along with colleagues have held several workshops and discussions with them. But certainly it is not as simple as this. As Eve Tuck and K. Wayne Yang write, decolonization is unsettling, and we must be wary of "settler moves to innocence" that "attempt to relieve the settler feelings of guilt or responsibility without giving up land or power or privilege. Without having to change much at all" (10). We must examine the policies, structures, curricula, and practices that remain in place to uphold colonialist ideologies, asking ourselves how we implicitly or explicitly recenter them despite the desire to decolonize. These are the deeper self-examinations that we all need to engage in and questions we need to ask.

Decolonial Conversations in Posthuman and New Material Rhetorics could not be more timely. The collection pushes us toward critical dialogue to provoke our complacency within our ivied walls. While reexamining several theoretical underpinnings through decolonial lenses, the editors and authors first consider their own social locations to examine the settler logics that are entrenched in our discipline. For some, this means moving into territory where their discomfort is evident. For others, it means bringing Indigenous intellectuals and stories to the forefront of their chapters. The collection presents academic theories of posthumanism and new materialism, then challenges them through the lenses of traditional ecological knowledge /

Indigenous knowledge, and it asks readers to question their own relationships with their scholarly practices. As editors Jennifer Clary-Lemon and David Grant write, "Our scholarship in rhetoric and composition can—and must—do better to situate ontological worldmaking truthfully, ethically, humanely, and with care" (2). Thus, the authors in this collection offer insights into their struggles to bring about decolonial work as insiders and outsiders to Indigenous ways of knowing. In her chapter, Christina Cedillo reminds us that "how we perceive and act affects everyone and everything because we are all materially and ethically conjoined" (98). The intra-weaving of citations from Zoe Todd, Robin Wall Kimmerer, Kim TallBear, and Eve Tuck are like the strands of sweetgrass Malea Powell and Andrea Riley Mukavetz carefully pick up as they make their braid that is central to the book. The collection does help us to *listen otherwise,* practice ethical relationships, and recognize the importance and impact of stories. I will use this book to help my colleagues and students unleash themselves from a reliance on settler colonial theories and "note the possibility of a productive tension" (Clary-Lemon and Grant 13, this volume) necessary to bring about new insights, understandings, and stories. I am grateful to the editors and authors for asking us to join in the braiding.

Works Cited

Mignolo, Walter. "Delinking: The Rhetoric of Modernity, the Logic of Coloniality and the Grammar of De-Coloniality." *Cultural Studies,* vol. 21, no. 2, 2007, pp. 449–514.

Tuck, Eve, and K. Wayne Yang. "Decolonization Is Not a Metaphor." *Decolonization: Indigeneity, Education, & Society,* vol. 1, no. 1, 2012, pp. 1–40.

INTRODUCTION

Working with Incommensurable Things

JENNIFER CLARY-LEMON AND DAVID M. GRANT

Neither of us had met the other until we were put together on a panel at Michigan State University for the third biennial Cultural Rhetorics Conference in 2018. We had submitted individual papers and were put together with Beau Philaja on a panel titled "Post/De-/Colonial Rhetorics." As a panel of three white scholars exploring new materialisms, ethics, settler narratives, and decolonialism, we wrestled with and were interrogated about our own positionality and applications of theoretical insights that were, after all, of Eurocentric origin and design, though graciously welcomed there on the ancestral, traditional, and contemporary lands of the Anishinaabeg, Odawa, and Potawatomi people. We are continually grateful for that chance to present. After our presentation, though, we found ourselves with more questions than we had started with, particularly about whether or not the decolonial could be held commensurate with the new material. As one respondent to our panel asked, why would decolonial scholarship have any need for new materialisms?

Even as we introduce this collection, we recognize that *need* is a strong word to describe the relationship between decolonial work and new material and posthuman scholarship. The point may be, instead, that new materialist and posthumanist projects need decolonial scholarship. Projects involving the ontological and extradiscursive in rhetoric can only be improved by an accountability to their own complicity in the settler colonial academy, one that proceeds as a global network of knowledge workers designed to further extractive and exploitative systems for the profit of a few selected largely on skin tone, ethnic status, and/or conformity to Euro-Western behavioral norms. Our task, then, is not one of finding analogies between the fields, nor of absorbing, adopting, and transposing decolonial theory and praxis into the terms of new materialisms or the posthuman. Our task, instead, is an attempt to position ourselves so as to invite change across the differences we recognize and alter the relations between the decolonial and the new material, each understood as broad and complex domains of rhetorical inquiry. This collection is the result of those conversations with one another, with our communities, and with a host of scholars doing the work to *listen otherwise* in addressing and responding to many of the criticisms of new materialist theory.

At the conference, David's talk explored how colonialism appropriates both knowledge and material being from the colonized, exemplified in Marisol de la Cadena's book *Earth Beings*, an examination of American tourists' extraction of spiritual ways from people indigenous to the Andes. As de la Cadena explains, this is a situation in which some informants participate in cultural and spiritual commodification for a host of complicated reasons and from within complex situations. Where, in such cases, David asked, is the line between taking and sharing? To take has connotations of theft and forceful removal, yet it also has deep etymological roots, such as connections to *nimble*, that may open relational avenues to equalize exchange, reciprocity, and processes that both give and take rather than unidirectional movements of extraction and colonization. Like de la Cadena's Andean spiritual laborers, David looked at an example from the roadside trade outside the Wounded Knee Massacre site, where colonial violence is still perpetuated because of the taking of 150 lives in 1890 and two more in 1973. David wanted to ponder if something different could be heard from the land's testimony to such a historical rupture.

As Jen came to the conference panel to present her talk on "Situating Rhetorical New Materialism as a Settler Narrative," it was with some chagrin that she saw three white people on a panel titled "Post/De-/Colonial Rhetorics," even as each thoughtfully parsed problematics of new materialism, whiteness, ethics, and settler colonialism. Her own talk questioned the written histories and citation practices of new material and posthumanist scholars who have tended to draw only from Euro-Western philosophy, to the exclusion of Indigenous and feminist scholarship. One takeaway from her talk was that our scholarship in rhetoric and composition can—and must—do better to situate ontological worldmaking truthfully, ethically, humanely, and with care.

But it was not only about trying to bring together incommensurable ways of being in a good way. It drew on the case of the Unist'ot'en camp of the

Wetsuwet'en people and their erection of a barricade as an act of resistance. They did so on the only logging road that provides access to unceded land that has been slated for construction of the Pacific Trails Pipeline corridor. This example, which blended human and nonhuman bodies of flesh and barricades, Indigenous and non-Indigenous people, decolonial refusal with colonial demands, roads and trucks and oil and land, was an example of the way that we can no longer hold in separate hands what might count as "ontological worldmaking," "settler colonialism," or "identity politics." The rhetorical *energia* in assemblages like those Jen described is created from ongoing struggle: for rights to Canadian land, from the unequal distribution of power to Indigenous people, and in the fossil fuel economy. In both presentations, whether examining struggle or reimagining rupture, what united them was the notion that the tensions between our frames and cosmologies are what give them the agency to move.

Freedoms of movement, self-determination, and sovereignty are what decolonization is about. These are not freedoms given obligingly by Europeans and viewable only with reference to Eurocentric notions of rights or norms of thinking about the world. Freedoms are crafted, expressed, and performed in the ongoing lives of people. Such people are individuals and community members acting in relation to times and places colonized and often brutally settled by Europeans. Our man-made systems of living can actively take freedoms from communities and in return give nothing of value back. Decolonization, then, to borrow from Tuck and Yang, is not a metaphor, but a continual work of recognition, as Victor Villanueva reminds us: "We do an injustice in acting as if a mutuality already exists" (99). Decolonization contains actions like ceding back lands, honoring treaties, and recognizing one's own settler moves to innocence. It is, as said by so many scholars, artists, and thinkers, also about doing things in a good way.

In "My Pink Powwow Shawl, Relationality, and Posthumanism," one such scholar, Kristin Arola, shares a story about animiiki, or thunderbird, "with a good heart" (388). Her story of animiiki allows her to make two points: first, that "humans and non-humans have relations with one another and always have," and second, "part of these relations include communication and unknowability" (389). She cites Vine Deloria's belief that "everything is alive and making choices that determine the future" and that while we may "call to communicate with things outside ourselves," we must still acknowledge "that we might not know if, or how, understanding is possible" (389). Such a position of unknowing, of sitting with the incommensurable, guides many of the conversations that we have had with one another, and many of the conversations in this volume. The point is to "know we are not the center" (389). As coeditors, we find within such radical decentering and unsettling—because *everything else* is also making choices that determine the future—the idea that there is no possibility to continue with things as they currently are.

To decolonize, then, as we understand it, is to understand the immanent rhetorical and embodied work set before us all as already emplaced and community-composed beings, and to hold ourselves as complicit in an unjust system of power that rests on invasion and seizure while also being held accountable to "Indigenous sovereignty and futurity" (Tuck and Yang 35). This can feel confrontational, as Tuck and Yang argue. They note that to embrace the decolonial beyond the metaphorical "will not emerge from friendly understanding, and indeed require[s] a dangerous understanding of uncommonality that un-coalesces coalition politics—moves that may feel very unfriendly" (35). Rather than paper over differences, we instead allow those differences to do their own, often incommensurable, work. The essays in this collection do some of that work, and all acknowledge that these are the first steps among many that need to be taken beyond the page. They force us to ask, can we—as settlers—be uncomfortable, *be unsettled,* in a good way?

One situated move of unsettling is to point out specific rather than generalized and generic modes of survivance. As Enrique Dussel points out with his concept of transmodernism, different Indigenous and colonized communities have different histories of and responses to being colonized. To revise relations is not a simple matter between European and Indigenous cultures or lifeways, but a far more complex differential between various European powers and local inhabitants, their histories, and legacies of sometimes multiple settler colonial invasions. Many Indigenous communities of North America have shared the pan-Indigenous concept of "all my relations." The vocal group Ulali produced a song with this title whose lyrics touch on both the easy and the hard aspects of relations, acknowledging connection to survivors, carriers of tradition, the damaged, and even those who cause the damage, both knowingly and not. The list of relations is set to the music of an Irish ballad, "Gary Owen," a favorite melody of George Armstrong Custer and "the regimental tune of the seventh cavalry" (Montague). It is a powerful song of decolonization and wisdom because it speaks in specificity about all relations, not just those apparently similar or affectively convenient. As editors, we heed the lesson of working to hear one's own position among the good and the bad while acknowledging the culturally and geographically specific differences between expressions of "all my relations": *mitakuye oyasin* (Lakota), *indinawemaaganidog* (Anishinaabe), *hozho* (Navajo/Diné), and others.

Bringing to the fore the relationally complex, rather than simple one-to-one notion of *all my relations* is a result of our understanding of decolonization, though we are not the first to attend to this in either decolonial or new materialist rhetorics. Donnie Sackey asks, for instance, "What happens when we consider CR and PR [cultural rhetorics and posthuman rhetorics, respectively] as constellated rather than unitary, totalizing bodies of knowledge?" (Sackey et al. 376). Sackey's question echoes the Cultural Rhetorics Theory Lab's "Our Story Begins Here: Constellating Cultural Rhetorics" and the scholarly publication *Constellations: A Critical Rhetorics Publishing Space.* Posthumanism and new materialism each encompass a variety of theories within them that, as Stacy Alaimo contends, "all insist upon the significance and agency of materiality and the inter- or intra-actions across the primary dualisms of western thought" (177). In an effort to make *constellated,* we hope to accord plurality to new materialisms as well as decolonial projects.

New materialisms co-emerged in the 1990s within the philosophy of science and the work of Manuel DeLanda, on the one hand, and the critical humanities and feminist theory of Rosi Braidotti on the other, both emerging broadly from the work of Gilles Deleuze (see Dolphijn and van der Tuin). We might think of new materialisms as existing under the umbrella of the posthuman, which rejects the conception of the human subject embraced by the Enlightenment: "a coherent, rational self, the right of that self to autonomy and freedom, and a sense of agency linked with a belief in enlightened self interest" (Hayles 85–86). To that end, there is much to like about any theory that brings matter back into an equation that has so long depended on only human agency: It distributes agency among actors and breaks down hierarchies; it speaks across disciplines; it incorporates a "yes—*and*" rather than a "no, but" approach to intellectual traditions (Dolphijn and van der Tuin). What we believe to be useful about the posthuman and new material frameworks through which to view rhetorical problems is its commitment to an ecological understanding of relationships between humans and nonhumans and their environments, an ontological understanding of this ecology, a disavowal of human exceptionalism, an acknowledgment of species interdependence, and an embrace of nonhuman agencies (Bignall and Rigney 159). In other words, the inclusivity of posthumanism houses its appeal: It allows for the agency and vibrancy of matter—animals, things, forces—to count in rhetorical conversations while working to unseat the Euro-Western commonplace that separates mind from body, culture from nature, logics from affects. We find the widening of frame to the ecological and energetic useful for rhetorical studies in particular to account for, in Nathan Stormer and Bridie McGreavy's terms, an increased rhetorical capacity among actors, an attention to the distribution of our and others' vulnerabilities in acting, and an emphasis on adaptability and change in engaging with other-than humans.

Yet, as Bignall and Rigney suggest in "Indigeneity, Posthumanism, and Nomad Thought," "the ideas expressed in posthumanism do not constitute a 'new paradigm,' and there is nothing especially new about the vibrant 'new materialism' presently gaining traction in the philosophical academy" (170). There is much that is exclusive about these theories as well. The "human" critiqued in posthumanism is one already beholden to a particular problematic logic. Bignall and Rigney respond to the varied ways that new materialism has been taken up across humanities disciplines in ways that do not acknowledge that the dualisms it wishes to unseat not only come from a universalized Euro-Western dogma, but "such dogmas originated in European societies involved in colonization, were globalized in and through colonial practices, and are currently given life in white supremacist settler societies" (Sundberg 36). Thus while we recognize that there is much promise held by new materialisms that situate themselves in feminist science studies and environmental justice—Bignall and Rigney specifically point to the work of Rosi Braidotti as one that advances a "nonimperial posthumanism" (160)—we also recognize that a claim to newness has historically erased marginalized bodies while "mak[ing] only certain forms of matter both legible and desirable" (Leong 24). This tension in particular is one that we wish to engage in this book—to examine directly the charge that for many, the relationship between the posthuman or new materialism and, for example, Indigenous theory and ways of knowing may be, as Alaimo contends, "awkwardly irrelevant or redundant" (187). Both new materialism and its posthuman umbrella are settler theories, despite their perceived usefulness or progressive-seeming tendencies.

Rather than cast this tension aside, we see instead an opportunity to question and engage—to converse—about potentialities for relevance and resilience instead of recalcitrance, in Stormer and McGreavy's (1) terms. Rather than acting *on* recalcitrant bodies, as Stormer and McGreavy point out, we aim to work *with* various bodies in ways that might foster "responsiveness, complexity, and adaptivity" in our own thinking and movement toward action. This requires relating differently. In Tuck and Yang's terms, we look to unsettle our own settler scholar assumptions and to not stop there while the settler colonialist academy continues to fail Indigenous, Mestiza, Black, Latinx, Asian, and former and current colonial subjects. We hope we might carry a small portion of the unacknowledged labor and responsibility toward decolonizing our settled spaces. That means detailing how a singular focus on Eurocentric ideas further perpetuates settler colonial erasure of those whose traditions have already developed from the same ideas and insights, often in ways far more nuanced and carefully material than anything produced by using Latour, Deleuze, or even Braidotti. Even pointing out our own Eurocentric gaze is no guarantee of solidarity. Tuck and Yang recognize how "solidarity is an uneasy, reserved, and unsettled matter that neither reconciles present grievances nor forecloses future conflict" (3). Yet we call to communicate with an uncertain and risky openness to others to answer, or not, and to choose their own manner and time of response.

Interdisciplinary Inquiries: The Places and Times for Rhetorical Response

As we began the work of trying to find ways to broaden these conversations beyond one panel, one conference, one space, one moment in time, we found ourselves facing these critical and urgent questions at a moment of immense ecological and social vulnerability. In the spring of 2020, the world was hit with the COVID-19 pandemic, a viral outbreak that scientists warn could become more frequent as humans push further into and fragment contiguous natural areas, coming increasingly into contact with highly mutable and communicable pathogens (see Everard et al.). Such events fall hardest on colonized people. The Navajo Nation, already suffering epidemics of obesity, diabetes, heart disease, and decades of economic and political neglect (Newton), experienced an outbreak in May 2020 that exceeded the per capita rate of New York City at its worst. While nations work to slow the spread of disease, these nations are also engaged in resource extraction, refinement, and transportation development in the forms of pipelines, fracking, and development on unceded land, disproportionately affecting colonized people (see Gómez-Barris). The shale oil, natural gas, and petroleum transport industries in central North America are more than #NODAPL's water protection from the Black Snake; they are also about ending the continued legacy of rampant sexual exploitation and trafficking raised by awareness campaigns such as #MMIWG2S (Schiano). Finally, as wealth is increasingly siphoned by the ultra-rich like iron filings to a magnet (see Collins et al.), such scenes of exploitation and abuse spill out from communities of color and onto a wider section of society, many of whom even in academia are asked to choose between their long-term bodily health and their paycheck (see Flaherty). And this is just the start of the fester 2020 exposed as long-standing societal ills. In reflecting on these legacies, we are all revealed as vulnerable.

The ways humans relate to nonhumans is squarely at the center of what concerns us—whether in viral load, the toxicity of topsoil, or the disappearance of kin species. What pushed us to move these concerns beyond a conference venue to this collection was one, ultimately, of critically thinking through how new materialisms and decolonial action can join most usefully as potentially partnered frameworks for action. We also wrestled with how relations play out in duration and time, wondering if, in part, differing conceptions of the temporal are at the heart of the disconnect between new materialisms and decolonial theories. As Mark Rifkin points out, European linear time may be detrimental to all sorts of non-chrononormative beings including queer, Indigenous, and colonized orientations to past, present, and future. Certainly reflecting on 2020 as the year that many epidemiologists saw coming but that caught us all in varied kinds of time—homeschooling children, living at work, being isolated in long stretches, not knowing the day, week, or month—challenged us all to think of time differently, as containing and exhibiting more rhetorical capacity than perhaps any of us have ever felt before. To consider this place, this time, and the many places and times that contributors to this volume position for readers is not just an expanded set of material relations, then, but as Jeff Corntassel makes clear, a kind of necessary and careful kind of activism: "Our stories need to be re-told and acted upon as part of our process of remembering and maintaining balance within our communities" (89). Relations change with time. There is rhetorical work to be done in generatively and creatively asking of new materialist rhetorics how they might grow to be theoretically richer by an overt acknowledgment of decolonial practices.

Such insights are just some of many we wrestled with as we constructed the call for this collection. While many fields in the humanities and social sciences have reframed their debates through lenses of the ontological and posthuman, the posthuman move has also been seen as reproducing an inequitable status quo. Zoe Todd famously pronounced her dissatisfaction with Bruno Latour for his failure to cite or even acknowledge contributions of Indigenous people who have coexisted with Arctic ecosystems for millennia. Similarly, Alison Ravenscroft argued that at the interface between posthumanist and postcolonial theory, the operative binary ceases to be nature opposed to culture but shifts instead to colonizer and native, with its implications for whose theories will and will not count. Importantly, these voices are not focused on condemning the questions about the relations between nature and culture posed by posthumanisms or new materialisms, but on firmly stating how such questions are products of Euro-Western thinking. The binaries they purport to question have never made sense to many non-Western people, so why would they want to be part of a conversation about them?

Yet questions about the relations between nature and culture, animal and human, or ontology and epistemology have already been part of a broad range of interdisciplinary scholarship that is not grounded in Eurocentric ways. This can be seen with Kim TallBear's work with the Dakota pipestone, Robin Wall Kimmerer's work with sweetgrass, Leanne Betasamosake Simpson's work with the beaver and both resistance and regeneration, and Sean Sherman's work with precolonial foods. We might add to this list highly intercultural studies like Marty Holtgren, Stephanie Ogren, and Kyle Whyte's work with lake sturgeon and the Anishinaabe people; Cleo Woelfle-Erskine's work with beaver and the Karuk people; and Rosi Braidotti's call for a robust framework to support a "critical post-humanities," which might provide some ethic for moving and working between reciprocal knowledges to tackle contemporary techno-social problems. We thus see the questions posed by these scholars as poised to take on Euro-Western limitations in ways that acknowledge relationality and reciprocity, thereby furthering dialogue, aiding decolonial efforts, and helping create new loci for tackling problems of knowledge and being. Further, we see scholars who are particularly well suited to take up this challenge as those who increasingly position themselves between the juncture of some form of new materialist and/or posthuman theory and theories of culture, society, and power, as contributors to *Rhetoric Review*'s 2019 symposium did. It is our hope that as you read others like them here, you will be convinced, as we were, about the ways that the researchers and scholars in this collection are creatively addressing some of the most problematic and difficult conversations the field currently wrestles with.

We see the contributors to this volume as positioned to dialogue with a host of others in rhetoric, composition, and communication studies. Many scholars are beginning to explore and intervene in crises of both equity and environment, contributing to the creation of a better world in all its relations, not merely in a narrowly defined, Euro-Western sense of discourse. We see their contributions as joining with other scholarship currently doing the work to provide alternative thinking-through, whether in tracing Indigenous technologies of communication to offer culturally specific alternative models unrecognized by settler colonial epistemologies (Haas; Grant); overtly engaging in practices of Indigenous new materialism and recognition in rhetorical studies (Clary-Lemon); situating making and crafting practices—working with things—as openings into embodied and storied worlds (Arola; Driskill); pushing us to redefine rhetorical possibilities outside of the monolithic and monologic European orbit (Garcia and Baca; Ruiz and Sánchez); drawing us into the intersections between visibility and vulnerability in conservation efforts (Propen); showing us the way that animals persuade (Bjørkdahl and Parrish); reimagining traditional terms and rhetorical paradigms (Rickert; Gottschalk Druschke); or noting the complex meaning-making activities that come with the acknowledgment of the entanglement between intersectional identity and specific objects in the world (Nicotra; Hallenbeck). *Decolonial Conversations in Posthuman and New Material Rhetorics* joins with this scholarship to gently and persuasively ask questions and to engage in healing. We hope that such exciting and cutting-edge scholarship will invite future conversations and interventions that extend the circulation of decolonizing

Euro-Western theoretical frameworks. Further, with this collection, we join in Braidotti's assertion about the life of theory: "You have to *do* something" with it (Braidotti and Regan 175).

Perhaps it should come as no surprise, then, the two main patterns that emerged as contributors sent us their scholarship: scholarship that engaged both the positional work of decolonized recognition and scholarship that engaged the place-based ecologies in which these practices may be enacted. These are the thematics that have also emerged in a field that has for so long creatively engaged in rhetorics of identification, relation, material, and ecology. This has manifested itself in the work of Malea Powell and the Cultural Rhetorics Theory Lab to understand rhetoric to be a process of weaving cultures out of constellations of people, animals, plants, places, things, objects, and relations; at the same time, such materiality and reciprocity is underscored by Jenny Rice's use of the same term to discuss agency, vulnerability, and risk as dynamically and perhaps vibrantly interconnected.

We recognize that rhetoric's contributions to new material, decolonial, and posthuman inquiry, as reflected here, uniquely belong to the field. Attention to recognition and ecology as rhetorical commonplaces are not reflected in contemporary philosophies of the new material, as Bruno Latour suggests in his 2017 interview with Lynda Walsh. In his words,

> You can say that all of the animal rights people, the feminist people, all the people who worked with post-colonial studies, all the subaltern studies people are doing rhetoric because they are inventing ways of making these voices heard, but I think that would be an appropriation of the field of rhetoric of a vast, immense domain where people have made the voices of voiceless entities heard, and that would be an abuse of terms. (qtd. in Walsh et al. 416)

For us, and for those whose voices contribute to this collection here, it is this very "abuse of terms" that we wish to reveal as the force through which our arguments about nonhuman agency must travel and that they do so through affective, relational, material, and discursive means. We believe that it is rhetoric's unique place to do so.

Orientation to Material Turning: The New Material, the Posthuman, and the Decolonial

In rhetoric, communication, and writing studies, projects that listen to and honor being otherwise are increasing in number and scope. Garcia and Baca's

Rhetorics Elsewhere and Otherwise: Contested Modernities and Ruiz and Sánchez's *Decolonizing Rhetoric and Composition Studies* are two recent cases in point. These collections build on past scholarship to redefine rhetorical possibilities outside of the monolithic and monologic European orbit. Ruiz and Arellano's "*La Cultura Nos Cura*: Reclaiming Decolonial Epistemologies through Medicinal History and Quilting as Method" (in Garcia and Baca) specifically develops an approach that blends new materialist and decolonial insights, while numerous works on embodied rhetorics in these collections and elsewhere point to the persistent truth that decolonial work has long been concerned with rhetorics beyond the scope of human culture or social construction.

That both of these works are collections rather than monographs is also important. Anthropologist Macarena Gómez-Barris argues that "studying multiply to decenter a singular eye has long been a modality of decolonial perception" (12). Collections offer such multiplicities, reminding us of the heterogeneity of both colonized groups and colonizers. To support consensus-based decision making, knowledge must be seen as constellated, and all its stars and their relations to each other must be heard. The very term *constellation* comes from the Latin *sidereus,* or group of stars, and that it is this term and not *astra,* or single star, is important. Such terminology is where we find the locus of consideration and care for multiple stances and their attendant dialogues. *Decolonial Conversations in Posthuman and New Material Rhetorics* thus follows a similar strategy to help unsettle and constellate rhetoric's posthuman and new materialist turns in scholarship. This is deliberately not just epistemic, but also ontological in forwarding modes of being and being multiply emplaced, rather than globally totalized.

At the same time, we recognize Aníbal Quijano's "colonial matrix of power" (cited in Mignolo, "Introduction" 156) that asks first for a recognition of one's own enmeshment with colonial modernity before a subsequent detachment from it. The purpose of detachment, as Mignolo describes in *The Darker Side of Western Modernity,* is an instantiation of a decolonizing move. Recognizing this forces us to ask not "Is this a project for two Anglo scholars who have benefited from settler colonial privilege?" but "What useful work can we take on as recipients of privilege?" Rather than see our role in editing this collection as one that furthers a move to innocence (borrowing from Tuck and Yang) that somehow negates our own culpability in enjoying the privileges of benefitting from a white supremacist culture, or conversely ignores the benefits such a collection will continue to contribute to our professional lives, we instead suggest, as final contributors Andrea Mukavetz and Malea Powell invite, that our role is one that enacts "white/settler harm reduction"

(Tuck and Yang 21). That is to say, we know that our own role in this work will not undo the privilege that is enacted by it, but we see it as one practice that may work toward reducing white settler harm, particularly for those who invoke new material and posthuman theory in rhetorical work now and in future—theories that have been criticized for being dominated by "White, heteronormative, patriarchal, settler-colonial discourse" (Ruiz 39) in particular. Importantly, we acknowledge Tuck and Yang's point that any harm reduction model is meant as a stopgap measure, and not the end goal. It is not the answer all must give in similar situations, but it is a particular answer born of our work at the Cultural Rhetorics Conference, working within colonized communities, and our relationships with scholars who do decolonial work in the field. We know that there is much more work to be done.

This reminds us to remain consistent with not just decolonial theory, but the legacy of new materialist theory as one with an avowedly feminist orientation, as Judy Holiday and Elizabeth Lowry also acknowledge in this volume. Donna Haraway, Jane Bennett, Karen Barad, and Rosi Braidotti ground their materialisms in a feminist embodiment in the world and a practice of Emma Lazarus's quote that "until we are all free, none of us are free." By bringing these voices into scholarship that complicates the relationship between the decolonial, the ontological, the new material, and the posthuman, we hope to engage to some degree in both historicist memory work that honors the role feminist science studies has made in this area, and reparative work that engages closely with the importance and centrality of feminist engagement in new material practice—and to also make room for feminist disavowal of many of the moves made in posthuman work, as Eve Tuck articulates in "Breaking Up with Deleuze."

Thus, part of our intention here is not only to invite a range of voices to the table who are finding ways through seemingly incommensurable worldviews and laying plain relations of power inherent in discussions of human and nonhuman agency. We also want, to some degree, to risk what it might mean to find "new ways to listen" (20), as Marilyn Cooper suggests elsewhere and as Ehren Pflugfelder and Shannon Kelly demonstrate (in this volume). Part of finding new ways to listen rhetorically, as Krista Ratcliffe suggests in the words of Jacqueline Jones Royster in the epigraph to *Rhetorical Listening*, is through "developing an appropriate response" to what we hear (1). Listening is material and embodied. And in some cases, that means recognition through resistance, a turning-away-from as a rhetorical move. What this means, in practice, is *not* that we do not value critical theory produced by a range of Euro-Western scholars and its contribution to a robust way of understanding the world in ways that are new to Euro-Western scholars. What it does mean is recognizing the use that comes from a listening stance of openness while also recognizing, as John Muckelbauer urges us to think of a heliotropic rhetoric of plant persuasion, that there are times to open toward the sun, and times to close. We note the possibility of a productive tension that emerges when we turn away from Latour, Bogost, Heidegger, Harman, Deleuze, and Guattari and toward a range of others. We ask that you practice this recognition, that you engage in rhetorical listening through resistance as well.

Divergent Ontologies: Citing Widely, Gathering Worlds

To demonstrate the incommensurable, it is important to note how European ontologies traditionally posit a single universe whose behaviors are governed by the immutable laws of physics, chemistry, biology, and other sciences, where time is unidirectional and animals follow humans in an ever-expanding and perfecting evolutionary progression of the Great Chain of Being. Yet subaltern ontologies posit radically different worlds, many of which conflict with what Eurocentric epistemologies consider "reality." How could persuasion happen without a common understanding of reality?

Rhetorical studies is not the first to grapple with this. Anthropologist Marilyn Strathern retells the coming together of traditional Pacific Islanders and Eurocentric academics within the European Consortium for Pacific Studies (ECOPAS). She focuses on the framing of rhetorical purposes in this endeavor—"knowledge exchange" rather than "knowledge transfer"—and the unspoken different assumptions of "What was to count as knowledge?" (27). She draws from Donna Haraway to view these different orientations toward knowledge as "never simply an issue of identifying preexisting interests but of appreciating the co-constitution of interests as they emerge in interchanges of all kinds" (27–28). Strathern argues that the ECOPAS encounter was not a difference of registers or epistemologies between Pacific Islanders and Europeans—a difference to be transversally bridged—but a cosmological difference, "a divergence in what people take relations to be" (28). Quite literally, how to start is open for debate. It was not simply a matter of respective positions and how they might fit together, but a matter of the co-constitutive emergence of a shared concern. Divergence, in this instance,

> is not "between" practices—a practice does not define itself in terms of its divergence from others, for each "produces itself." Insofar as divergence is

> constitutive, then, it allows no domaining; practices appearing juxtaposed to one another are not divisions of the same world, do not occupy the same environment. (29)

We believe that the possibility of such radical heterogeneity along with shared concern for sustained, if asymmetrical, reciprocity brings forward the worthiness of the endeavor put forward by the contributors to this volume.

Part of what we hope to offer in this collection is such a juxtaposition of perceived incompatible positions in order to help an emergence of shared concerns that can lay the groundwork for future writers and thinkers to follow. The processes of proposing, reading, collecting, responding to, and rationalizing this collection have also come from the need to situate our methods otherwise—to, as Stephanie Springgay and Sarah Truman articulate it, queer the trail. While we may not be able to physically move through a geography, we do move through and sense particular academic territories and their boundaries. As we sense and move, we intra-act with that territory and have engaged in Springgay and Truman's "research-creation," an inventive activity born of both relation and divergence, and cognizance of "speculative middles" (2). To that end, we also recognize the organizing function that much new material theory has in terms of research methodology (van der Tuin). In this collection, we embrace research-creation as a different kind of collecting and arranging, one that recognizes that citation and curation practices are a meaningful gathering of ancestors: Stories, plants, walls, and smoke are all data that "glow" (MacLure 228).

We have therefore turned to a kind of methods-thinking to organize this collection that engages recognition, decolonization, and ecologies. We focus on Springgay and Truman's shift toward thinking about methods as "becoming tangled in relations" (2), in which methods themselves may be defined within experience and movement, giving way to their material effects. As a reader makes their way through this collection, we encourage them to think through the terminologies, sites, and practices used and cited here to shape their own research in ways that are generative, reflexive, and experimental. We note, too, that many figures in this book both function generatively and serve as contentious theoretical figures; for example, Jane Bennett has been both praised for her work on vital materiality and critiqued for her Eurocentric worldviews, something contributors here take up (see Cedillo; Whitaker, both in this volume). While we have arranged these pieces to move a reader through particular juxtapositions, possibilities, affects, ecologies, and cases, we see such organizational cues as those that will ultimately, as our final contributors Andrea Mukavetz Riley and Malea Powell encourage, demonstrate lessons out of collective strands of care.

We begin with two pieces that encourage us to think critically about the importance of recognition in work engaging decolonial humans, nonhumans, and posthumans. Robert Lestón argues in "The Politics of Recognition in Building Pluriversal Possibilities: Posthumanism, *Buen Vivir,* and Zapatismo" that various posthumanisms are inadequate for accounting for "the multitude of knowledges, cosmologies, and ways of living and being that are outside a Eurocentric framing" (25). Lestón draws instead from the *buen vivir* movements in their particularity among Ecuadorians and Zapatistas to make a connection between epistemic delinking and recognizing the more-than-human upon which any thought of human recognition depends. Lestón asks us to foreground our conceptual apparatus to ask how its framing as otherwise might engender different relations and, hence, different possibilities.

Similarly, in "Performing Complex Recognitions: (De)Colonial (Mis) Recognitions as Systemic Revision," Kelly Medina-López and Kellie Sharp-Hoskins examine practices of recognition in academic work, not just as a political matter, but also as a relational and constitutive one in academic mentorship. They advance a notion of "performing complex recognitions as a methodology capable of acknowledging differential bodies (human and nonhuman) and practices that disrupts closed loops (of recognition) by invoking the revisionary potential of decolonial misrecognitions as part of systemic revision" (50). In both of these starting chapters, the affordances of continually and regularly attending to the *otherwise possible* orientations in any human gathering is of central concern.

In their contribution "Listening Otherwise: Arboreal Rhetorics and Tree-Human Relations," Ehren Helmut Pflugfelder and Shannon Kelly take that *otherwise possible* to a case that is concrete and material, thus emphasizing the complexity added when we attune to the more-than-human in our gatherings. They look to a local forested area and encourage us to listen to and think with trees in order to cultivate ethical relations through an "arboreal rhetorics" centered on the nonhuman. In this, trees and their ecological continuance depend on a listening that acknowledges more than the discourse of ecological science and human timescales. It recognizes the ways we already think with trees and how they hold serious consequences for what may be.

Extending a lens on the local, in "Smoke and Mirrors: Re-Creating Material Relation(ship)s through Mexica Story," Christina V Cedillo works from a Mexica framework provided from the creation story of Tezcatlipoca, or Smoking Mirror, to look at environmental racism in the petrochemical industry of

Houston, Texas. Cedillo brings together thinkers in feminist science studies with Mexica storytelling to engage with new possibilities for entanglement and relation, possibilities that allow us to engage with a whole that "includes a both and sometimes either, both and sometimes neither, because everything is the Everything" (99). Her rhetorics recognize the disproportionate damage borne by brown and black bodies along the western Gulf Coast.

A. I. Ramírez similarly recognizes contemporary, state-sanctioned violence in her essay, "Perpetual (In)securities: (Re)Birthing Border Imperialism as Understood through *Facultades Serpentinas*." Ramírez looks at border wall murals along Mexico's border with the US to trace out the broader connections to what she calls the "global border industrial complex" (GBIC). Employing a "serpentine research method, theory, and practice of writing," Ramírez argues that border wall murals are not just visual representations of resistance, but more fully sensual and "generate the capacity to confront the dominant narrative and material realities" of the GBIC, opening responses to both good and bad (127). Where recognizing and listening to the biological may offer one strand with which to view our material collective, Cedillo and Ramírez point also to the industrial and technical operations of profit and control that perpetuate contemporary colonial violence. They also diverge in their similar methods. Each moves through Mexica theory in her own way, demonstrating not a unified body of knowledge, but a highly situated yet locally grounded panoply of methods and resources.

Through colonization, the land is often a proxy to control human beings. Matthew Whitaker examines how the very existence of Ponka corn is itself both testament to and organizing feature of decolonial resistance. "Corn, Oil, and Cultivating Dissent Through "Seeds of Resistance": A Case Study on Rhetorics of Survivance and the Protest Assemblage," examines possibilities for activism and advocacy in an interspecies rhetoric. Acknowledging, like Cedillo, the centrality of corn-human *being* for many Indigenous people, Whitaker takes readers through a braiding of corn-people-ceremony, where land is reclaimed and resacralized as an act of resistance to the prophesied Black Snake. In "Top Down, Bottom Up: Ecological Restoration, Rhetorical Resistance, and Decolonization," Judy Holiday and Elizabeth Lowry consider possibilities for "ideal cohabitation" among humans and nonhuman landscapes with an explicitly feminist grounding in abolition politics that align with Indigenous values. Examining the case of expanding legal personhood to include the Colorado and Whanganui Rivers, Holiday and Lowry argue that rather than reconsecrating territory, nature's personhood reenvisions possibilities for ecological recognition and the otherwise possible.

To these different (mis)recognitions, divergences, and intertwined strands of the decolonial and posthuman, we offer a final reflection that Springgay and Truman might call "a future provocation on thinking-making-doing" (5). Andrea Riley Mukavetz and Malea Powell's "Becoming Relations: Braiding an Indigenous Manifesto" offers a proposition to establish difficult common ground between the varied theoretical forces at work within and among the pieces here, offering up a situated hope with a good heart. Riley-Mukavetz and Powell braid together diverse strands of body, place/space, and culture in order to "trace a particular orientation to materials and traditions in which Indigenous knowledge is circulated and constellated" (195). Like our overall selection and curation for this collection, they turn away from the pressures of the Eurocentric knowledge-producing paradigm because they affirm that knowledge is not objectively out there, but in relation with us. While this collection makes helpful contributions to recognition, listening, and divergence, Riley-Mukavetz and Powell remind us that "the plants are talking whether we choose to listen" or not (196).

Throughout these contributions and matrices of thinking pluriversally, there is a deliberate tendency to focus on North America, not because the rest of the world is less important, but because that is where contributors live. We have tried to include perspectives from many different geographies of the academy in North America, though we could not include all. A most glaring omission is the absence of Black voices and perspectives, which we acknowledge as both a limitation of this collection and a clear call for what still needs to be done. Scholars such as Tiffany Lethabo King draw our attention to how and why Black and Indigenous academics may turn away from posthuman and new material theory, and we recognize that this refusal is both warranted and generative. There is still much work to be done to acknowledge a pathway through the limitations of Western critical theory that, as both King and Zakiyyah Jackson note, are predicated upon "colonial myths and racial hierarchy" (Jackson 1). The difficulty of this pathway in our own discipline has been eloquently captured by the work of Iris Ruiz, who notes that much critical scholarship in rhetoric and composition emerges out of "traditions of Whiteness" (39). We can't, thus, unyoke Western critical theory from these traditions, but we can both acknowledge them and call on scholars in the field to examine not only what a refusal to engage might mean, but also how we might unseat both whiteness and totalizing ideas that sit at the center of what King calls "Deleuzoguattarian thought" (173). We acknowledge that the unjustified killing of Black men, women, and children and the social and material infrastructure of surveillance and control of black and brown bodies that encourages those killings will not be undone by theory. Yet we see the potential in conversing along new material and decolonial lines not to blithely and blindly tout a progressive or savior theory—in King's words, to attempt "self-critique and self-correction in the name of justice for humanity" (165–66)—but to engage what is possible and acknowledge the very limits of theory itself. The ultimate limit of posthuman and new material theory may be its Enlightenment and colonial legacies. Yet as King reminds us, refusal itself is a rhetorical choice, one of many "modes of engagement that are uncooperative and force an impasse in a discursive exchange" (164). It is our hope that scholars can read *Decolonial Conversations* alongside scholarship such as Alexander Weheyile's *Habeas Viscus,* Kathryn Yusoff's *A Billion Black Anthropocenes or None,* and Michelle Wright's *Physics of Blackness: Beyond the Middle Passage Epistemology,* and decide to what extent they wish to engage or refuse the intellectual commitments proffered by what Tuck and Yang term an "ethic of incommensurability" (35). It is our hope that such commitments might be taken up within fields of rhetoric, composition, and communication, among many others.

We can only hope that the ways contributors to *Decolonial Conversations in Posthuman and New Material Rhetorics* nod in the directions toward which we are all held accountable in our relations, by writing *with* the inhabitants and legacies with whom they are entangled and to whose inhabitants and legacies they are accountable. If there is a point where the incommensurable lines between posthumanist and decolonial writing touch on one another, this may be it. Writing out of our own entanglements, temporal orientations, and communities, we are also beholden to them. We must be silent in order to listen to our entanglements and the constellations we comprise. Our own editorial method embraces the local and particular ecologies in which we live and work, as do the contributions here. We strive to balance the ways we take certain meanings, spaces, and care with a reciprocal sharing and giving back, mindful that any mistakes are our own. May you, too, be unsettled in a good way.

Works Cited

Alaimo, Stacy. "New Materialisms." *After the Human: Culture, Theory, and Criticism in the 21st Century,* edited by Sherryl Vint, Cambridge UP, 2020, pp. 177–91.

Arola, Kristin. "My Pink Powwow Shawl, Relationality, and Posthumanism." *Rhetoric Review,* vol. 38, no. 4, 2019, pp. 375–401.

Barad, Karen. *Meeting the Universe Halfway: Quantum Physics and the Entanglement of Matter and Meaning.* Duke UP, 2007.

Bennett, Jane. *Vibrant Matter: A Political Ecology of Things.* Duke UP, 2010.

Bignall, Simone, and Daryle Rigney. "Indigeneity, Posthumanism, and Nomad Thought." *Posthuman Ecologies: Complexity and Process after Deleuze,* edited by Rosi Braidotti and Simone Bignall, Rowman International, 2018, pp. 159–81.

Bjørkdahl, Kristian, and Alex C. Parrish, editors. *Rhetorical Animals: Boundaries of the Human in the Study of Persuasion.* Rowman and Littlefield, 2017.

Braidotti, Rosi. "A Theoretical Framework for the Critical Posthumanities." *Theory, Culture, and Society,* vol. 36, no. 6, 2019, pp. 31–61.

Braidotti, Rosi, and Lisa Regan. "Our Times Are Always Out of Joint: Feminist Relational Ethics in and of the World Today: An Interview with Rosi Braidotti." *Women: A Cultural Review,* vol. 28, no. 3, 2017, pp. 171–92.

Clary-Lemon, Jennifer. "Gifts, Ancestors, Relations: Notes Toward an Indigenous New Materialism." *enculturation,* vol. 30, 12 Nov. 2019, http://enculturation.net/gifts_ancestors_and_relations.

Collins, Chuck, et al. *Billionaire Bonanza 2020: Wealth Windfalls, Tumbling Taxes, and Pandemic Profiteers.* Institute for Policy Studies, 2020.

Cooper, Marilyn. "Listening to Strange Strangers, Modifying Dreams." *Rhetoric, through Everyday Things,* edited by Scot Barnett and Casey Boyle, U of Alabama P, 2016, pp. 17–29.

Corntassel, Jeff. "Re-Envisioning Resurgence: Indigenous Pathways to Decolonization and Sustainable Self-Determination." *Decolonization: Indigeneity, Education & Society,* vol. 1, no. 1, 2012, pp. 86–101.

de la Cadena, Marisol. *Earth Beings: Ecologies of Practice across Andean Worlds.* Duke UP, 2015.

Dolphijn, Rick, and Iris van der Tuin. *New Materialism: Interviews & Cartographies.* Open Humanities Press, 2012.

Driskill, Qwo-Li. *Asegi Stories: Cherokee Queer and Two-Spirit Memory.* U of Arizona P, 2016.

Dussel, Enrique. *The Invention of the Americas: Eclipse of "the Other" and the Myth of Modernity.* Translated by Michael D. Barber, Continuum, 1995.

Everard, Mark, et al. "The Role of Ecosystems in Mitigation and Management of Covid-19 and Other Zoonoses." *Environmental Science and Policy,* vol. 111, Sept. 2020, pp. 7–17.

Flaherty, Colleen. "Faculty Diversity Fell in Time of Crisis." *Inside Higher Ed,* 18 Oct. 2021, https://www.insidehighered.com/news/2021/10/18/study-shows-faculty-diversity-took-hit-time-crisis. Accessed 10 Jan. 2022.

Garcia, Romeo, and Damian Baca, editors. *Rhetorics Elsewhere and Otherwise: Contested Modernities, Decolonial Visions.* NCTE, 2019.

Gómez-Barris, Macarena. *The Extractive Zone: Social Ecologies and Decolonial Perspectives.* Duke UP, 2017.

Gottschalk Druschke, Caroline. "A Trophic Future for Rhetorical Ecologies." *enculturation,* 2017, n.p. http://enculturation.net/a-trophic-future.

Grant, David M. "Writing Wakan: The Lakota Pipe as Rhetorical Object." *College Composition and Communication,* vol. 69, no. 1, 2017, pp. 61–86.

Haas, Angela. "Wampum as Hypertext: An American Indian Intellectual Tradition of Multimedia Theory and Practice." *Studies in American Indian Literatures,* vol. 19, no. 4, Winter 2007, pp. 77–100.

Hallenbeck, Sarah. "Objects, Material Commonplaces, and the Invention of the 'New Woman.'" *Rhetoric, through Everyday Things,* edited by Scot Barnett and Casey Boyle, U of Alabama P, 2016, pp. 197–211.

Haraway, Donna. *Staying with the Trouble: Making Kin in the Chthulucene.* Duke UP, 2016.

Hayles, N. Katherine. *How We Became Posthuman: Virtual Bodies, in, Cybernetics, Literature, and Informatics.* Chicago UP, 1999.

Holtgren, Marty, et al. "Renewing Relatives: Nmé Stewardship in a Shared Watershed." *Tales of Hope and Caution in Environmental Justice,* 25 Apr. 2016. SSRN: https://ssrn.com/abstract=2770100.

Jackson, Zakiyyah Iman. *Becoming Human: Matter and Meaning in an Antiblack World.* New York UP, 2020.

Kimmerer, Robin Wall. *Braiding Sweetgrass: Indigenous Wisdom, Scientific Knowledge, and the Teachings of Plants.* Milkweed, 2014.

King, Tiffany Lethabo. "Humans Involved: Lurking in the Lines of Posthumanist Flight." *Critical Ethnic Studies,* vol. 3, no. 1, Spring 2017, pp. 162–85.

Leong, Diana. "The Mattering of Black Lives: Octavia Butler's Hyperempathy and the Promise of New Materialism." *Catalyst: Feminism, Theory, Technoscience,* vol. 2, no. 2, 2016, pp. 1–35.

MacLure, Maggie. "The Wonder of Data." *Cultural Studies <-> Critical Methodologies,* vol. 13, no. 4, 2013, pp. 228–32.

Mignolo, Walter. *The Darker Side of Western Modernity: Global Futures, Decolonial Options.* Duke UP, 2011.

———. "Introduction: Coloniality of Power and De-colonial Thinking." *Cultural Studies,* vol. 21, no. 2–3, Mar./May 2007, pp. 155–67.

Montague, Tony. "Ulali Combines Tradition with Contemporary Flair." *The Georgia Straight,* 10 Mar. 2005, https://www.straight.com/article/ulali-combines-tradition-with-contemporary-flair.

Muckelbauer, John. "Implicit Paradigms of Rhetoric: Aristotelian, Cultural, and Heliotropic." *Rhetoric, through Everyday Things,* edited by Scot Barnett and Casey Boyle, U of Alabama P, 2016, pp. 30–41.

Newton, Creede. "Why Has Navajo Nation Been Hit So Hard by the Coronavirus?" *Al-Jazeera,* 27 May 2020, https://www.aljazeera.com/news/2020/05/navajo-nation-hit-hard-coronavirus-200526171504037.html.

Nicotra, Jodie. "Rhetorical Assemblages at Speed: The Case of Phage Therapy." Rhetoric Society of America Conference, 2 June 2018, Minneapolis, Minnesota. Panel presentation.

Powell, Malea. "Rhetorics of Survivance: How American Indians Use Writing." *College Composition and Communication,* vol. 53, no. 3, Feb. 2002, pp. 396–434.

Powell, Malea, et al. "Our Story Begins Here: Constellating Cultural Rhetorics." *enculturation,* 25 Oct. 2014, http://enculturation.net/our-story-begins-here.

Propen, Amy. *Visualizing Posthuman Conservation in the Age of the Anthropocene.* The Ohio State UP, 2018.

Ratcliffe, Krista. *Rhetorical Listening: Identification, Gender, Whiteness.* Southern Illinois UP, 2005.

Ravenscroft, Alison. "Strange Weather: Indigenous Materialisms, New Materialism, and Colonialism." *Cambridge Journal of Postcolonial Literary Theory,* vol. 5, no. 3, Sept. 2018, pp. 353–70.

Rice, Jenny. "How Can an Ecosystem Have a Voice?" Forum: Bruno Latour on Rhetoric. *Rhetoric Society Quarterly,* vol. 47, no. 5, 2017, pp. 403–62.

Rickert, Thomas. *Ambient Rhetoric: The Attunements of Rhetorical Being.* U of Pittsburgh P, 2013.

Rifkin, Mark. *Beyond Settler Time: Temporal Sovereignty and Indigenous Self-Determination.* Duke UP, 2017.

Royster, Jacqueline Jones. "When the First Voice You Hear Is Not Your Own." *College Composition and Communication*, vol. 47, no. 1, Feb. 1996, pp. 29–40.

Ruiz, Iris D. "Critiquing the Critical: The Politics of Race and Coloniality in Rhetoric, Composition, and Writing Studies Traditions." *Race, Rhetoric, and Research Methods*, by Alexandra Lockett et al., WAC Clearinghouse, 2021, pp. 39–79.

Ruiz, Iris, and Raul Sánchez, editors. *Decolonizing Rhetoric and Composition Studies: New Latinx Keywords for Theory and Pedagogy.* Palgrave, 2016.

Sackey, Donnie, et al. "Symposium: Perspectives on Cultural and Posthumanist Rhetorics." *Rhetoric Review*, vol. 38, no. 4, 2019, pp. 375–401.

Schiano, Chris. "'No More Stolen Sisters' Demonstration Blockades DAPL Man Camp; 25+ Arrests." *Unicorn Riot*, 16 Nov. 2016, https://unicornriot.ninja/2016/no-stolen-sisters-demonstration-blockades-dapl-man-camp-25-arrests/

Simpson, Leanne Betasamosake. *As We Have Always Done: Indigenous Freedom through Radical Resistance.* U of Minnesota P, 2017.

———. *A Short History of the Blockade: Giant Beavers, Diplomacy, and Regeneration in Nishnaabewin.* U of Alberta P, 2021.

Springgay, Stephanie, and Sarah K. Truman. "On the Need for Methods beyond Proceduralism: Speculative Middles, (In) Tensions, and Response-Ability in Research." *Qualitative Inquiry*, 2017, pp. 1–12.

Stormer, Nathan, and Bridie McGreavy. "Thinking Ecologically about Rhetoric's Ontology: Capacity, Vulnerability, and Resilience." *Philosophy & Rhetoric*, vol. 50, no. 1, 2017, pp. 1–25.

Strathern, Marilyn. "Opening Up Relations." *A World of Many Worlds*, Marisol de la Cadena and Mario Blaser, Duke UP, 2018, pp. 23–52.

Sundberg, Juanita. "Decolonizing Posthumanist Geographies." *Cultural Geographies*, vol. 21, no. 1, 2014, pp. 33–47.

TallBear, Kim. "An Indigenous Reflection on Working beyond the Human/Not-Human." *GLQ* vol. 21, no. 2–3, 2015, pp. 230–35.

Todd, Zoe. "An Indigenous Feminist's Take on the Ontological Turn: 'Ontology' Is Just Another Word for Colonialism." *Journal of Historical Sociology*, vol. 29, no. 1, 2016, pp. 4–22.

Tuck, Eve. "Breaking Up with Deleuze: Desire and Valuing the Irreconcilable." *International Journal of Qualitative Studies in Education*, vol. 23, no. 5, 2010, pp. 635–50.

Tuck, Eve, and K. Wayne Yang. "Decolonization Is Not a Metaphor." *Decolonization: Indigeneity, Education, & Society*, vol. 1, no. 1, 2012, pp. 1–40.

van der Tuin, Iris. "Neo/New Materialism." *The Posthuman Glossary*, edited by Rosi Braidotti and Maria Hlavajova, Bloomsbury, 2018, pp. 277–78.

Villanueva, Victor. "Subversive Complicity and Basic Writing across the Curriculum. *Journal of Basic Writing*, vol. 32, no. 1, 2013, pp. 97–110.

Walsh, Lynda, et al. "Forum: Bruno Latour on Rhetoric." *Rhetoric Society Quarterly*, vol. 47, no. 5, 2017, pp. 403–62.

Weheliye, Alexander. *Habeas Viscus: Racializing Assemblages, Biopolitics, and Black Feminist Theories of the Human.* Duke UP, 2014.

Woelfle-Erskine, Cleo. "The Watershed Body: Transgressing Frontiers in Riverine Sciences, Planning Stochastic Multispecies Worlds." *Catalyst: Feminism, Theory, Technoscience*, vol. 3, no. 2, 2017.

Wright, Michelle. *Physics of Blackness: Beyond the Middle Passage Epistemology.* U of Minnesota P, 2015.

Yusoff, Kathryn. *A Billion Black Anthropocenes or None.* U of Minnesota P, 2019.

CHAPTER 1

The Politics of Recognition in Building Pluriversal Possibilities

Posthumanism, Buen Vivir, *and Zapatismo*

ROBERT LESTÓN

Decoloniality is not an academic area of research. Decoloniality is not an academic trend. Decoloniality is not a movement. Decoloniality is not a discipline. Contrary to what the editors at Wikipedia say, decoloniality is not a form of critical theory applied to ethnic studies. Decoloniality is not a study. Decoloniality is the struggle. The so-called intellectual most certainly has a role to play, but the struggle does not belong to the intellectual. The struggle belongs to those who have suffered the most under 500 years of colonization, whom Frantz Fanon called "les damnés."

From the perspective of well-meaning, conscientious whites who grew up in stable households in the globe's wealthiest and most powerful country, this struggle may at first be hard to grasp. In the US, the internet is fast and ubiquitous. We drive cars. Our roads are paved. Public toilets have seats. Trash is collected. Mexicans, Caribbeans, and Central Americans landscape public spaces. They take care of white people's children. They plant, grow, and harvest the food that fills the shelves of grocery stores that are everywhere. The condemned are more important than *pinche* Wegmans.

Despite the Foxconn suicides working for Apple, we academics open our MacBooks and set to work—reading writing, citing. This work, though—the decolonial project—feels different. It's not done to make a name for yourself or even to get tenure. Decoloniality is about the interconnected global struggle of peoples who have been trying to stand despite a boot pressing on their necks for hundreds of years. Decolonial thinking in Fanon's time, in Malcolm's time, was too often misconstrued as violence, as revolution. To put down the dog that bites you, "by the ballot or the bullet." But even then, the primary thrust of decolonial thinking was epistemic "delinking," or what Aníbal Quijano has called *desprenderse,* to unattach yourself from the Euro-Western history of thought. With Fanon and Malcolm X, Quijano reminds us that while it often appears and is presented as universal, Euro-Western thinking is limited to a geopolitics of knowledge that through colonial and economic conquest has come to dominate the globe (Quijano et al. 68). For Fanon, only the actions of the condemned have the power to bring about a more just order, but first the mind itself must be decolonized. Fanon saw the role of the intellectual as a supporter and constant reminder that the only way colonial heteropatriarchy can be overcome is through the actions of the condemned.

Given that many of the writers and readers of this volume are employed at institutions of higher ed in the Global North, we might ask ourselves what role intellectuals in the Global North can have in helping *les damnés de la terre* wrestle back what belongs to them given the significant tools—and potential influence—we have at our disposal. One of my arguments is that we should follow Fanon's footsteps. As researchers and educators, we should serve as advocates and facilitators for those peoples, knowledges, and cultures that have been excluded from mainstream Western society—not in order so they can be absorbed and assimilated by what Quijano has called the "coloniality of power" (more below), but rather so that the West itself can be made more just by being transformed by their influences (533). The second argument is that we can begin decolonizing the portion of the educational and economic sphere to which we have been entrusted, and that is, quite literally, the courses we teach, the curriculums we design, and the programs we coordinate. As with any professional development that we might introduce to new cadres of teachers and graduate students, it is incumbent upon rhetoric and writing scholars to get to work helping those communities who have ancestral, border, and non-Western cultural knowledges become contributors to transforming what we do and teach at the college level. Catherine Walsh has called upon decolonial practitioners to look for the "cracks" in the colonial patriarchy of higher ed, to identify them, and to begin filling them in with pluriversal knowledges—that is, ways of doing and being that come from a plurality of different epistemic and cultural centers (Mignolo and Walsh 20).

One of the reasons why Walsh calls upon decolonial practitioners to look for fissures and tactical opportunities within the university system rather than arguing for wholesale systemic change is that she is keenly aware of the kinds of failures that can occur when demands for recognition are made at the institutional level. As such, this essay discusses two examples concerning what is often called "the politics of recognition," a line of inquiry that has a long and robust history, one that figures prominently in Fanon, Sylvia Wynter, and liberation thinkers from every stripe. Here I discuss two separate social movement encounters, the *buen vivir* movement in Ecuador and just a small but significant piece of the revolution of thought connected to the Zapatista uprising, both taking place within the past twenty years. The essential difference between the Zapatistas and *buen vivir* is that the constitutional revolution in Ecuador received statewide sponsorship, while the Zapatista revolution put no trust in the state and thus had no desire for statewide recognition or assistance. Largely inspired by the six Declarations of the Lacondón Jungle issued by the Zapatistas (1993–2006), Ecuador wrote into its 2008 constitution some of the strongest legislation the globe has seen concerning human and natural rights. It elevated the rights of plants, animals, water, and earth to a status equal to that of humans and featured Indigenous rights and cosmologies as central to a pluriversal identity. And yet, even a self-declared, anti-imperialistic, culturally pluriversal country has not been able to resist the forces of capitalism in the forms of globalization and natural resource extraction, conditions that have led Ecuador to default on its constitutional promises to its people. But a state not being able to uphold its constitutional promises comes as no surprise. We see the same scenario from other countries of the Latin American "pink tide" also buckling under the pressure to fund themselves by exploiting their own natural resources for global markets. For scholars in rhetoric and writing studies interested in pluriversal starting places as they set forth the task of decolonizing the university, the cases of *buen vivir* and the Zapatistas offer examples of cosmovisions that are outside the paradigm of Western thought that can readily be incorporated into curricula. This analysis, to which I will return at the end of the essay, underscores the ultimate failure of looking for recognition from the state, and lets us locate hope for a pluriversal future in the eyes of living, breathing people.

Before that discussion, this collection seeks to analyze the relationship between recent developments of posthumanism and new materialism and their intersection with decolonial critique. Let me get some preliminaries out of the way so that I can frame this discussion the best I can.

- First, although the posthuman and new materialist discourses have much in common with each other, I will focus my discussion primarily on the posthuman to keep the legacy of the human and its relationship to colonialism in the forefront. As I will explain, one of the problems of the "posthuman" is that it does not problematize what is meant by "human."

- Not always, but often, knowledge production in the Western academy follows a myth of progress that has been constructed from modernity's unilinear notion of time. This is reflected in the act of naming domains that carry prefixes such as "post-," "new-," neo-," and so on. When these discursive conventions appear, there is a high likelihood that those intellectuals are working within a Eurocentric tradition, citing other Westernized scholars and writing for the Western academy. In this regard, while there is an affinity between postcolonial and decolonial scholars, postcolonial scholars are seeking to influence and change academic work in the West, whereas:
- The decolonial project is grounded on the prospect of advancing those knowledges that have been occluded by the totalizing and universalizing narratives of Western modernity. Decolonial projects seek to rupture the fabric of the unilinear temporality of progress and in so doing to reveal or invent worlds that follow multiple anti-colonial trajectories, ways in which subjugated peoples are revalued and different ways in which they seek recognition for being human.

I begin, then, with a discussion of posthumanism within rhetorical studies and explain why, in its current configuration, I see it as necessarily limited in its ability to provide a meaningful framework for how to go about instituting the kind of praxis of pluriversal knowledges I advocate here. While posthumanism and decolonialism share affinities in removing the Euro-Western human from the center of concern, posthumanism's assemblages—whether vegetal, animal, or machinic—do not account for the multitude of knowledges, cosmologies, and ways of living and being that are outside a Eurocentric framing.

This kind of thinking, I would argue, reveals what Mignolo has called a specific "loci of enunciation," the time and place from which a writer writes ("Delinking" 492). Looked at from a global and historical scale, where both "modernity" and "humanity" are European constructs, such loci become an entire "geopolitics of knowledge," founded on an order of rationality embedded within the notion that posthumanism is an advancement over humanism rather than an extension of it. I unpack this below.

Posthuman Approaches and Decolonizing the Academy

Posthumanism altered the course of analyses provided by techno-humanists of the twentieth century—Walter Ong, Lewis Mumford, Langdon Winner, and

Marshall McLuhan, among others—who interrogated the impact new and ever-renewing technologies had on the organization of social, political, and ecological life. Their central concerns often questioned the relationships that humans had with what Mumford, Bernard Stiegler, and Don Ihde called technics, what might be reframed in Heideggerian terminology as "the question concerning technology," an exploration into the human historical relationship with studying how various technologies have altered what is man/being/civilization, all from within a humanistic and colonial epistemic frame (Heidegger 307).

The so-called first wave of posthumanism was often concerned with moving what Friedrich Kittler liked to call "so-called man" from the center of what passed for humanistic research in the Western tradition (16). Posthumanism's symbolic awakening came when epistemic genealogist Michel Foucault provocatively pronounced that the "recent invention" that was man would soon wash away like a "face drawn in the sand at the edge of the sea" (387). The next moment came with the rise of the machine in the 1990s. From that time period, one can recall Donna Haraway's cyborg, Latour's *We Have Never Been Modern,* Hayles's concerns with information and embodiment, and Marilouise Kroker and Arthur Kroker's "flesh-eating 90s." This turning toward the machine intersected with the rise of the internet, hypertext, and the pop of cyberpunk writers such as Gibson, Sterling, and Stephenson, among others, culminating in one of its best articulations in pop culture just before the turn of the millennium with *The Matrix.* In the field of rhetoric, Richard Lanham's *The Electronic Word* was published in 1993. By 1996, Victor Vitanza's *Cyber-Reader* was a popular undergraduate anthology and the journal *Kairos* was founded. Soon after, Bolter and Grusin were attending to "remediation" in "late age of print," visual rhetoric was becoming a serious area of inquiry, and it seemed that just about every grad student and their grandma was learning how to code HTML. Students interested in what had not yet been widely accepted as "new media" gravitated toward posthuman studies.

In the humanistic tradition, "human" most always meant white, heteronormative, European man, as anyone other was an afterthought or of no consequence. In its attempt to become the "post" of the human, posthumanism intends to remove the human from the center of thought, usually not in order to replace it with something else, another "master signifier," but rather to extend what is meant by "human" to include nonhuman others. Most frequently, this extension is made to our interaction with media machines and applications in contemporary Western culture. More recently, the rise of other discourse networks in the past twenty years that include domains in new materialisms, animal studies, studies in the Anthropocene, and other developments has brought renewed attention to objects of our attention—plants, animals, things, and other nonhuman entities—so that we might think differently about nonhuman others if we attempt to think about them through a perspective whose goal is to see them not as beings or things who are put into the service of the human, but as worth thinking about in their own right insofar as they are part of a larger self-organizing ecology.

This renewed attention to the material world that now falls under the diverse title of "new materialisms" forcefully argues that "matter matters," and positions itself as overcoming the period of postmodern discourses that spent too much energy focusing on issues related to language. Here we can see the false narrative of academic progress rearing its head. Posthumanism looks toward the future, but it does not look backward or laterally to concern itself with central issues concerning the genre and hierarchy of the human as it relates to colonized others. Most typically, however, and this is especially true in rhetorical and writing studies, posthuman discourse is deployed to more adequately describe distributed agency of the human. In other words, the seat of the will of the human, the place from which rhetorical invention might occur, for instance, is not within the writer's own personhood or subjectivity, but seeks to assert the primacy of how the agency of the human is entangled with vital and self-organizing nonhuman assemblages.

Thomas Rickert's work in ambient rhetoric can be read as posthuman insofar as it draws our attention to the ambient background where all of these entities live and comingle with each other into many different assemblages, where the hum and rhythms of the world take place and produce our identities and subjectivities. For Rickert, this condition makes music and sound especially important because they can become a relay that provides the opportunity to engage our ambient condition on different levels of attention. Different musics and sounds can be designed so that our attention can be brought to engage different levels of being in diverse ambient spaces (28). Other scholars in rhetoric working from the posthuman have a tendency to focus more on human-technological assemblages.

Justin Hodgson's recent work draws upon the posthuman to draw our attention to the notion that "to be" a part of contemporary "Western culture" means to be "mediated—to relate to the world in mediated ways" (18). The consequences are that screen technologies have altered human action by introducing many different ways not only for how people act but also for how "people think about" and articulate their actions (18). In these and related discourses, the posthuman is often invoked to draw attention to human-machine assemblages while always continuing to problematize anthropocentric notions of agency that were part of so much work that happened during the period of social constructivism. Today, subjects are mediated, assembled, ecological, and ambient. Our subjectivities are thrown to the wind and dispersed like pollen in April, although many other metaphors might suffice.

From the perspective of progress and developing a body of scholarship that accounts for how bodies become mediatized in network culture, these developments have been important and essential. And still, the central question concerning this study is, In what ways may posthuman approaches aid in the project of decolonizing the academy? It certainly can be said that posthumanism throws into question the practice of the Western human as being an essentialist ontological category. When I read, for instance, the work of Lewis Mumford mentioned earlier, I cannot help but appreciate the scholar's erudition, his love for organic life, and his fear for ever-expanding technological progress and how the development of technological apparati threaten the future of human existence. Simultaneously, I feel tossed into a time warp, in that all references to mankind are concerned with men and the thoughts of other men. Women, communities of color, and Indigenous peoples, if addressed, are held in a binaric opposition to and against "man." To the problematizing of this category of man, the posthuman promotes our entanglements and relationships with other creatures and things, and so the posthuman does indeed share a common interest with decolonial critique as it draws our attention to those beings that have been "objectified, muted or rendered passive by a certain manifestation of anthropocentrism or human exceptionalism" (Zembylas 254).

It is not questionable, however, whether decolonial critique and posthumanism have different priorities. They begin from different origins, and that makes all the difference. I see two primary difficulties of posthuman critique / new materialisms / postcolonialisms or any knowledge discourse in the contemporary academy able to do the work of decolonial critique. The first involves the locus of annunciation of any scholar working in and trained in the West. This locus of annunciation as it applies to any single writer necessarily limits their frame of reference. Second, on both a historical and global scale, these loci become an entire geopolitical apparatus that creates knowledge on the foundations of the Western academy that reaches well beyond Europe and North America (Mignolo, "Delinking" 460).

The posthuman condition takes up battles for the sake of those othered others already living within a social episteme that is primarily the so-called first world. The moving away of a self-obsessed narcissistic category of man implies a concern for the well-being and social justice for all beings and creatures that reveals a general affinity with decolonial critique. I would like to speculate that most everyone working in the field of posthuman studies would be sympathetic with the efforts to decolonize the academy, but I would nonetheless echo Zakiyyah Iman Jackson's point that there is "much humanity, and even humanism, that posthumanism theory has yet to pass through" (676).

When buried narratives of definitions of the human are ignored, scholars working in the (post)humanities unwittingly risk perpetuating structural and historical racism. The traditions of black liberation intellectuals and decolonial theorists have established that the "color line" introduced by Du Bois in 1903 needs to be further incorporated not just into posthumanism or new materialism, but into all the intellectual work we do. Twenty-plus years after New York City policemen unloaded forty-one rounds into unarmed Amadou Diallo, we only need to look at routine traffic stops to see how the color line remains the primary problem of the twenty-first century in the US. The diagnosis made by Du Bois, Fanon, and others, that the act of territorial and epistemic colonization often causes terror in the streets and in the minds of the colonized, is no joke. That black folk continue to be murdered, experience existential terror, and internalize the false narratives that they are inferior to whites reveals how these legacies of subhuman status persist.

Posthumanism's concern with mediatized and cyborg bodies, its concerns with the subject's entanglements with other nonhumans, and its desire to overcome the linguistic turn all express a unilinear temporal order that remains firmly rooted in the epistemological locus of the West. It should come as little surprise that the target audience of posthuman discourses, just as for postcolonial discourses, is other scholars working in the Global North. These discourse networks are framed by numerous boundaries: geographic boundaries that contain first-world populations; linguistic boundaries that are primarily English, but extend to French and German, that leave out entire swaths of thinkers working in different languages; and geopolitical boundaries that duplicate and continue colonial, Eurocentric epistemologies.

One of the central tenets of decolonial thinking in any number of threads, whether from Latin America (Dussel, Quijano), the Caribbean (Wynter, Césaire), or Africa (Mbembe, Thiong'o) is that modernity in the European sense could not have occurred without the global atrocities of colonialism and slavery. It is for this reason that much decolonial critique pairs modernity with coloniality, as in "modernity/coloniality," so they can be simultaneously expressed. Modernity's foundation is European imperial territorial expansion, "African enslavement, Latin American conquest, and Asian subjugation" (Wynter 263). Embedded within coloniality is genocide, slavery, and cultural genocide (epistemicide). Like the modernity/coloniality pair, it is not possible to have the category of the human without the other orders of subhuman status: the slave, the Indian, the savage, and the peasant. The posthuman still works within a tradition that is founded on a humanism that is part and parcel of modernity and a humanity that is anything but humane. Mignolo and Walsh put the matter succinctly:

> Postmodernity came into the picture as a critique of many assumptions of the modern imaginary, chief among them the need of macronarratives. Postmodern critiques of modernity, however, did not originate in China or Namibia, Uzbekistan or Bolivia. They originated, as should be expected, in the same place the word modernity appeared first: France. But postmodernity did not and does not refer only to a critical stance toward North Atlantic modernity. It asserts that all of us, "we," on the planet are also living in postmodern times, as typified by Jean-François Lyotard's concept of postmodernity and Fredric Jameson's theory of the logic of late capitalism. In other words, the West's particular ontology of history continues to assert its universality. One of the latest consequences is the universality of posthuman, which presupposes that all on the planet is posthuman when, in reality, modernity has reduced the majority of the population to quasi-human. (119)

Consequently, posthuman and related discourses suffer from several ethical blind spots: They do not problematize that they emerge from a Euro-Western tradition that has sought to universalize its knowledge production across the globe through a colonization of thought in the academy; they do not acknowledge that the tradition to which they belong has always closed its doors to thinkers outside of the West; and they do not seek to expand beyond arguments and audiences who are firmly rooted in so-called first-world problems.

It is also worth noting a fourth blind spot. Karsten Schulz has explained, in the context of environmental degradation, that new materialism does not take historical materialist conditions into account: "Considering how coloniality intersects with a global system of production, consumption, finance and labor that generates growing environmental degradation and social inequalities, it is nevertheless questionable whether the ethical attunement to matter that characterizes the new materialism is sufficient to fully account for these predicaments" (133). The materiality of new materialism does not begin with the material conditions of survival. Global systems of finance, debt, development, extractivism, dependency, and technocapitalism are the tools of continued coloniality as it is expressed through global development and technological propagation. Posthuman scholars spend time discussing how technologies mediate our bodies, but outside of academic circles, at the borders and at the colonial peripheries, what matters is that there is colonization and daily recolonization operating through global systems of domination. Each morning as day breaks and trucks roll out, another day of recolonization takes place, from the cigarettes smoked by government officials sidelining as human traffickers, or metrosexuals in Mexico City sporting the latest fashion made by girls under the age of twelve working in spinning mills in South India, or the 600 to 700 Wayuú Indigenous children who die every year of thirst in La Guajira, Colombia, because big mining corporations are stealing water from communities to increase mining extraction (Sherrif). For many authors (Wallerstein, Giddens, Habermas), including many working from a decolonial perspective, there is "no outside of modernity" or the global world capitalist system. In a book on Indigenous culture and development, Timothy MacNeill writes: "Ideas such as *progress, development,* and *gross domestic product* are entrenched in the culture of modernity and are ubiquitous in our globalized world. There is no escape, or outside vantage-point from which to gaze on these complex perceptions" (4).

Insofar as arguments are made important to the intellectual work that is being done in the academy, posthumanism needs to be held to account for what it can see and what it cannot. This is not to say, however, that there are no affinities between the decolonial and posthumanistic projects. There are many. Arturo Escobar has grouped fields such as new materialism, posthumanities, decolonial critique, animal studies, assemblage theory, systems theory, affect theory, feminist new materialisms, ecocriticism, disability studies, and critical race theory under the category of what he calls "transition discourses," discourse communities that actively create pathways toward imagining democratic systems after capitalism ("Degrowth" 452). From this perspective, posthumanism / new materialism and decoloniality will have much to say in support of each other so long as the foundations that gave rise to modernity and humanism are put into question.

Pregutando Caminamos

There is one thing that theorists of recognition agree upon. All human beings have a deep-seated need to be recognized and validated. What they don't agree upon is from whom that recognition should come. They likewise agree that economic equality is not a substitute for mutual recognition. The history of the colonial matrix of power and all of its constituents—conquest; genocide; slavery; linguistic imperialism; patriarchy; economic and environmental degradation; the massive discursive networks that categorically transform human beings into barbarians, savages, animals, and other nonhuman forms based on appearance or sexual orientation—have led to historical wounds that cannot be undone. Appeals made to the state to increase opportunity for those who have been excluded in the forms of recognized racial, sexual, and gender equality and greater access to employment, housing, education, and social services cannot undo the trauma inflicted by histories of colonial injustices. As Fanon pointed out, even if freedom is granted to the slave from the master, that only confirms the master's superiority to the slave. Likewise, it is an important gesture when state programs are put in place to grant greater access to those whose ancestors have suffered humiliation and exploitation, but it does little to overturn the social order.

Glen Coulthard has argued persuasively, from the perspective of Canadian Indigenous groups, that most models of liberal reform call for a transaction of land, capital, and political power to be moved from the state toward Indigenous communities in recognition of their sovereignty through a variety of different legislative and economic agreements. His historical and cultural analysis reveals, however, that instead of "ushering in an era of peaceful coexistence grounded on the ideal of reciprocity or mutual recognition, the politics of recognition in its contemporary liberal form promises to reproduce the very configurations of colonialist, racist, patriarchal state power that Indigenous peoples' demands for recognition have historically sought to transcend" (3).

If recognition in the form of reciprocity and economic concessions does little to stop exploitative social structures, then perhaps recognition can come from different sources. The establishment of the Zapatista communities after the uprising that took place in 1994 is the premier exemplar of a community who has sought to build "un mundo donde quepan muchos mundos" (a world where many worlds fit; my translation). In contrast to MacNeill's mentioning above that there is no outside of modernity, the Zapatistas didn't try to build a world outside the global hegemonic system; they sought to build worlds inside it.

By removing state influence in its communities that number over 300,000, the Zapatistas have carved out of the Chiapas mountains autonomous spaces where they have built communities complete with schools, hospitals, and their own direct, horizontal forms of government in the form of their *caracoles y juntas de buen gobierno* (municipalities and meetings of good government). The Zapatistas have established a movement that stretches far beyond its own community members that is global in reach, they have restored dignity to the Mayan groups that live within their communities and identify as Zapatistas, they have resisted the influences of the *mal gobierno,* and they have, in the words of John Holloway, "changed the world without taking power" (*Change*).

Of value for rhetoric and writing studies scholars and teachers is the way in which the Zapatistas have incorporated Indigenous (Maya) ways of knowing/feeling into their own Zapatista rhetoric. When the core group of the Zapatista revolutionary forces were first forming in the 1980s, they then identified as members of the FLN, the Forces of National Liberation, and were not unlike many other Marxist guerilla groups in Central America. During the 1970s and '80s, the FLN had training facilities stationed in the jungles throughout various states in southern Mexico. This was a time in Mexico known as the *guerras sucias* (the dirty wars), where thousands of people were surreptitiously disappeared and murdered at the hands of the government. One of the government's campaigns was to eliminate the FLN, which they set about doing and successfully accomplished. After the raids on the FLN training facilities, six remaining members regrouped in Chiapas and ascended the mountains in what would become a decade-long campaign to convince Indigenous communities that they join forces and take up arms against the Mexican government.

It was during these years, however, when the rebels themselves were transformed by the cosmovision of the Indigenous communities. Subcomandante Marcos, the articulate spokesperson for the Zapatistas during their formative years, recalls that when they went into the mountains to explain their Marxist-Leninist-Guevarist cause and the need to take up arms, they were met with "tu palabra es muy dura, no la entendemos" (your word is very hard. We don't understand it; my translation; qtd. in Higgins 364). Consequently, what followed was what Mignolo has called the "theoretical revolution of zapatismo" ("Zapatista's") as there were a variety of different reasons why the highland Indians in Mexico could not understand the Marxist language of revolution. In traditional revolutionary politics, the first order of business is changing the consciousness of the masses, but explaining what is wrong with the world and what needed to be done did not resonate with the communities in Chiapas. Rather than talking, Marcos and the others started listening to the people in the communities and came to realize that the goal was not to change consciousness, but to restore the dignity that the people had lost since the onset of colonization. In a 1994 letter written to the Zapatista organization, they explain the importance and meaning of restoring dignity:

> Then that suffering that united us made us speak, and we recognised that in our words there was truth, we knew that not only pain and suffering lived in our tongue, we recognised that there is hope still in our hearts. We spoke with ourselves, we looked inside ourselves and we looked at our history: we saw our most ancient fathers suffering and struggling, we saw our grandfathers struggling, we saw our fathers with fury in their hands, we saw that not everything had been taken away from us, that we had the most valuable, that which made us live, that which made our step rise above plants and animals,

> that which made the stone be beneath our feet, and we saw, brothers, that all that we had was DIGNITY, and we saw that great was the shame of having forgotten it, and we saw that DIGNITY was good for men to be men again, and dignity returned to live in our hearts, and we were new again, and the dead, our dead, saw that we were new again and they called us again, to dignity, to struggle. (EZLN 122)

Once dignity rather than changing consciousness becomes the goal, then, as Holloway puts it, "the whole tonality and style of political action" changes ("Zapatismo"). And it is from here where we get one of the central principles of the Zapatista organization: *preguntando caminamos,* "asking we walk," a way of learning from Indigenous people that meant that moving forward could only come from listening to the people, and what they wanted was not to take up arms but to restore dignity. As I mentioned in the introduction to this chapter, we should follow Fanon's principle that only the "wretched of the earth," the condemned and colonized, have the power to bring about a more just order. Here, the revolutionaries went into the mountains and in so doing had their *palabra dura* undergo an involution, a decolonization, bringing about a way of living that made real another of Fanon's principles, that the last should be first.

Many members of highland communities preserve their identity through language, dress, and custom, where Castilian Spanish is often a second language after one of the variants of Mayan languages spoken in Chiapas: Tzetzal, Tsotsil, Chol, and Tojolábal. As Mignolo outlines, much of the "theoretical revolution" came from learning from Indigenous people that included finding a way to allow the Spanish language to receive an inflection that comes from other Mayan languages that have no correspondence to Latin- or Greek-based languages. This can partly account for why the speeches and writings of the Zapatistas are often poetical in nature—two incompatible languages are being worked over together to reorganize thought into the colonizer's language. We can find examples throughout the writings, fables, and parables of Marcos as well as in this passage below, taken from the 1997 International Zapatista *Encuentro* and made by one of the movement's founding women, Major Ana Maria:

> We were born war with the white year, and we began to trace the path that took us to the heart of yours, the same that today took you to our heart. The voice which arms itself so that it can make itself heard. The face which hides itself so that it can be seen. The red star that calls to humanity and the world, so that they will listen, so that they will see, so that they will name. The

> tomorrow that is harvested in the yesterday. Behind our black face, behind our armed voice, behind our unspeakable name, behind the we that you see, behind we are you. (qtd. in Mignolo, "Zapatista's" 254)

The original Spanish in the last line is "Detrás estamos ustedes," which in itself is a linguistic impossibility. There are various reconfigurations that would make linguistic sense, such as "detrás estamos nosotros" (we are behind), "detrás están ustedes" (you are behind), or "estamos detras de ustedes" (we are behind you), but none of these are being said here. We can locate a distinct epistemic feature that is being articulated in this phrase "behind we are you" as well as "the tomorrow that is harvested in the yesterday" that has no correspondence to Greek, Latin, or the so-called Romance languages. Ana Maria's first language is Tojolábal, a language that does not use or have a subject-object correlation as a way of expression, but rather uses a grammar structured in the correlation between subjects. From this perspective, one completely natural to Ana Maria, "behind we are you" can be taken at face value. Behind the face, the voice, the name, we are you. The Zapatistas have accomplished other theoretical revolutions, but finding ways to open a language to other ways of thinking is what Catherine Walsh has called a crack in the colonial matrix of power. The struggle comes "from and within modernity/coloniality's borders and cracks, to build a radically distinct world. Decoloniality is not a new paradigm or mode of critical thought. It is a way, option, standpoint, analytic, project, practice, and praxis" (Mignolo and Walsh 5). Of the numerous lessons that can be learned from the Zapatistas, finding ways to change the mode of thinking attached to a colonizer's discourse, I would argue, is a significant accomplishment.

In *preguntando caminamos,* Zapatismo puts front and center the cultural richness of Indigenous communities so it is the people who lead and the leaders who obey, as expressed in another principle, *mandar obedeciendo* (lead by obeying); in so doing, recognition and value are immediately granted to the people in order to restore the dignity that had been stripped away by years of oppression. But this recognition is not granted from the state. They have turned toward a self-recognition and affirmation, and over a period of almost thirty years, have resisted state intervention.

Buen Vivir (Sumak Kawsay)

The constitutional reform that took place in Ecuador in 2008 can be attributed to the suasive force of its primary social movement, a united federation of different Indigenous groups that goes by the acronym CONAIE (Confederation of Indigenous Nationalities of Ecuador). The number of Indigenous peoples living in Ecuador is contested, but CONAIE has claimed that Indigenous and Afro-Ecuadorian peoples together compose approximately 40 percent (Yashar 40; Becker 48). As any federation of distinct peoples attempts to come together, the differences between Indigenous groups can often be prohibitive toward establishing solidarity. Although the numbers of Indigenous in the US are a considerably smaller part of the population than in the South, alliances among autonomous nations in the US have not been able to overcome their differences in order to form an organization that can speak on behalf of Indigenous people in the US (notwithstanding much of the hopeful solidarity that emerged from the Dakota Access Pipeline Protests in 2016 and 2017).

CONAIE is a coalition of Indigenous organizations that includes three federations, fourteen distinct Indigenous groups, and is organized at the national scale. The three federations correspond to the three primary geo-ecological territories of Ecuador—the Amazon lowlands, the highland Andes, and the coast. The Indigenous peoples include the Shuar, Achuar, Siona, Secoya, Cofán, Huaorani, Záparo, Chachi, Tsáchila, Awá, Epera, Manta, Wancavilca, and Quichua. It is considered to be the longest-standing and among the strongest Indigenous movements in all of Latin America. CONAIE is a formidable force with which to be reckoned. It has extreme popular support and over the years has come to be known for its ability to mobilize massive popular uprisings through direct actions.

By the time the 2006 election arrived, CONAIE was ready to implement the constitutional reform known as *buen vivir,* most easily translated as "living well." In Western capitalism, "living well" typically resonates with such images of "living the dream," "living large," or other similar images that invoke people who have tons of cash and spend it by throwing lavish parties on yachts in Ibiza; it invokes images of lifestyles of the rich and famous with their Hollywood mansions or Manhattan apartments that rent for 52,000 dollars a month. For the Indigenous in Ecuador, to live well carries considerably different connotations. It is typically associated with the Quechua concept of *sumak kawsay.* As the Uruguayan sociologist and activist Eduardo Gudynas explains it, *sumak kawsay* invokes a sense of a fullness of living in community both with other persons and with nature:

> The richness of the term is difficult to translate into English. It includes the classical ideas of quality of life, but with the specific idea that well-being is only possible within a community. Furthermore, in most approaches the community concept is understood in an expanded sense, to include Nature. *Buen vivir* therefore embraces the broad notion of well-being and cohabi-

> tation with others and Nature. In this regard, the concept is also plural, as there are many different interpretations depending on cultural, historical and ecological setting. (441)

As mentioned in the above discussion concerning modernity/coloniality, Western approaches to thinking about time invoke a unilinear mode and myth of progress, a sense that "one can never go back." These positions criticize looking back to the innocence of an earlier time as romantic and naive. Keeping that in mind, it is fitting to recall the image of the *caracol* (conch, nautilus) used by the Zapatistas to name their autonomous councils of good government that I mentioned earlier. There is an important Mayan archeological site in Belize that carries the name, but the *caracol* is an icon that appears frequently throughout all of Central America—on murals, in museums, in street art, on restaurant menus, in the names of shops, and so on. One might think of the ancient Mayan astronomical knowledge that formulated different cycles of time into each other in their interwoven calendars. It's also fitting that the *caracol* is also the primary exemplar of the Fibonacci pattern.

Bolivian activist Pablo Solón offers a helpful way to approach the cosmovision that is embedded in the concept of *buen vivir.* As Solón explains it, it is essential to approach *buen vivir* from the desire to grasp a sense of the whole, what to those from the Andes would appear as *pacha.* Often *pacha* is translated as "nature" or "earth," and *pacha mama* as "Mother Earth," but these translations fail to invoke the cultural connotations that go along with the notion, in particular the way that "nature," if we think merely of *naturaleza,* does not invoke the sense of the universe or cosmos. "*Pacha* is a much broader concept," writes Solón, "that includes the indissoluble unity of space and time" ("Pablo").

> *Pacha* is the whole in constant movement, it is the cosmos in a permanent state of becoming. *Pacha* refers not only to the world of humans, animals and plants but also to the world above (Hanan Pacha), inhabited by the sun, the moon and the stars, and the world below (Ucu Pacha), where the dead and the spirits live. ("Is Vivir")

Thinking about *buen vivir* as a return to an earlier, simplistic, and more primitive time misrepresents what the concept, conceived from an Andean perspective, essentially entails. *Buen vivir* is distinct from Western knowledges rooted in progress and modernity as they are conceived upon a logic of linear development. Rather than conceiving of *buen vivir* as an antiquated approach to thinking about progress, it is the other way round: Linear development is a form of thinking that needs to be dispensed with. *Buen vivir* is not a return to "a distant, Andean past" of "pre-colonial times. It is not a static concept but an idea that is continually being created" (Gudynas 443).

Its dynamic quality makes *buen vivir* an essential kind of epistemological thinking that should be opened up in the Westernized academy. Rather than there being a linear past, present, and future, the Andean vision of time sees the past, present, and future as coexistences that interrelate dynamically. They have nothing to do with Newton's mechanics that state that time is a coordinate independent of space but rather echo Einstein's famous statement that the distinction between past, present, and future is "only a stubbornly persistent illusion" (qtd. in Dyson 193). Within the cosmovision of *buen vivir,* the future blossoms with the past even as the past is remade by it (Solón, "Is Vivir").

It follows that time and space follow the cyclical pattern of the *caracol.* Solón explains that the "lineal notions of growth and progress are not compatible with that vision. Time advances in the form of a spiral. The future is connected with the past. In any advance there is a return and any return is an advance. Hence, as the Aymara say, 'let us walk with our backs toward the future and our eyes on the past'" ("Is Vivir"). In this way, the good life never arrives; it is always being made and remade. Far from a desire to return to a distant or even a recent past, *buen vivir* invokes a present where the past and future are always present, all acting on each other. Turning to living a good or beautiful life, then, is not a turning back to a more innocent time but is an advancement in thinking and acting. Given the continued and increasing environmental devastation resulting from ceaseless economic growth, this nonlinear conception of temporality recognizes that there are better ways of thinking about our futures rather than continually trying to overcome our present.

Vivir Bien and the Constitution

This dynamic way of thinking about living a good life that is in balance with nature is not in any way isolated to epistemologies born from the Andean region or from other epistemologies of the South. In fact, even in the US there are local communities that have attempted and others that have succeeded in granting rights to nature. What is unique to the Ecuadorian constitution is that it frames *sumak kawsay* as a set of inalienable rights. Chapter 2 in the Ecuadorian Constitution of 2008 is entitled "Rights of *Buen Vivir*" and includes sections on water; food security; a healthy environment where *sumak kawsay* is mentioned; information and communication; culture and science; education; housing and habitat, which includes a right to decent housing regardless of income; health; and labor and social security. Chapter 7, entitled "Rights of Nature," includes statements that nature has the right to be respected for its existence, that it has the right to be maintained, that it has the right to have its life cycles and evolutionary processes regenerated and restored, and that those who take it upon themselves to restore nature will be compensated by the state. It includes statements for the protection of species and ecosystems and holds that citizens have the right to enjoy and live in harmony with nature.

In 2008, the constitution was put to a popular vote and passed easily. For a brief period of time, Ecuador, along with Bolivia, which passed a similar constitutional reform, was both a leader and a beacon for natural and pluriversal rights. From the beginning, however, other forces of the legacy of coloniality in the form of globalization were continuously at work, undermining the constitution even as it was being written. As Ecuadorian decolonial scholar Catherine Walsh has mentioned, "the project's decolonial shifts and movements never really got off the ground" (Mignolo and Walsh 66).

But the lesson here isn't one of remorse. It is no surprise that the pluriversal, constitutional rights of people and nature have been abrogated to usher in continued development and resource extraction, regardless of what the letter of the constitution stipulates. For Ecuador to grow and develop, environmental destruction will continue; as the primary framer of the constitution explains, this "is accepted as the inevitable cost of achieving development," and "since this is not questioned," it is most convenient to simply pretend not to remember the achievement in forming the 2008 constitution (Acosta 62). "There is no doubt that audacity with a large dose of ignorance and well-programmed amnesia in society," writes Alberto Acosta, "goes hand in hand with arrogance" (62). And in addition, let us not forget that all these discourses and propaganda work to instantiate, support, and continue practices where environmental destruction is accepted as the inevitable cost of feeding the North's insatiable appetites.

Even as the Indigenous concept of *sumak kawsay* was being written into the Ecuadorian constitution, it was already being undermined by other state actors. When it comes to the question of recognizing the dignity of Indigenous populations and their lands, plenty of ink was spilled, but at the end of the day, the people's and nature's sovereignty were not honored, respected, or recognized by the state of Ecuador. This pattern has been historically true wherever you look concerning aboriginal people and their relationship with the state.

Conclusion

Along with Glen Coulthard mentioned above, we must ask, Who has the power to ensure that nature has its rights so that it can survive? Who has the power to restore dignity to the peoples who have been violated, who continue to be seen and treated as less than human? To return to my primary exemplar, since 1994, the Zapatistas have organized themselves to restore dignity to the 300,000 members of their communities, and they have done so through self-recognition and self-affirmation.

The powerful and political act of a community's self-recognition is by no means limited to the case of the Zapatistas, however. There is a 500-year-long history of communities bonding together in attempts to define the praxis for how their worlds will be constructed. As Kaqchikal Mayan activist Aura Cumes reminds us, "Anti-colonial and decolonial struggles have existed ever since Colombus and Pedro de Alvarado set foot on our lands" (qtd. in Clavo). In the colonial context, the definitions of the hierarchical genre of the human that Wynter and others unveiled set about defining the ideal man, and in so doing defined that man against the subhuman savage and slave. From the Incan rebellion of Tupac Amaru in 1572, to the second great transcontinental rebellion led by Tupac Amaru II in 1781, to the famous barricades of the Paris Commune and the moneyless Spanish Revolution, to the lesser-known cases of runaway slave communities in the Great Dismal Swamp, the 2006 Oaxaca Commune, the Abahlali baseMjondolo autonomous community in Durban, South Africa, and countless other self-organizing decolonial insurrections, rebellions, and resurgences, the global capitalist world system is replete with fissures and cracks where the assembly of new worlds and new definitions of those worlds become possible.

"¿Escucharon? Es el sonido do su mundo derrumbándose. Es el del nuestro resurgiendo. El día que fue el día, era noche, Y noche ser el día que será el día" (Did you hear? It is the sound of your world falling apart. It is of ours resurging. The day that was day was night. And night will be the day that will be day; my translation; Marcos). These words by Marcos may be inspirational, but they can only hold true so long as communities continue to turn to their own definitions, resources, traditions, and knowledges (as well as their alliances and affinity groups) rather than looking for validation and acceptance from the colonial legacy responsible for their othered status. In *Red Skin, White Masks,* Coulthard works through the politics of recognition as they relate in Fanon's thought, and he analyzes three essential achievements that are key to thinking about the politics of recognition that will help as we proceed here toward a conclusion.

Coulthard's analysis precedes by showing that recognition between the colonized and the colonizer is typically predetermined by the power relations that ultimately serve the interests of the colonizer. Second, following Fanon, Coulthard unpacks how colonized populations often develop "psychoaffective" or ideological attachments to the colonizer's false narratives that the colonized are inferior. Third, decolonization can take root when internalized forms of colonial recognition are converted toward self-empowerment. When colonized groups turn away from external recognition and toward a reclamation of their own personal dignity, they begin a process of healing that finds resources in their own group identity, a "reclamation and revitalization of precolonial social relations and cultural traditions" (153). Hasana Sharp calls this movement "transubstantiation," where the colonized must free himself from the struggle not only with the external other but "with the internal other who denies his core humanity" (157).

Coulthard's move is to seize upon this moment by bringing Canadian First Nation voices into the conversation; he spends considerable time reading through two influential voices, those of Mohawk political scientist Taiaiake Alfred and Anishinaabe feminist Leanne Simpson. Here are some quotes that echo some of my sentiment here about political self-validation and recognition that I find helpful.

> "We [must] choose to turn away from the legacies of colonialism and take on the challenge of creating a new reality for ourselves and for our people." (Alfred, qtd. in Coulthard 154)

> "Decolonization requires that Indigenous communities reorient our collective labor from attempts to transform 'the colonial outside into a flourishment of the Indigenous *inside*.'" (Simpson, qtd. in Coulthard 154)

> "We need to decolonize on our own terms, without the sanction, permission or engagement of the state, Western theory or the opinions of Canadians." (Simpson, qtd. in Coulthard 154)

> "We have a responsibility to recover, understand, and preserve these values, not only because they represent a unique contribution to the history of ideas, but because renewal of respect for traditional values is the only lasting solution to the political, economic, and social problems that beseech our people." (Alfred, qtd. in Coulthard 154–55)

Some principles that can be garnered here are the following: (1) Turning away from colonialism constitutes creating a "new reality"; (2) rather than dealing with the "bad government" (to borrow from Zapatista lingo), a turning inward, toward the community itself, is necessary in order to flourish; (3) decolonization must take place on the terms defined by the community; and

(4) reviving and drawing from local traditions is key for building new epistemologies that lead toward new worlds within which the communities can thrive. The key step toward building these "new realities" or pluriversal worlds is to turn away from outside recognition toward self-affirmation. This is the first step of decolonization, a process of "delinking" from the narrative logics of coloniality/modernity. But we must ask, What comes after delinking? Not only are Alfred and Simpson delinking, but they are also seeking to *relink* with their communities' traditional ways of being and living that open toward plural epistemologies and ontologies. Each shared dream of the Anishinaabe and ceremony of the Mohawk opens toward other ways of receiving knowledge and being together.

While the process of delinking is essential for self-recognition, the process of delinking is never enough. Stopping there opens potential dangers in the decolonial project. For one, delinking does not imply the absence of coloniality, as coloniality is sure to always be present. This also means that decoloniality is not another discourse that fits into the linear progress of academic development that leads to some further "enlightenment" (Mignolo and Walsh 99). This kind of thinking has the potential for the decolonial project to be co-opted by academic discourse and commodified in the academic sphere as a means toward individual advancement without connection to praxis and struggle.

By way of relinking, then, let me offer some commentary concerning the meshing of the decolonial project and my earlier discussion of the Western academy and posthumanism. As I suggested earlier, there is an affinity between postmodern related discourses and the decolonial project, and these affinities can be traced to the disruptions and countertraditions to Western modernity from within the Eurocentric paradigm. This counterhegemonic Eurocentric tradition, to my mind, includes Nietzsche and Spinoza as well as those they have influenced, who in turn influenced contemporary theorists like Elizabeth Grosz and Rosi Braidotti. From one perspective or another, many thinkers in this tradition can be read as having an affinity with posthumanism. Another common thread is the shared philosophy of immanence in this tradition. For Braidotti, a "critical posthumanities is a neo-Spinozist monistic ontology that assumes that radical immanence, i.e., the primacy of intelligent and self-organizing matter" (1). This autopoiesis that Braidotti mentions not only applies to nonhuman worlds, but Spinozist-inspired monism offers an alternative to external recognition that is consistent with the politics of self-recognition that has been discussed above. Stemming from Spinoza's doctrine that there is no transcendence, that god is self-perpetuating nature (thus, we are all god), someone who thinks from immanence thinks from a countermodern tradition where what is put in relation are the elements that serve self-perpetuation and becoming, whether that self is a human, a community, or a discourse. In contrast, as de Beauvoir suggests in the *Second Sex*, the duality of transcendence is marked by overcoming war, patriarchy, hierarchy, subordination, and self-immolation for the sake of the illusion of some superior other.

Posthumanism and decoloniality appear to share an affinity based on non-anthropocentrism and self-perpetuation, but the affinity begins to break down when what counts as human has not been sufficiently theorized, and working within a radical European tradition still remains a European tradition. Just as one example, the decolonial project asks: What of the precolonial ways of living and being and their legacies that have undergone erasure? As Maldonado-Torres has shown, the *cogito ergo sum* that founds much of secularized modernity/coloniality was originally denied to those who were conquered. The "I" is attributed to those who are human, and so since the conquered peoples of Africa and the Americas were less than human, they were unable to attain the status of the I. Consequently, they did not think. And unable to complete the second half of the proposition, they were denied being. *I do not think therefore I am not* (Maldonado-Torres 252). Consequently, as Linda Alcoff notes, "the progressivist teleology of Europe which sanctions its expansion by a belief in its own superiority is not the natural by-product of a culture on the rise but the result of false narratives, occluded histories, burned books, and murdered scholars" (60).

What of the knowledges of the Maya, the Aymara, the Quechua, and the Nahuatl, whose languages, civilizations, and subjectivities supply a multitude of cosmovisions and different approaches to perceiving our relations with nature and each other to which the rest of the world is oblivious? Burned books and murdered scholars. At this stage, the comments that I made in my opening paragraph, that we need to follow Fanon in that the decolonial project is a struggle that belongs to "les damnés," should now be seen as an ethical imperative.

Concerning our own intellectual contributions, the decolonial project pursues the disclosing of plural modes of being, feeling, thinking, and living that come from traditions that have been struggling for air since the onset of the totalizing narratives of modernist discourse. We have already seen several examples of building pluriversal possibilities in the case studies of the Zapatistas, *buen vivir*, our reflections on temporality, the CONAIE movement, and so on. One possible avenue is to follow the same process of unattaching oneself from the totalizing discourse of colonial narratives and to look for the "fissures and cracks" that open multiple and plural epistemologies and ontologies. Delinking and then relinking would require a shift in perspective that would take the Western false value of "universal personhood and humanity" and convert it to "pluriversal personhood and humanity," so that what is heard when we attend and listen to the sounds coming up from the cracks and fissures is that the occluded worlds are resurging, and there are many. While driven by their own local self-definitions, they share the common purpose in their own self-validation, their dignity, and their mutual support. The role of the intellectual is *pregutando caminamos,* asking we walk: to unlearn, to listen, to relearn, and maybe, to teach again.

Works Cited

Acosta, Alberto. "Extractivism and Neoextractivism: Two Sides of the Same Curse." *Beyond Development Alternative Visions from Latin America,* edited by Miriam Lang and Dunia Mokrani, translated by Sara Shields and Rosemary Underhay, Fundación Rosa Luxemborg, 2011, pp. 61–86.

Alcoff, Linda Martín. "Philosophy, the Conquest, and the Meaning of Modernity." *Human Architecture: Journal of the Sociology of Self-Knowledge,* vol. 11, no. 1, Fall 2013, pp. 57–66.

Becker, Marc. *Pachakutik: Indigenous Movements and Electoral Politics in Ecuador.* Rowman & Littlefield, 2012.

Bolter, Jay David, and Richard Grusin. *Remediation: Understanding New Media.* MIT P, 1999.

Braidotti, Rosi. "A Theoretical Framework for the Critical Posthumanities." *Theory, Culture & Society,* May 2018, pp. 1–31.

Clavo, María Íñigo. "Conversation with Aura Cumes on Maya Epistemology, Postcolonial Theory and the Struggle for Identity." *Re-Visiones,* no. 7, Dec. 2017. *re-visiones.net,* http://re-visiones.net/index.php/RE-VISIONES/article/view/239.

Coulthard, Glen Sean. *Red Skin, White Masks: Rejecting the Colonial Politics of Recognition.* Langara College, 2017.

de Beauvoir, Simone. *The Second Sex.* Translated by Constance Borde and Sheila Malovany-Chevallier, Vintage Books, 2009.

Dyson, Freeman. *Disturbing the Universe.* Basic Books, 1981.

Escobar, Arturo. "Degrowth, Postdevelopment, and Transitions: A Preliminary Conversation." *Sustainability Science,* vol. 10, no. 3, July 2015, pp. 451–62.

EZLN. *Chiapas: La Palabra De Los Armados De Verdad y Fuego: Entrevistas, Cartas y Comunicados Del EZLN.* Ed. Del Serbal, 1994.

Fanon, Frantz. *The Wretched of the Earth.* Translated by Richard Philcox, Grove Press, 1963.

Foucault, Michel. *The Order of Things.* Vintage Books, 1970.

Gudynas, Eduardo. "Buen Vivir: Today's Tomorrow." *Development,* vol. 54, no. 4, Dec. 2011, pp. 441–47. https://doi.org/10.1057/dev.2011.86.

Haraway, Donna Jeanne. *Simians, Cyborgs, and Women: The Reinvention of Nature.* Routledge, 1991.

Hayles, N. Katherine. *How We Became Posthuman: Virtual Bodies in Cybernetics, Literature, and Informatics.* U of Chicago P, 1999.

Heidegger, Martin. *Basic Writings: Ten Key Essays, Plus the Introduction to Being and Time.* Edited by David Farrell Krell, HarperCollins, 1993.

Higgins, Nicholas. "The Zapatista Uprising and the Poetics of Cultural Resistance." *Alternatives: Global, Local, Political,* vol. 25, no. 3, 2000, pp. 359–74.

Hodgson, Justin. *Post-Digital Rhetoric and the New Aesthetic.* The Ohio State UP, 2019.

Holloway, John. *Change the World without Taking Power: The Meaning of Revolution Today.* Pluto Press, 2019.

———. "Zapatismo." *John Holloway,* 30 July 2011, www.johnholloway.com.mx/2011/07/30/zapatismo/.

Jackson, Zakiyyah Iman. "Animal: New Directions in the Theorization of Race and Posthumanism." *Feminist Studies,* edited by Kalpana Rahita Seshadri et al , vol. 39, no. 3, 2013, pp. 669–85.

Kittler, Friedrich A. *Gramophone, Film, Typewriter.* Translated by Geoffrey Winthrop-Young and Michael Wutz, Stanford UP, 1999.

Kroker, Arthur, and Marilouise Kroker. *Hacking the Future: Stories for the Flesh-Eating 90s.* New World Perspectives, Montreal, 1996.

Latour, Bruno. *We Have Never Been Modern.* Harvard UP, 1993.

MacNeill, Timothy. *Indigenous Cultures and Sustainable Development in Latin America.* Palgrave, 2020.

Major Ana María. *Chiapas 3—Discurso Inaugural de La Mayor Ana María.* https://chiapas.iiec.unam.mx/No3/ch3anamaria.html. Accessed 14 Oct. 2019.

Maldonado-Torres, Nelson. "On the Coloniality of Being: Contributions to the Development of a Concept." *Cultural Studies,* vol. 21, nos. 2–3, Mar. 2007, pp. 240–70.

Marcos, Subcomandante. "Comunicado del Comité Clandestino Revolucionario Indígena-Comandancia General del Ejército Zapatista De Liberación Nacional del 21 de diciembre del 2012." http://enlacezapatista.ezln.org.mx/2012/12/21/comunicado-del-comite-clandestino-revolucionario-indigena-comandancia-general-del-ejercito-zapatista-de-liberacion-nacional-del-21-de-diciembre-del-2012/. Accessed 26 Apr. 2021.

Mignolo, Walter D. "Delinking: The Rhetoric of Modernity, the Logic of Coloniality and the Grammar of de-Coloniality." *Cultural Studies,* vol. 21, no. 2–3, Mar. 2007, pp. 449–514.

———. "The Zapatista's Theoretical Revolution: Its Historical, Ethical, and Political Consequences." *Review (Fernand Braudel Center),* vol. 25, no. 3, 2002, pp. 245–75.

Mignolo, Walter D., and Catherine E. Walsh. *On Decoloniality: Concepts, Analytics, and Praxis.* Duke UP, 2018.

Quijano, Aníbal (2000). "Coloniality of Power, Eurocentrism, and Latin America." *Nepantla: Views from the South,* vol. 1, no. 3, 2000, pp. 533–80.

Quijano Aníbal, et al. *Aníbal Quijano: Textos De fundación.* Ediciones Del Signo, 2019.

Rickert, Thomas. *Ambient Rhetoric: The Attunements of Rhetorical Being.* U of Pittsburgh P, 2013.

Schulz, Karsten A. "Decolonizing Political Ecology: Ontology, Technology and 'Critical' Enchantment." *Journal of Political Ecology,* vol. 24, no. 1, Sept. 2017, pp. 125–43. https://doi.org/10.2458/v24i1.20789.

Sharp, Hasana. *Spinoza and the Politics of Renaturalization.* U of Chicago P, 2011.

Sherrif, Lucy. "Colombia: Dying of Thirst, Wayuu Blame Mine, Dam, Drought for Water Woes." *Mongabay Environmental News,* 1 Nov. 2018, https://bit.ly/3dvd9hu.

Solón, Pablo. "Is Vivir Bien Possible? Candid Thoughts about Systemic Alternatives." *Links International Journal of Socialist Renewal,* 30 Sept. 2016, links.org.au/pablo-solon-vivir-bien-beyond-capitalism-development.

———. "Pablo Solon on 'Vivir Bien': Going beyond Capitalism?" Translated by Richard Filder. *Links International Journal of Socialist Renewal,* Sept. 2016, links.org.au/pablo-solon-vivir-bien-beyond-capitalism-development.

Thiong'o, Ngũgĩ wa. *Devil on the Cross.* Penguin Books, 2017.

Vitanza, Victor J., editor. *CyberReader.* Pearson Longman, 1996.

Wynter, Sylvia. "Unsettling the Coloniality of Being/Power/Truth/Freedom: Towards the Human, After Man, Its Overrepresentation—An Argument." *CR: The New Centennial Review,* vol. 3, no. 3, 2003, pp. 257–337.

Yashar, Deborah J. "Contesting Citizenship: Indigenous Movements and Democracy in Latin America." *Comparative Politics,* vol. 31, no. 1, Oct. 1998, pp. 23–42. https://doi.org/10.2307/422104.

Zembylas, Michalinos. "The Entanglement of Decolonial and Posthuman Perspectives: Tensions and Implications for Curriculum and Pedagogy in Higher Education." *Parallax,* vol. 24, no. 3, July 2018, pp. 254–67.

CHAPTER 2

Performing Complex Recognitions

(De)Colonial (Mis)Recognitions as Systemic Revision

KELLY MEDINA-LÓPEZ AND KELLIE SHARP-HOSKINS

It was spring 2014. Kellie was a second-semester tenure-track faculty member and Kelly a second-year doctoral student at New Mexico State University (NMSU). Kelly's doctoral coursework was nearly over, and comprehensive exams loomed in her future. She nervously set an appointment with Kellie with one goal in mind: convince her to be her doctoral advisor. Perhaps it was something to do with being *tocayas,*[1] but during that meeting Kelly and Kellie found that they shared interests and commitments adequate to justify mentoring: "But let's keep this on the down-low for now?" Kellie said, alluding to her misgivings about her preparedness to advise a student when she was only one year out of graduate school herself. "Absolutely," Kelly replied, exposing her suspicions about a field in which she didn't see herself represented. The following fall, the *tocayas* submitted the departmental paperwork that made their advising relationship official, and Kelly began the process of drafting exam reading lists for review and approval by Kellie. Kelly drew on coursework and training to create lists that reflected rough shapes of rhetoric and composition as it had been presented to her. She was not particularly energized by the lists, but that did not seem to be the point of comprehensive exams, anyway. She

1. Spanish for "namesake," although without the same connotations as one who is named for another and instead meaning two friends who share the same name. *Tocayo/a/x* is commonly used as a friendly greeting, nickname, or term of friendship: "Hola tocaya!" or "Conoces a mi tocaya?"

was proving that she was in the field and could be recognized as such. Kellie also recognized the field as represented by the lists (dominated by a narrowly defined Western canon) and questioned her own participation in corroborating it through courses she had taught the previous year. She did not, however, recognize Kelly in the lists. She saw none of Kelly's research commitments to Chicanx epistemologies or decolonial methodologies reflected but, instead, pages and pages of bibliographic entries that Kellie knew Kelly to be wary of. Although they were nominally comprehensive, Kellie did not just want Kelly to go through the motions of the exams but to search out the scholarship in which she would recognize herself and feel seen and heard by the field, not despite, but because of her history, identity, and ethics. With some training in decolonial theories but without a strong background in Chicanx rhetorics specifically, Kellie nonetheless knew they existed in the field. And so began the process of Kellie mentoring Kelly to look for the scholars and scholarship that affirmed her sense of place in the field. Without denying the pull of the canon or the disciplinary politics that prioritize it, Kellie encouraged Kelly to find the scholarship in which she would recognize herself, see her values being reflected, and feel seen.

A little over three years later (and now in her first semester of her own tenure-track job at California State University, Monterey Bay—CSUMB), Kelly was approached by one of her students about the academic options narrated to her (by the course catalog and academic advisors) as the right fit for her research interests: Chicanx studies classes.[2] "The Chicanx studies classes are frustrating," Itzel said, pausing to gauge Kelly's body language; "I appreciate the message, but I'm an Indigenous Maya Guatemalan. They don't have any classes for us. We can minor in Chicanx studies but that doesn't really help me do what I want to do." Kelly, who had unproblematically called herself a Chicana ever since her dad explained the term while hanging the United Field Worker's flag in the living room, nonetheless understood this as misrecognition—Itzel's research interests were (mis)recognized as her name, language, history, and body were interpreted in institutional terms, and Chicanx itself was (mis)recognized as a catchall for relations among the Americas. "I can see that," Kelly said, and then with less certainty, "What should we do about it?" "That's why I'm here." Itzel grabbed a handwritten list from her bag. "These are the grad schools I'm applying to." After reviewing the list together, Kelly had a question: "Itzel, why these schools? Some of them don't really match with your interests so much?" Itzel already had an answer: "Because if I say I

2. Itzel is a pseudonym. This story is shared with her permission.

went to these schools people will pay more attention to me. They'll think I'm smart. They'll listen."

Kelly understood Itzel's critique of Chicanx studies as a field and followed the logic of her solution—she sought to change the terms of recognitions by participating in their formulation as vetted, as an expert. This was, after all, how Kelly had been mentored and how she was redressing recognition politics in her own field, (un)settling its terms and (un)settling its limits by participating in it (as a professor, as a researcher, as a teacher, as a mentor). But the idea that Itzel's contribution to such terms and limits could only come *after* she had been vetted didn't seem to hold up. After all, Itzel's frustration itself was already changing how Kelly thought about and talked about Chicanx studies (especially in relation to her campus and its specific history). Not only as a politically inclusive, progressive term for a coalition of identities, histories, and projects, but—and simultaneously—an institutional term capable of overwriting difference. It was changing how she thought about and talked about academic choices. It was changing the questions she asked Itzel and other students: What seemed to be given? In which spaces did they find fit? And crucially, where was there misfit? The misrecognition was thus not merely shoring up the boundaries of recognition, but shifting its terms, changing its politics.

We begin with these brief stories from our shared history to center the complicated rhetorical function of recognition that shapes and constrains possibilities for mentoring, which necessarily invokes the politics of seeing and being seen. As we argue in this chapter, these politics are not confined only to issues of individual or institutional power (i.e., where an academic mentor structurally exerts more power than her mentee), but traffic with larger material histories of bodies, knowledges, and spaces and how they can be recognized—or not—within institutional, department, disciplinary, cultural, and colonial discourses. Mentoring someone to be seen by or to recognize themselves as participants in (even when critics of) an academic conversation requires negotiating boundaries of acceptability, whether they are marked explicitly or not. Framed in this way, mentoring recognition is a name for how one individual (an advisor, for example) gives advice to another (an advisee), narrating terms of materiality (how concepts, methods, scholarship, and even scholars themselves come to matter in the field). And indeed, as reflected in our opening stories, mentoring is often conceptualized as individual, intentional, and directional, moving from one person to another. But our story also surfaces the problematics of mentoring based on recognition, wherein assumptions about identities, commitments, and goals can overwrite the complexity of the system in which recognition emerges.

As a rejoinder to mentoring recognition, in this chapter we propose performing complex recognitions as a methodology capable of acknowledging differential bodies (human and nonhuman) and practices that disrupts closed loops (of recognition) by invoking the revisionary potential of decolonial misrecognitions as part of systemic revision. Important to our contribution to a collection on decolonial conversations in posthuman and new materialist rhetorics, we seek a rhetorical methodology capable of intervening in the directionality of recognition in order to shift possibilities for its uses. More specifically, we consider how bringing complex, systemic thinking (Jung; Mays; Gómez-Barris) into conversation with social and cultural theories that challenge the boundaries of the colonial imagination (Haas; Ríos; Sandoval) can facilitate a more robust decolonial ethics of recognition, where colonial expectations of reciprocity and directionality are radically (re)contextualized in terms of their emergence in complex historical and material relations. Predicating our understanding of theories of complexity on a belief that complex systems are neither discrete nor fixed (Connolly) but rather always (even when not acknowledged as such) in conversation with theories of oppositional consciousness (Sandoval), we argue for a more complex understanding of recognition that does not preexist or supersede relations but emerges as the effect of "fluctuating influences," co-constituted within systems, and "affect[ing] and affected by" all other elements in the system (Sandoval 77). Understanding recognition in this way means we can pay attention not only to who is recognized and by whom—as if recognition merely exists and can be practiced or not—but to *how* it emerges within geopolitical, sociocultural, and materio-discursive relations.

With this stated goal, we also acknowledge the limitations of claiming a "decolonial ethics" for our work, attuned to the risk of using decolonization as an ambiguous metaphor for social justice or settler futurity (Tuck and Yang 2). Specifically, we acknowledge that our argument can easily function as what Eve Tuck and K. Wayne Yang refer to as "colonial equivocation," which "gesture[s] towards Indigenous people without addressing Indigenous sovereignty or rights, or forward[s] a thesis on decolonization without regard to unsettling/deoccupying land" (19). In place of vague equations or abstractions, we propose that a more complex articulation of recognition fundamentally and materially impacts and intervenes in whose and how bodies settle, unsettle, occupy, and deoccupy land. Similarly, and in this collection, Robert Lestón argues for a more complex understanding of decoloniality that reaches past a theoretical flattening of decoloniality as simply an area for research, academic trend, theoretical movement, discipline, or critique, but rather more robustly articulated as "the struggle" of the colonized. Following Tuck and Yang and

Lestón, we extend and leverage our understanding of decoloniality and the project of decolonization to account for the material realities of colonized bodies and lands and "the struggle" to unsettle and deoccupy. Further, and in tandem, we guide our decolonial ethics following Linda Tuhiwai Smith, who asserts that while "questions of imperialism and the effects of colonization may seem to be merely academic . . . sheer physical survival is more pressing" (4), and we thus apply this methodology to cases of mentoring, where the stakes determine who is allowed to survive (in) the academy and how they must do so.

We begin this work with a review of scholarship on recognition that acknowledges its complications and theoretically grounds our proposed methodology before situating it in more complex, material terms. More than providing simple scholarly context, this review synthesizes interdisciplinary Indigenous, decolonial, new materialist, and rhetorical systems scholarship to build a methodology adequate to the complexity of systemic revision. While not all of these theories are always gathered under the explicit rubric of complexity, we propose that complexity rhetorics as theorized in the West have too often been disarticulated from the complex thinking that characterizes Indigenous epistemologies and decolonial projects. By drawing disparate voices together, however, we offer a methodology capable of accounting for and intervening in the complexity of recognition, broadly conceived. Thereafter, to demonstrate the affordances of this methodology, we return to our stories above, foregrounding the decolonial possibilities of the *mis*recognitions always already at work. When such misrecognitions are understood in complex relation with their conditions of emergence, we argue, we can shift possibilities for recognition itself, radically decolonizing its institutional function. Performing complex recognitions, we show, productively collates scholarship from Indigenous, decolonial, and Western traditions to disarticulate recognition from its conceptual basis in individual volition, reciprocity, or directional causality and reimagine its function as emerging in (complex) relations of land, bodies, and colonization.

Recognition Matters

Discussions of recognition politics, which have been central to many recent explorations of racial violence, racial justice, human rights, and Indigenous survivance, leave us with a complicated understanding of the intersectional and juridical powers of recognition. In one articulation, recognition is a vehicle for social action, a forced witnessing of the invisible power structures that predetermine lived realities. Given this understanding, recognition for the rights and sovereignty of people is paramount to their social, cultural, and material livability (Taylor), and thus "charged with emancipatory promise" (Fraser). Accordingly, Glen Sean Coulthard acknowledges that "the struggle for recognition has become a central catalyst in the international Indigenous rights movement" (2). Demands for political, juridical, and economic recognition come in the context of the historical and ongoing violence that subtends misrecognition—that is, when the lives, bodies, experiences, and knowledges of Indigenous peoples are elided, discounted, or appropriated in service to ongoing colonization. As Kelly Oliver argues, "recognition is a matter of seeing. The stakes are precisely the unseen in vision—the process through which something is seen or not seen" (*Witnessing* 158). And the stakes of being seen—or not—could not be higher, including human rights (Hesford, *Spectacular*), grievability (Butler), and survivance itself (Powell).

From another perspective, however, recognition is itself a predetermining structure, a sociopolitical tool that limits the power of marginalized groups by setting terms of recognizability and replacing equity with simple inclusion (Ahmed, *On Being*). Accordingly, Coulthard's account of First Nations peoples' demands for recognition gives way to a radical critique of its adequacy to "transform the colonial relationship between Indigenous people and the . . . state" (3). Grounded in the "ideal of *reciprocity* or *mutual* recognition," Coulthard critiques recognition in "its contemporary liberal form [which] promises to reproduce the very configurations of colonialist, racist, patriarchal state power that Indigenous peoples' demands for recognition have historically sought to transcend" (3). When framed through Ahmed and Coulthard as a predetermining structure of inclusion or mutual reciprocity, recognition emerges as a project in commensurability, a colonial relationship that aims to measure Indigenous and settler peoples by Western metrics of visibility, legibility, and livability.

Indeed, scholars from Charles Taylor to Nancy Fraser to Judith Butler provide liberal genealogies of recognition that begin with Hegel, who, according to Butler, "requires that each partner in the exchange recognize not only that the other needs and deserves recognition, but also that each, in a different way, is compelled by the same need, the same requirement" (44). While Fraser critiques conceptualizations of recognition articulated in individual terms, then, and Butler seeks accounts of differential recognition, both nonetheless engage its Western Hegelian tradition of individual reciprocity and a politics of commensurability. As Butler argues explicitly in *Precarious Life,* "we are not separate identities in the struggle for recognition but are already involved in a reciprocal exchange" (44).

Contra the Hegelian tradition of recognition, Coulthard draws on the work of Frantz Fanon to reject its formulation in terms of "freedom and dignity for the colonized," and asserts recognition "*as the field of power through which colonial relations are produced and maintained*" (Coulthard 17). Indeed, as Fanon writes of the effect of colonial recognition on the consciousness of Black men in *Black Skin, White Masks,* "The environment has shaped him . . . has torn him apart" (190). To understand this conceptualization, we can also turn to Aníbal Quijano's theory of *colonialidad del poder,* or the "colonial matrix of power." Building on Quijano, Walter Mignolo theorizes the colonial matrix of power as operating through the unified work of the rhetoric of modernity and the logic of coloniality, where "one is constantly named and celebrated (progress, development, growth) and the other silenced or named as problems to be solved by the former (poverty, misery, inequities, corruption, commodification, and dispensability of human life)" (vxiii). This naming work creates visibility and value for some at the expense of others, allocating recognition through its "racial and patriarchal foundation of knowledge," which controls economy, authority, gender and sexuality, and knowledge and subjectivity writ large (8). Although Mignolo doesn't specify recognition as the modus operandi of the matrix, its very figure suggests a framework through which recognition is bestowed. And indeed, it is this directional work of recognition, in which it is bestowed rather than exchanged, that reveals the inadequacy of imagining recognition as reciprocity. Figured as reciprocity, an ethics of commensurability predicated on Western ideologies of modernity and progress overlooks the coloniality of power in which settlers will always broker the criteria by which colonized peoples are expected to become visible and legible. Or, as Wendy Hesford puts it, "recognition affords legibility to certain bodies and social relationships and not to others" ("Surviving" 539).

Whereas the scholarship cited above considers the effects of equating recognition with visibility and legibility within a colonial matrix of power, Kelly Oliver attends to the "affects of oppression" more explicitly to account for the role of recognition in *The Colonization of Psychic Space* (87). Building on Fanon, she asserts that "the need for recognition from the colonizer is a symptom of the pathology of colonization. . . . The colonized suffer from an obsession with gaining love and recognition from the harsh dominators" (53). For Oliver, affect is at once social and psychological and she thus characterizes its function in terms of "psychic infection" through which "colonial affects are deposited in the bodies of the colonized at the same time that the colonial prohibitions against affect infect them" (*Colonization* 59). Primarily theorized through psychoanalytic and social theories, Oliver's work alerts us to the importance of affect to understanding the relationships between colonization and recognition. What Butler might call the "scenes of address" of recognition thus include, following Oliver, the materiality, energy, and resonance of affect. Infection, in other words, is not only a useful metaphor for the linguistic or psychological work of affect to distribute (or withhold) recognition but might also be understood to characterize *how* affect travels: circulating materially between bodies and through the air, landing unequally on the inoculated and predisposed.

Considering the role that affect plays in recognition corroborates the inadequacy of conceptualizing recognition-as-reciprocity, grounded, as discussed above, in visibility. Writing from a feminist new materialist understanding of affect—where affect does not "stand[] apart or ha[ve] autonomy . . . [but] begin[s] with the messiness of the experiential, the unfolding of bodies into worlds, and the drama of contingency, how we are touched by what we are near" (Ahmed, "Happy" 31)—Sara Ahmed demonstrates as much in her study of the politics of recognition at play when institutions conduct diversity work. She contends that the hypervisibility of people of color showing up in an institutional "sea of whiteness" does not guarantee equitable participation or valuation by institutions. Rather, affective orientations frame expectations of who will "show up" as well as how they can do so. In institutional spaces, she explains, "whiteness is produced as a host, as that which is already in place or at home" (*On Being* 43). This requires paradoxical performances of people of color: to simultaneously embody "diversity" (through hypervisibility) without disrupting the affective milieu of the institution. In Ahmed's words, "If whiteness is what the institution is oriented around, then even bodies that do not appear white still have to inhabit whiteness" (41). Or, as she explains elsewhere, "bodies do not arrive in neutral . . . *how* we arrive, *how* we enter this room or that room, will affect what impressions we receive" ("Happy" 36, 37; emphasis added).

This phenomenon is well documented by Angela Mae Kupenda in her contribution to *Presumed Incompetent,* as she recounts an early career scolding at an annual review, during which her white male administrator called her out for being "too private," ultimately yelling, "You must trust us more if you want to succeed here; there are no spooks behind the door!" (20). Followed up by stories that revealed invitations and demands for Kupenda to smile more, to be more likeable, to change grades of students, to support gender parity but not discuss racial equity, and to dismiss experiences of explicit racism, this insistence on trust confirms not only the directionality of expectation and recognition but its fundamental ties to affect. As evidenced by this case, Kupenda is only measured, can only be recognized, when she acquiesces to the demands of commensurability, when her hypervisibility is made more affectively palatable through practices of self-styling that include smiling, silence, and submission.

Drawing affect into an account of the colonial matrix of power (as precipitated by Fanon, tacitly explored by Oliver and Ahmed, and documented by Kupenda) contextualizes the function of racial and patriarchal knowledge in creating expectations for who will show up, how they must do so, and what will be expected of them on arrival. Colonial recognitions depend not only on visibility, but on a more complex sense of fit or fitness (see Dingo): Bodies are recognizable when they fit affective expectations. In the colonial matrix of power, these affective expectations are the criteria that settlers broker, the metric that measures nonwhite bodies as (in)commensurate with white bodies. As Ahmed explains, "In this sense recognition produces rather than simply finds its object; recognition produces the boundaries of what it recognizes as given" (*On Being* 45). Or, as put by Indigenous rhetorician Scott Lyons: "He who sets the terms sets the limits" (452).

Toward a More Complex Recognition

As suggested by our brief review, far from a simple issue of visibility or reciprocity, recognition is entangled in complex social, material, and affective relations that create expectations for which and how bodies emerge as sayable, legible, measurable, and livable. To intervene in recognition politics—the reproduction of specific forms of knowing, living, and being at the expense of others—thus requires attention to complexity and its participation in boundary-making. That is, as Ahmed reveals, the boundaries that attend recognition are not merely negative, and neither do they preexist relations. Rather, boundaries make recognition possible, a claim that resonates with accounts of complexity that might disarticulate recognition from its simple, directional premises. To clarify, we do not seek to resuscitate or depoliticize colonial recognition but want to consider why, how, and to what end we might leverage its complexity to practice a decolonial ethics.

With precedents in the field much earlier, in the last two decades complexity has emerged explicitly in rhetoric and composition studies to counter what Jenny Edbauer calls its "elemental frameworks" (5), in which discrete elements ground the theories, methodologies, and methods of the field at the expense of acknowledging their interrelations (see, for example, Cooper; Hawk; Jung; Mays; Rice; Yood). Whereas elemental frameworks foreground "linear causality" (DeLanda) or "efficient causality" (Connolly 179)—where preexisting elements (people, objects, belief systems, etc.) collide to create effects—complexity theories consider "emergent causality" as better suited to describe how "new forces can trigger novel patterns of *self-organization* in a thing, species, system or being, sometimes allowing something new to emerge from the swirl back and forth between them: a new species, state of the universe, weather system, ecological balance, or political formation" (Connolly 179–80).

Following this trend in the field (and interdisciplinary posthumanisms more broadly conceived) to engage complexity, we argue it as distinct from difficulty, intricacy, or complication and better understood to characterize systems that emerge in relation to their environments and self-organize in unpredictable ways. The conceptual affordance of this particular definition is significant to our project: By naming relations as complex and emergent, we can reimagine how the boundaries of recognition emerge and, importantly, how they might emerge differently. Whereas a Hegelian tradition flattens and individuates recognition, figuring it as an act that exists directionally between people, cultures, or nations, a more complex articulation suggests that it emerges and gets marked in relation or, to put a finer point on it, in complex relations. Julie Jung's articulation of systems rhetoric helps us delineate between simple, countable, or causal relations and complex relations. Discussing complexity as represented by second-order systems theory, she explains, "A complex system cannot be understood by reducing it to its component parts, since it's the *interaction* among parts and not the sum of their individual properties that produces macrolevel behaviors attributable to the system as a whole." This is corroborated by Chris Mays's articulation of rhetoric systems, where "every movement of one of the [system's] elements affects and is affected by all of the others, and each of these linkages contributes to the stability of the whole."

As stated, and cited, these definitions draw on and invoke a specific tradition of complexity and emergence in the West (for a helpful overview, see DeLanda; Hayles). But non-Western and decolonial rhetorics of complexity, we argue, offer yet more opportunities to move toward the robust configuration of complexity that we seek to employ. Macarena Gómez-Barris, for example, uses a decolonial femme methodology focused through Andean phenomenology to theorize the role of complexity in shifting trajectories of activist work in what she names "extractive zones," or majority Indigenous regions in South America with capitalistic histories of extraction and exploitation of natural resources. Central to her argument, Gómez-Barris analyzes "the complexity of social ecologies and material alternatives proposed and proliferated by artists, activists, movements, submerged theorists, and cultural producers" in relationship to the subtle, entrenched capitalism that allows exploitation and extraction to continue (xv). Juxtaposing "subtle capitalism" against complex activisms, she substantiates the "importance of epistemological autonomy and embodied knowledge as necessary to pushing away from a paradigm of mere resistance into the more layered terrain of potential" (xv). Leveraging complexity through non-Western terms allows Gómez-Barris to "[abandon] the epistemology of measure for something much more tenuous, reaching toward addressing the complexity and entanglements of potential" (11).

Resonating with the concept of emergent causality and its uptake in systems and complexity rhetorics, Gómez-Barris's work shifts our attention away from preexisting elements of reciprocity and recognition and toward "novel [patterns] of *self-organization*" (Connolly). But her work likewise calls attention to what Santiago Castro-Gómez calls the "*hubris of the zero point*" of posthumanisms: an epistemological orientation toward detachment or neutrality that haunts Western articulations of how meaning is produced and reproduced. That is, although Western systems scholars conceptually reject "zero points," they often discount the "importance of epistemological autonomy and embodied knowledge" (xv) and unwittingly reinscribe commensurate, neat, and measurable Western standards of recognition. By considering complexity in Gómez-Barris's terms, however, we are better able to account for the incommensurate: the places where bodies and epistemologies are not bounded by discrete, predetermined settler criteria of visibility and legibility, but instead allow a "novel [pattern] of *self-organization*" to emerge that does not resettle settler futurity but rather unsettles possibilities for pluriversal futures (see also Lestón, this volume). This is particularly true when Western theories of complexity in complex systems are brought into conversation with the social and cultural theories that emerge in/with/from Indigenous epistemologies and decolonial projects.

In addition to drawing on the conceptual affordance of complexity as theorized in complex systems, and in line with Gómez-Barris, we also characterize as complex the social and cultural theories that direct attention away from simple, even when multidirectional, causality or discrete, existing contexts and features and toward the conditions of possibility that allow such to emerge and be marked accordingly, affirming that complexity rhetorics as theorized in the West have too often been disarticulated from the complex thinking that characterizes Indigenous epistemologies and decolonial projects. Angela M. Haas demonstrates this phenomenon as she identifies "Wampum as Hypertext"—a sophisticated, multimedia technology overlooked in the colonial imagination. In the specific case of posthumanist rhetorics, Gabriela Raquel Ríos argues that the field has yet to contend with the complexities of Indigenous relationality even as it pursues ecologically motivated projects. For Ríos, "Indigenous relationality recognizes that humans and the environment are in a relationship that is co-constituted and not just interdependent. Additionally, Indigenous relationality recognizes the environment's capacity to *produce* relations" (64). Despite the conceptual resonances between her work and that of systems rhetoric, Ríos reminds us of a critical difference: "This Indigenous concept relies on a relational ontology at the level of *kinship* quite literally" (64).

Explicitly citing Ríos's work in introduction to their collection on *Feminist Rhetorical Science Studies,* Amanda K. Booher and Julie Jung remind us that "the fact that human and nonhuman animals, objects, and lands are enmeshed is not a recent Western 'discovery'" (7). This disarticulation and misrecognition can be understood more broadly in terms of what Chela Sandoval calls "intellectual apartheid," wherein Western cultural theories emerge in complex, unacknowledged relation to theories of oppositional consciousness articulated by women of color (78). By following Gómez-Barris, Haas, Ríos, and Sandoval to posit a multivalent genealogy of complexity, we propose that we can (re)consider recognition, drawing out its implication in complex colonial politics of reciprocity more explicitly.

Emerging from different traditions, these perspectives each emphasize the interactions and movements that sponsor emergence of and give definition to discrete elements within a complex system, a perspective that resonates with what Sandoval calls rearrangement and reformatting. In *Methodology of the Oppressed,* she explains how the possibility of positioning power hinges on "constant rearrangement" of paradigmatic and syntagmatic dimensions in which "subjectivity is continually redetermined by the fluctuating influences and those powers that surround and traverse us" (77). She continues, "It is in the shifting conjuncture between the paradigmatic and the syntagmatic that new combinatorials emerge, through an ongoing form of semiotic life reading that places the subject differentially inside power" (77). We propose that collating Sandoval's claim with the definitions of complexity and relationality offered by Jung, Mays, Haas, Ríos, and Gómez-Barris offers a more complex understanding of recognition, one that emerges at the "shifting conjuncture" of "fluctuating influences" and is "affect[ing] and affected by" all other elements in the system (Sandoval 77). This allows us to move past simple conceptualizations of recognition that only consider it as a practice of mutual reciprocity, legibility, or commensurability, and instead to theorize how recognition emerges within incommensurate geopolitical, sociocultural, and materio-discursive relations.

Understanding recognition in these complex terms also means we can reconsider misrecognition, which, as an effect of what its dictionary definition refers to as a case of mistaken identity ("Misrecognition"), functions as "social subordination" by "put[ting] moral pressure on individual members to conform to a given group culture" (Fraser). Contra an identity-based model of recognition (which Fraser herself contests), a complex model of recognition makes space to imagine how—and with what effects—misrecognitions participate in the conditions of possibility of recognition as well as the conditions of its revision. In a complex model, as Mays argues, even systems that seem stuck (immune to outside influences) must nonetheless account for, through internal reorganization and adjustment, perturbations. Likewise, misrecognitions stand to provoke systemic revision: perturbing the frames of vision and legibility by "mistaking" identity, missing their mark.

As we return to our opening stories below, we argue that a complex understanding of misrecognitions, which corroborate, assume, and assert ("mistaken") identities through the colonial matrix of power, might be leveraged to identify and shift decolonial possibilities for (de)occupying institutions. As Ahmed and Kupenda attest, this work is not without differential effects, and the changes it provokes are not guaranteed to move toward positive outcomes. But performing complex recognitions, we argue, calls attention to how land has been and continues to be occupied, whose and how bodies show up there, and how we might unsettle expectations for who and what is given.

Mentoring Misrecognition

To illustrate how we see performing complex recognitions as holding revisionary potential to direct attention away from sovereign, human agents who bestow recognition and to dramatize a broader range of relations and bodies that contribute to (de)colonial (mis)recognitions, we return to our stories of mentoring. Like in our stories, academic mentoring is often narrated as an individual relationship of trust and care (a narrative we value) predicated on directional recognitions, where mentors are entrusted to articulate how mentees can become recognizable, demonstrating their fit (or, Rebecca Dingo might say, fitness) within an institution or field. Mentoring recognition, then, operates from elemental premises, precluding accounts of how such elements emerged and became recognizable. Moreover, the focus on the future—how mentees can demonstrate fit and recognizability—is yoked to a stable and continuous articulation of the past: Who and what have been recognizable set the terms (and limits) for who and what can be recognizable. Holding these complicated intersections of past, present, and futurity in mind, we consider mentoring in more complex terms, accounting for how misrecognitions might participate in who becomes given and how they do so.

Performing complex recognitions considers how recognizability (or fitness) emerges by attending to the relations that produce it, including material relations between land and bodies that come to occupy institutional spaces.

Focusing on occupation, on the land that our institutions settle, mobilizes decolonization not as metaphor (Tuck and Yang), but as a politics of unsettling. That is, performing complex recognitions requires us to ask what histories of settling, unsettling, occupying, and deoccupying give way to the current geographies of our institutional spaces, and how those geographies and histories materialize as bodies in our classrooms.

To demonstrate the affordances of this methodology, we return to our opening stories of mentoring and (re)considering the institutions and land from which they emerged. Both NMSU and CSUMB share political histories as settler institutions. Like many US colleges and universities, NMSU—which occupies the ancestral lands of the Manso and traditional lands of the Piro–Manso–Tiwa and the Mescalero and Chiricahua Apache peoples—is a land-grant institution, meaning the US federal government gifted land to what was then the territory of New Mexico to establish a university to meet the changing workforce demands of the industrial revolution (New Mexico State University). CSUMB, although not a land-grant institution, similarly moved from being federal land, Fort Ord Military Base, to public university (California State University, *CSUMB*), occupying the traditional land of the Ohlone people. Key to a decolonial understanding of the emergence of these two institutions is a critical questioning of how and to whom land was assumed (by the US federal government) and bestowed (also by the federal government), and how those similar political histories overwrite tribal sovereignty. Both NMSU and CSUMB, in marking these government-sanctioned settlings of land as their origin point, also settle the terms by which bodies can and do become recognizable in their classrooms.

Thinking through how the colonial histories of settler institutions are predicated on government-afforded (mis)recognitions of the kinds of bodies that can and should materialize in classrooms, we can work toward a more complex understanding of how the colonial matrix of power sets and limits terms of recognizability. These two institutional histories, as specific examples of geographical, material, colonial, and political relations that both produce and limit recognition, also set expectations about whose bodies fit on their campuses. Examining the institutional histories of both NMSU and CSUMB further indicates how these colonial (mis)recognitions allowed for our mentoring experiences to emerge. NMSU, for example, was founded in 1888, when New Mexico was still a territory and negotiating its relationship to the US (largely prompted by the arrival of the railroad in 1879), which placed the land into direct conversation with US imperialism for the first time (after extended contact with Spanish and Mexican imperialism). As Jennifer Ramirez Johnson, Octavio Pimentel, and Charise Pimentel show, New Mexico's close association to imperial Mexico was an obstacle to white settlers looking to exploit the natural resources of the state and bring more white bodies—and capitalism—to the territory (217). Settlers thus embarked on a campaign, largely leveraged through immigration propaganda pamphlets, that articulated New Mexico not as "barren and inhabited by superstitious racial inferiors who were alternately lazy or deadly," as previous white settlers had done (Johnson et al. 217), but as "sleeping, waiting for enterprising Americans to wake her from her slumber so she might give up her resources for their benefit" (Johnson et al. 218).

Understanding NMSU as emerging in this specific historical context of settling land and bodies allows us to see how Kelly, identifying as a fifth-generation New Mexican with Indigenous ancestry, might have also felt hailed to articulate her own relationship to her institution and field in similar colonial terms. As Johnson et al. corroborate, "textual representations of New Mexico reproduce racist constructions of native New Mexicans and represent whiteness as the norm" (212). To be legible, visible, and measurable as a body that *could* graduate with a PhD from NMSU, Kelly felt urged to show her fitness with the white Western canon so as not to be marked as a "superstitious racial [inferior]." Kellie, on the other hand, who is not from New Mexico and whose whiteness circumscribes different relations to its institutions and land, elided this history with her mentoring advice, focusing on how Kelly could *become* (future tense) recognizable within rhetoric and composition studies rather than how NMSU's occupation was already shaping Kelly's work, sponsoring what emerged. She, in effect, settled the institutional land yet again by invoking a disciplinary way of seeing. By attending to this colonial (mis)recognition now, however, and tracking it in complex terms of settler ecological, material, colonial, and political systems, we see opportunities for unsettling the colonial narratives of both the institution and rhetoric and composition, directing attention not just toward who is recognized by whom, but, again, toward how recognition itself emerges.

Kelly and Itzel's story likewise reverberates with colonial histories. Unlike NMSU, with its institutional history longer than New Mexico's statehood, CSUMB is a newer university, founded in 1994. The university emerged after, and as a response to, the civil rights movement and increased scholarship on identity politics of the 1960s to 1990s, particularly diverse peoples of California and, more specifically, the agricultural basin of the Salinas Valley. This is affirmed in the CSUMB "Founding Vision Statement," which commits the campus to "serving the diverse people of California, especially the working class and historically undereducated and low-income populations," and to "multilingual, multicultural, gender-equitable learning." It is further reified by the founding faculty, many of whom are pillars of the Chicanx community: Luis Valdez, father of Teatro Campesino and author of *Zoot Suit*; artist Amalia Mesa-Bains; and Rina Benmayor, testimonialista and founding member of the Latina Feminist Group. The actively Chicanx, social justice roots of CSUMB run parallel to the campus's history as a military base, and as federal land bestowed to the state for the purposes of establishing a university. They allow Chicanx studies to emerge as a legible, legitimate field of study. But they also allow for it to be flattened and normalized as part of the complicated system of recognition—or in Itzel's example, (mis)recognition—that circulates on the campus. In other words, because the campus history is tightly woven together with histories of Chicanx studies, the terms and limits of how bodies become recognizable in the institution are set by material boundaries of whose bodies count as Chicanx. For Itzel, these limits emerged as a (mis)recognition, where the campus was hailed to recognize her in terms of Chicanidad, an identity that doesn't fit.

Itzel's (mis)recognition emerged in relation to the colonial history of the land that CSUMB is settled on as well as Chicanx itself as a settler colonial identity. Indeed, Itzel's institutional (mis)recognition echoes key contemporary conversations in the field of Chicanx studies, where contentious patterns of recognizability and acceptability are rapidly changing. As Nicolás Cruz of the Seattle University chapter of Movimiento Estudiantil Chicano de Aztlán or MEChA (Chicanx studies' oldest student group) wrote in early 2019, "As a political identity, Chicanx doesn't have to be tied to Mexico as a national identity. But what if the historical roots of Aztlán and its use in the Chicanx power movement *are* tied to Mexican nationalism?" (2).

With this question, Cruz directs attention temporarily away from struggles for institutional recognition *of* MEChA and toward the settler colonial and imperial systems of recognition that support and encourage subtle nationalism *by* MEChA, encouraging students like Itzel to feel at once both hailed by the political and theoretical goals of the group and (mis)recognized by its structuring discourse. By analyzing the history of naming Aztlán as the Chicanx homeland, Cruz highlights the term's entanglement with Mexica imperialism that ignores the Indigenous ancestry of those not of Mexica descent from Mexico, Central America, and South America. It is thus Itzel's identification as an Indigenous Mayan Guatemalan that exposes the inability of Chicanx studies to (fully) account for the historic and ongoing relations between (colonized) land and (Indigenous) bodies at CSUMB. But, we argue, it also shifts those very relations—rearranging and reformatting which and how bodies can matter there. In the same way, Cruz's question centers misrecognition as fundamental to rearranging and reformatting colonial recognitions, not as a causal agent with linear effects but as a glitch that creates new combinatorials and new effects.

For Itzel, the early realization that the university wasn't actually the center of all knowledge (as it had been presented), or even adequately prepared to teach students like her (for that matter), allowed her to make more pointed choices about her studies and her future. With Kelly's help, she more carefully planned what classes she would take and figured out how she could make the labor of those classes serve her learning goals on her terms rather than through the terms that were narrated to her. She assumed the role of expert and agent, capable of designing her learning for herself. And she headed to a top graduate program with the same disruptive and revisionary potential, ready, willing, and eager to use her embodied experience as a counterstory not just to her classroom learning but also to the institution itself. In a mentoring relationship ostensibly designed to help Itzel become recognizable, we propose that focusing on this glitch in the system by mentoring misrecognition can itself change the system of recognition. By showing up in a way that wasn't expected, Itzel perturbs recognition and provokes reformulation. New patterns of recognition can emerge, Itzel can experience her relationship to the institution (and her intended field of study) differently, and Itzel and Kelly can better strategize how to move forward in an institution that did not account for her arrival. Not only materially impacting Itzel's relationship to her studies and plans for her future, the named misrecognition also affects patterns of recognition more broadly. Kelly's expectations for who shows up in her classes and how they do so is affected (and affecting). How she identifies and teaches and talks about and writes Chicanx rhetorics are affected (and affecting).

Similarly, the *tocayas* relationship is affected: more attuned to embodied histories in relation to specific land histories and embodiments. Kelly was able to define the field in a way that matched her ways of knowing and being, rather than fitting her scholarly attachments to a narrowly shaped Western canon. This opened a different possible future, which led to a mentoring relationship capable of recognizing Itzel and the misrecognition that was frustrating her studies. Kellie's possibilities for mentoring are affected (and affecting)—not only her expectations for who will show up and how but how she has shown up, and with what effects.

Conclusion(s)

In this chapter, our stories of mentoring reveal the complex recognitions that necessarily limit how bodies emerge in institutional systems. To counter, we offer performing complex recognitions as a methodology that disrupts closed loops of recognition through decolonial misrecognitions, which necessarily perturb systems and sponsor systemic revision. We argue that performing complex recognitions disrupts reifications of colonial group identities, instead encouraging mentoring that leverages misrecognition as a catalyst of emergence to shift the possibilities of recognition itself and decolonize its institutional function. By reframing recognition not as individual volition, reciprocity, or directional causality and instead as part of a complex system that considers land, bodies, and colonization, we shift its possibilities of emergence.

Ultimately, we reject the idea that performing complex recognitions be taken up as reconciling any feelings of settler guilt or rescuing settler futurity (Tuck and Yang). Rather, we adopt an "ethics of incommensurability" (Fanon; Tuck and Yang), where we acknowledge that recognition as reciprocity and reconciliation forecloses on the potential to unsettle institutional systems and ignores the material, land-based goals of decolonization. Instead, we embrace messy and contingent decolonial (mis)recognitions as unsettling and disruptive without bending to settler anxieties about what happens next. To quote Tuck and Yang, "Decolonization is not an 'and.' It is an elsewhere" (36). Our critical mentoring on performing complex recognitions encourages our respective mentees to (re)define that elsewhere for themselves by pushing back against the limits of how they are (mis)recognized by/through/in institutional systems. In other words, we purposefully abandon a recognition that is synonymous with commensurability, and instead embrace one that is purposefully contradictory, uneven, and uncertain to evoke a theory of systemic revision predicated not on settler futures, but unsettling possibilities.

Works Cited

Ahmed, Sara. "Happy Objects." *The Affect Theory Reader*, edited by Melissa Gregg and Gregory J. Seigworth, Duke UP, 2010, pp. 29–51.

———. *On Being Included: Racism and Diversity in Institutional Life*. Duke UP, 2012.

Booher, Amanda K., and Julie Jung, editors. Prologue. *Feminist Rhetorical Science Studies: Human Bodies, Posthuman Worlds*, Southern Illinois UP, 2018, pp. 1–18.

Butler, Judith. *Precarious Life: The Powers of Mourning and Violence*. Verso, 2004.

California State University–Monterey Bay. *CSUMB History Archive*. https://csumb.edu/about/history/. Accessed 29 Sept. 2019.

———. "Founding Vision Statement." 27 Sept. 1994, https://csumb.edu/about/founding-vision-statement. Accessed 29 Sept. 2019.

Castro-Gómez, Santiago. *La Hybris del Punto Cero: Ciencia, Raza e Ilustración Nueva Granada, 1750–1816*. Pontificia Universidad Javeriana, 2005.

Connolly, William E. "Materialities of Experience." *New Materialisms: Agency, Ontology, Politics*, edited by Diana Coole and Samantha Frost, Duke UP, 2010, pp. 178–200.

Cooper, Marilyn. "Rhetorical Agency as Emergent and Enacted." *College Composition and Communication*, vol. 62, no. 3, 2011, pp. 420–48.

Coulthard, Glen Sean. *Red Skin, White Masks: Rejecting the Colonial Politics of Recognition*. U of Minnesota P, 2014.

Cruz, Nicolás. "Reflections on Aztlán and Its Role in the Chicanx Student Movement." MEChA, Seattle University Chapter, https://docs.google.com/document/d/1FxWRb9b1JmObzslxe_-mZYLhXNPfAJbHn-k3rBnWoMY/edit. Accessed 29 Sept. 2019.

DeLanda, Manuel. *Philosophy and Simulation: The Emergence of Synthetic Reason*. Continuum, 2011.

Dingo, Rebecca. *Networking Arguments: Rhetoric, Transnational Feminism, and Public Policy Writing*. U of Pittsburgh P, 2012.

Edbauer, Jenny. "Unframing Models of Public Distribution: From Rhetorical Situation to Rhetorical Ecologies." *Rhetoric Society Quarterly*, vol. 35, no. 4, 2005, pp. 5–24.

Fanon, Frantz. *Black Skin, White Masks*. 1952. Translated by Richard Philcox, Grove Press, 2008.

Fraser, Nancy. "Rethinking Recognition." *New Left Review*, vol. 3, 2000, pp. 107–20. https://newleftreview.org/II/3/nancy-fraser-rethinking-recognition. Accessed 30 Sept. 2019.

Gómez-Barris, Macarena. *The Extractive Zone*. Duke UP, 2017.

Haas, Angela M. "Wampum as Hypertext: An American Indian Intellectual Tradition of Multimedia Theory and Practice." *Studies in American Indian Literatures*, vol. 19, no. 4, 2007, pp. 77–100.

Hawk, Byron. *A Counter-History of Composition: Toward Methodologies of Complexity*. Pittsburgh UP, 2007.

Hayles, N. Katherine. *How We Became Posthuman: Virtual Bodies in Cybernetics, Literature, and Informatics*. U of Chicago P, 1999.

Hesford, Wendy. *Spectacular Rhetorics: Human Rights Visions, Recognitions, Feminisms*. Duke UP, 2011.

———. "Surviving Recognition and Racial In/justice." *Philosophy and Rhetoric*, vol. 48, no. 4, 2015, pp. 536–60. https://doi.org/10.5325/philrhet.48.4.0536. Accessed 29 Sept. 2019.

Johnson, Jennifer Ramirez, et al. "Writing New Mexico White: A Critical Analysis of Early Representations of New Mexico in Technical Writing." *Journal of Business and Technical Communication*, vol. 22, no. 2, 2008, pp. 211–36.

Jung, Julie. "Systems Rhetoric: A Dynamic Coupling of Explanation and Description." *enculturation*, vol. 17, 2014, http://enculturation.net/systems-rhetoric. Accessed 30 Sept. 2019.

Kupenda, Angela Mae. "Facing Down the Spooks." *Presumed Incompetent: The Intersections of Race and Class for Women in Academia*, edited by Gabriella Gutiérrez y Muhs et al., Utah State UP, 2012, pp. 20–28.

Lyons, Richard Scott. "Rhetorical Sovereignty: What Do American Indians Want from Writing?" *College Composition and Communication*, vol. 51, no. 3, 2000, pp. 447–68.

Mays, Chris. "From 'Flows' to 'Excess': On Stability, Stubbornness, and Blockage in Rhetorical Ecologies." *enculturation*, vol. 19, 2015, http://enculturation.net/from-flows-to-excess. Accessed 30 Sept. 2019.

Mignolo, Walter D. *The Darker Side of Western Modernity: Global Futures, Decolonial Options*, Duke UP, 2011.

"Misrecognition." *Oxford Reference*, https://www.oxfordreference.com/view/10.1093/oi/authority.20110803100201836.

New Mexico State University. "Our Heritage." https://www.nmsu.edu/about_nmsu/Our-Heritage.html. Accessed 19 Sept. 2019.

Oliver, Kelly. *The Colonization of Psychic Space: A Psychoanalytic Social Theory of Oppression*. U of Minnesota P, 2004.

———. *Witnessing: Beyond Recognition*. U of Minnesota P, 2001.

Powell, Malea D. "Rhetorics of Survivance: How American Indians *Use* Writing." *College Composition, and Communication*, vol. 53, no. 3, 2002, pp. 396–434.

Quijano, Aníbal. "Colonialidad del Poder, Eurocentrismo y América Latina." *La Colonialidad del Saber: eurocentrismo y ciencias sociales*, CLASCO, 2000, pp. 201–46.

Rice, Jenny. *Distant Publics: Development Rhetoric and the Subject of Crisis*. U of Pittsburgh P, 2012.

Ríos, Gabriela Racquel. "Cultivating Land-Based Literacies and Rhetorics." *Literacy in Composition Studies*, vol. 3 no. 1, 2015, pp. 60–70.

Sandoval, Chela. *Methodology of the Oppressed*. U of Minnesota P, 2000.

Smith, Linda Tuhiwai. *Decolonizing Methodologies: Research and Indigenous Peoples*. Zed Books, 1999.

Taylor, Charles. "The Politics of Recognition." *Multiculturalism: Examining the Politics of Recognition*, edited by Amy Gutmann, Princeton UP, 1994, pp. 25–73.

Tuck, Eve, and K. Wayne Yang. "Decolonization Is Not a Metaphor." *Decolonization: Indigeneity, Education & Society*, vol. 1, no. 1, 2012, pp. 1–40.

Yood, Jessica. "Gateway to Complexity: The Adjacent Possible of Beginning Writing." *Composition Forum*, vol. 30, 2014, http://compositionforum.com/issue/30. Accessed 30 Sept. 2019.

CHAPTER 3

Listening Otherwise

Arboreal Rhetorics and Tree-Human Relations

EHREN HELMUT PFLUGFELDER AND SHANNON KELLY

When Oregon was granted statehood in 1859, Congress earmarked a large portion of land specifically to fund public education. Comprising 80,000 acres of mostly old-growth forest south of the Umpqua River in the Oregon Coast Range, what became known as the Elliott State Forest has been owned and controlled by the state continually since that time and used to feed the Oregon Common School Fund. While the Confederated Tribes of the Coos, Lower Umpqua and Siuslaw Indians (CTCLUSI), along with Grand Ronde, Siletz, Coquille, and Cow Creek tribes, were all resident in portions of this forest, ancestral land titles have not been resolved since settler arrival in much of the region in the mid-1800s. Instead, the state has understood their "ownership" as stewardship, a slippery term with varying meanings, frequently deployed for multiple colonial purposes (Druschke 30). Much of this "stewardship" has resulted in a series of sometimes aggressive timber removal policies, the profits from which have funded state education. When endangered species–related court rulings in the 1990s curtailed many logging practices, these timber harvests began to slow, and the forest is now unable to generate the funds required by the state. Rules put in place to protect wildlife have shrunk the Elliott Forest timber harvest from 40 million board feet per year to approximately 15 million per year (Portland Audubon). Now mostly managed as a wildlife habitat, in order to protect the northern spotted owl, marbled murrelet, coho salmon, and other threatened and endangered species, the forest is cautiously up for sale (Public Lands Interpretive Association). Several interested parties have come forth to inquire about the land, but the most likely sale could be to the largest university in the state—Oregon State University (OSU).

Whether and how OSU's School of Forestry would manage and care for the Elliott State Forest is still unknown, as the university appears to first raise the quite substantial sum of $121 million in order to transfer the land. Like the other forests owned by OSU, the Elliott would likely be a managed space, and the land would probably be integrated into existing timber harvest, teaching, research, and outreach activities. No longer contributing to the Oregon Common School Fund, the 80,000 acres would still contribute to education through OSU's academic programs in forestry, fisheries and wildlife, and earth science, among others. What would happen to tribal interests concerning the forest has also yet to be decided, though several Indigenous groups desire to regain stewardship of this culturally and economically significant land (Oregon Consensus). In this complex set of stakeholders and relations, we argue there is a unique opportunity to do something different with a major mixed-growth Pacific Northwest forest by one of the best forestry programs in the country. Specifically, there is an opportunity to slow down or halt timber harvests, focus on habitat restoration and carbon sequestration, provide land rematriation to Indigenous groups, and integrate some of the goals of higher education into long-term ecological planning. In short, there is the option to listen to the land, the trees, and all their relations in ways less often practiced in the Euro-Western world.

This chapter considers the Elliott State Forest as a location where rhetorical listening to trees and forests could be practiced—that is, a location for listening to traditional environmental knowledges (TEKs) and scientific plant communication studies in order to learn from and practice ethical relations. Existing rhetorical considerations of interspecies communication (Haraway) and plant-oriented rhetorics have been suggestive about these same relationships. For example, Malea Powell, George Kennedy, and John Mucklebauer have already considered the persuasive structure of plant rhetorics. Our work builds from these studies, as well as others in Indigenous critical theory and new materialist thought, to complicate the dismissal of plant communication research projects from the 1970s that created a prohibition in Euro-Western science. While scientific practice is now catching up with Indigenous knowledge and reconsidering plant communication in terms of memory, intelligence, and associative learning (Wohlleben; Trewavas; Gagliano, "The Mind"), we are ultimately concerned with moving away from the scientific study of plant communication toward the recognition of tree-human relations in order to explore a potential and tentative arboreal rhetorics In doing so, we take seriously Lisbeth Lipari's ideas about listening as a means for these relations. For Lipari, ethics are second to listening, specifically a "listening to otherness while maintaining a commitment to proximity" that does not reduce or subsume any other (188). This position toward listening stands in distinction to other theories of rhetorical listening (Ratcliffe, "Eavesdropping") and in contradistinction from rhetoric as a study of remedying misunderstanding. In order to articulate this admittedly tentative arboreal rhetorics, we focus on "listening otherwise," a position of not-knowing that we expand to resist anthropomorphizing, and that works toward what we are naming *arboreal rhetoric* (Lipari 177). Such a practice allows us to illustrate a listening that is not predicated on understanding trees, but in recognizing the precarity of species we may never fully understand but nonetheless reside with and are responsible to. In other words, this listening practice avoids dependence upon Euro-Western communication expectations, where human creatures do not have to listen to species that communicate differently or otherwise.

Listening otherwise for an arboreal rhetoric also—and we suggest this cautiously—can be a parallel methodology to TEKs and Indigenous practices of listening that resist colonial legacies and Euro-Western assumptions in both scientific observations and communication studies. As such, we refrain from positioning our work thoroughly within a new materialist rhetorical approach, in part to avoid placing such practices solely within a Western ontology, where an arboreal rhetorics could become an extension of material rhetorics in much the same way that TEKs have been appropriated by Western scientific voices. To avoid perpetuating appropriation of Indigenous knowledge, we offer arboreal rhetoric as an anti-colonial methodology to listen beyond the human, and to disrupt Euro-Western colonial knowledge production. As white scholars working in higher education, our goal in this chapter is to amplify Indigenous approaches (see Mckoy) and listening otherwise while also working from our "located accountability" (Haas, "Race") and our particular relations, responsibilities, and complicity. That is, we do not consider arboreal rhetoric to be decolonial in that our work does not directly benefit Indigenous peoples and communities (Itchuaqiyaq and Matheson), and while we suggest that listening otherwise can be a tool to advocate for the return of Indigenous land to Indigenous people, our work currently does not move beyond decolonization as a metaphor (Tuck and Yang). In defining our terms, then, *anti-colonial* better describes our positionality and relations, and our attempt to disrupt and redress colonial influences on plant communication and listening practices. As Angela Haas argues, "for decolonial ideologies to emerge, new rhetorics must be spoken, written, or otherwise delivered into existence" (288). In this regard, we consider arboreal rhetoric as an anti-colonial complement to decolonial ideologies. To illustrate this methodology, we hypothesize what listening otherwise could mean for a space like the Elliott State Forest and consider whether the Long-Term Ecological Reflections project currently ongoing at a different forest site in Oregon would be appropriate as a means to pursue such an arboreal, rhetorical listening.

The Dismissal of Plant Rhetorics

Euro-Western research into plant communication and plant-human relations was jump-started by two empirically oriented books published in 1973: Peter Tompkins and Christopher Bird's *The Secret Life of Plants* and Dorothy Retallack's *The Sound of Music and Plants.* Tompkins and Bird wrote about a wide array of plant communication, from current studies to earlier quasi-scientific research and paranormal plant perception experiments, to claim that plants have feelings and can engage in a kind of extrasensory perception. They also suggested that this intelligence might originate in the supernatural. The authors recounted a 1968 experiment performed by Cleve Backster, an interrogation specialist for the CIA, who connected a small shrub to a polygraph machine and set about attempting to prove that plants recognize pain. Backster's other macabre experiments involved recording data from the polygraph machine while burning the plant, and then later killing small shrimp in an adjacent room. In the latter experiment, Backster tried to prove that plants were capable of sensing whether the nearby shrimp were dying. This research was published and vetted by peers, albeit in the *International Journal of Parapsychology.* Other studies of the same period were only somewhat more mainstream.

Tompkins and Bird's book on plant communication helped to popularize beliefs about human-plant relations, as they claimed that singing to plants could assist in their growth—now a fairly commonplace belief. In their chapter "The Harmonic Life of Plants," they recount several ad hoc experiments conducted over the years, including Charles Darwin's attempt to cause his touch-me-not plant (*Mimosa pudica*) to contract by playing his bassoon at it, and T. C. Singh's live music experiments where he observed the microscopic streaming speed of plant protoplasm. Retallack likewise showed that plants react to music, though she focused on identifying the qualities and effects of specific genres of music. An organist and professional musician, Retallack conducted research during her undergraduate project at Temple Buell College where she played different music to plants in a controlled setting. A 1971 *New*

York Times article noted that her plants leaned sharply away from "Led Zeppelin, the late Jimi Hendrix or the now disbanded Vanilla Fudge," but that "when she plays them Bach, or 'La Paloma,' or, especially, Ravi Shankar's classical Indian music, they flourish, with petunias turning their trumpet-like flowers toward the source of the music and even reaching their leaves out to hug the loudspeakers" (Ribley 64). Neither Retallack's nor Tompkins and Bird's book showcased careful, experimental research performed by scientists interested in identifying objective values, though Retallack readily acknowledged that her work never attempted "pure science."

While some lauded these quasi-scientific attempts as the innovative work of "outsider scientists," or enthusiastic citizen science, most of the scientific community reacted with extreme prejudice. When the books became popular, many scientists reacted like Dr. Cleon Ross, who called the work "pure garbage" (Ribley 64). According to Michael Pollan, while almost all of the science in *The Secret Life of Plants* has been rejected or discredited, "the book had made its mark on the culture. Americans began talking to their plants and playing music for them, and no doubt many still do. This might seem harmless enough; there will probably always be a strain of romanticism running through our thinking about plants." Pollan also describes the long-reaching effects from these publications on professional and academic botanists. *The Secret Life of Plants, The Sound of Music and Plants,* and similar books, including *The Power of Prayer on Plants* (Loehr), caused a backlash against the unverifiable scientific claims that plants were just like people, beings that shared the same emotions and cognitive powers. Their popularity led to a kind of "self-censorship" throughout the field of botany, and researchers who developed hypotheses or came to interesting conclusions about plant behavior, intelligence, and communication shied away from pursuing those possibilities for fear of being silenced by their peers.

Modern plant communication research goes by a few different names, and the results have again made a big splash in popular culture, in books like Peter Wohlleben's *The Hidden Life of Trees,* Stefano Mancuso's *The Revolutionary Genius of Plants,* and Monica Gagliano's *Thus Spoke the Plant.* These works, and a host of others, tell part of the story of current scientific work on plant communication, or what is controversially called "plant neurobiology." First introduced in a 2006 article in *Trends in Plant Science,* the term attracted renewed scientific and popular interest in how integrated signaling occurs within and between plants, and how the transport of chemicals and long-distance electrical signals functions under the provocative title of "neurobiology"—provocative because plants are not believed to have a neural network (Brenner et al.). In reaction to these claims, Pollan notes that "many plant scientists have pushed back hard against the nascent field," including a pretty dismissive letter, also in *Trends in Plant Science,* entitled "Plant Neurobiology: No Brain, No Gain?" The authors argued that "there is no evidence for structures such as neurons, synapses or a brain in plants. The fact that the term 'neuron' is derived from a Greek word describing a 'vegetable fiber' is not a compelling argument to reclaim this term for plant biology. . . . We maintain that plant neurobiology does not add to our understanding of plant physiology, plant cell biology or signaling" (Alpi et al. 135–36). While the Society for Plant Neurobiology has been renamed the Society for Plant Signaling and Behavior, mirroring the journal of *Plant Signaling & Behavior,* the research area has proven to be a flourishing one for plant and molecular biologists.

Stefano Mancuso, professor of plant science at the University of Firenze, is one of the leading researchers in the emerging field of plant intelligence and director of the International Laboratory of Plant Neurobiology. Working with Alessandra Viola, he has argued that plants escaped our (scientific) attention because of what they call "a problem of tempos" (38). Essentially, Euro-Western cultures typically live at a very different pace than most plants—in some fundamental ways. Humans live shorter lives than many plants, and certainly than most trees. For something that can grow over hundreds or thousands of years, within seasonal cycles, a human life feels oddly brief. As Mancuso and Viola articulate, it is possible that our senses "don't perceive plants moving, so we act as if they are inanimate objects. It makes no difference that we know they grow and therefore move; to us they're motionless because their movements escape our sight, and thus our deep understanding" (38). Recognizing the different scale and scope of plant life and behavior has led researchers to some spectacular insights over the last decade—and like Wohlleben's, Mancuso's, and Gagliano's work, these studies have attracted significant attention. One notable study, conducted by Suzanne Simard, a professor of forest ecology at the University of British Columbia, determined the extent of trees' underground mycorrhizal networks. As she described in her TED Talk and elsewhere, these fungal networks transferred water, carbon, nitrogen, and other materials, essentially linking forests of trees together—and sometimes going by the name the "Wood Wide Web" (Macfarlane). As Simard explained on the podcast *RadioLab,* "It's just this incredible communications network that, you know, people had no idea about in the past, because we couldn't, didn't know how to look" ("From Tree"). However, the "we" referenced here is also significant in that it represents a Euro-Western scientific inability to look to different creatures as knowledgeable and communicative. This difficulty in learning from others also extends to different ways of making knowledge, because, as Robin Wall Kimmerer reminds us, any experiment is only "a kind of conversation with plants," not a determination (*Braiding Sweetgrass* 158).

Traditional Ecological Relations

The forms of knowing that precede and exceed modern-day plant communication experiments include an array of traditional environmental knowledges, also sometimes referred to as traditional Indigenous knowledges. Martha Johnson's definition of the term frames TEK as "a body of knowledge built up by a group of people through generations living in close contact with nature. It includes a system of classification, a set of empirical observations about the local environment, and a system of self-management that governs resource use" (4). TEKs are not static in origin, and what is considered to be "traditional" about a TEK is not the age of the knowledge, but how it is passed down through a culture. As the Four Directions Council has noted, "the social process of learning and sharing knowledge, which is unique to each Indigenous culture, lies at the very heart of its 'traditionality.' Much of this knowledge is actually quite new, but it has a social meaning, and legal character, entirely unlike the knowledge Indigenous peoples acquire from settlers and industrialized societies" (5). Traditional and Indigenous knowledges have often been dismissed in modern scientific studies because they are largely qualitative, exist in oral traditions, are collective, and can be deeply connected with (and indeed be part of) specific cultural cosmologies. These features often fail to align with the tenets of modern scientific practice. For example, where Euro-Western science would refer to a localized ecosystem or habitat, a TEK might recognize the complex entanglement of beings infused with spirit, inhabiting a specific place, and possessing unique agencies and capacities. As Vanessa Watts explains, this Indigenous "place-thought" can represent different relations that are often at odds with, and can be inscrutable from, scientific assumptions. She argues that "habitats and ecosystems are better understood as societies from an Indigenous point of view; meaning that they have ethical structures, inter-species treaties and agreements, and further their ability to interpret, understand and implement. *Non-human beings are active members of society*" (23; emphasis added). When (what are often referred to in material rhetorics as) nonhumans are bracketed off by means of the ontological differentiations of Euro-Western modernity, scientific studies are able to ignore and thus misunderstand TEKs.

When a species is ontologically bound up with a cosmological system, the relationship between people and that species can (and does) preclude Euro-

Western obliviousness for how plants operate on different temporal planes of existence. Examples of this abound: For the Plains Cree, trees can be animate, because they have power; for the Quichua, some trees can become people when experienced through a hallucinogenic plant; for the Rarámuri, all plants alive today are cousins to humans. But perhaps the main reason as to why Euro-Western science has ignored TEKs, and thus plant and tree communication, for so long concerns issues of agency. Jarrad Reddekop explains this problem, noting that the larger issues that stem from a Euro-Western resistance to recognizing shared agency are also ethical problems that echo out in many directions. Reddekop claims that

> empathy, respect, and reciprocity—which seem to belong most fully to the domain of relationships between persons—obtain a pre-eminence in Indigenous relations to the non-human, the land, etc., in ways that are profoundly circumscribed if not outright precluded in [Euro-Western] habitual lifeways. Within the space of these alternate ontologies, we also gain a more positive sense of how non-anthropocentric relations with the non-human might be possible, and what it might mean not only to profoundly (and non-subjectively) rethink the problem of "agency" but to understand non-human others as also being agents. (205)

When agency is denied to beings like plants, it is hardly surprising that their existence is similarly discounted or fails to accord with Euro-Western experiences of time and growth. In many TEKs, plant agency and human agency are deeply intertwined, and in Indigenous worldviews, this interplay of relations means that human intervention is vital to the ecosystems in which we dwell (Kimmerer, "Native Knowledge").

A large body of work by Indigenous scholars discusses human relations with the more-than-human world around us. However, as non-Indigenous scholars, we both want to recognize the ways Indigenous knowledge has shaped our understanding of arboreal relations and offered us possibilities for listening, while also being mindful that we come to Indigenous knowledge as outsiders. Shannon is a white scholar originally from the Pacific Northwest, now working in the Midwest, and Ehren is a white scholar originally from the Rust Belt, now working in the Pacific Northwest. As white scholars working in rhetoric and science communication, we are also wrestling with the complexities of working in higher education while advocating for anti-colonial knowledge production. In our efforts to center Indigenous knowledge here, we do not mean to speak for or over Indigenous scholars, and we are also aware of the limitations of our white perspectives. We approach this work tentatively, and with the awareness that privilege is woven throughout our work. Our intention is to illustrate the connection between Euro-Western scientific thinking's dismissal of tree communication and the state of our contemporary human-tree relations, and to amplify scholarship and narratives that represent different relational possibilities. In these efforts, we hope—in some small way—to add to larger efforts that decenter colonial cosmologies. In writing with Indigenous knowledges, as we do here, we are mindful of Eve Tuck's question: "How do I as one person account for the interface of these concepts without falling into the traps put in place by the colonizers' and academy's long history of exploiting, romanticizing, and mining of Indigenous knowledge?" (646). We also want to be careful not to assume relations to Indigenous knowledge we do not actually have or practice, while being mindful of Zoe Todd's point that Indigenous knowledge is practiced by "peoples with whom we all share reciprocal duties as citizens of shared territories (be they physical or the ephemeral)" (17). With this caution comes the constant reminder that any rhetorical theory-building that we attempt is necessarily done in relation with our own cultural histories, the ontological relations embedded into those frameworks, and epistemologies to which we seek further connection. While our intention is to do this work with care, we also recognize that our impact could be otherwise.

With the above context, we want to point out that in contrast to a Euro-Western cosmology that emphasizes human dominion over nature, Indigenous critical theory (Cordova; Deloria; Lyons) does not recognize the same separations between humans and the natural world. A focus on the relatedness of the human and nonhuman suggests that the goal is not to create better relationships, but instead recognize how humans and nonhumans have always been related. Gabriela Raquel Ríos explains that Indigenous relationality, and thus Indigenous materiality, begins from an acknowledgment that humans and land are co-constituted, and so she identifies how a Euro-Western environmental rhetoric separates humans and nature. Ríos instead argues for nature "as a primary force in the creation of relations" and argues that land-based material rhetorics recognize that nature *produces* relations. The purpose of identifying these complex relations is not to, as Rosiek et al. describe, "leave in place the traditional enlightenment dichotomy between knowledge and values," but instead to explore what "specific performances of an ethical reciprocity with non-human agents would look like" (336). These performances are difficult for a Euro-Western ontology/cosmology to make sense of, and we see the evidence in critical theory; current Western new materialist theory is focused on identifying nonhuman agency, but "a greater portion of Indigenous scholarship focuses on working out specific performative and ethical implications of agent ontologies on their own terms. This difference makes the Indigenous studies literature on agent ontologies illegible to some scholars of Western philosophy," and is evidence for the same Euro-Western frame that produced our current, dominant human-nature relations (Rosiek et al. 336). Indigenous philosophy that works from the always-already related requires different ways of dwelling with our nonhuman relations.

In constructing a material-, relational-, and listening-based methodology for human-tree relations, Robin Wall Kimmerer's work has been particularly useful. She suggests that our relationship with land and the more-than-human will not heal until we hear their stories (*Braiding Sweetgrass* 9). She asks, "But who will tell them?" to which we add, "How will we listen?" In her work on material rhetorics, Marilyn Cooper tackles a similar question, asking, "How do we listen to and be persuaded by—or . . . persuade ourselves in response to—encounters with these others [that we share the world with]?" (17). Her answer is that a new ontology of persuasion should be grounded upon the idea that because "humans have for far too long assumed that nonhumans are nonconscious automatons or inert material," we need to begin paying "due attention to strangers whose opinions can infect us with new propositions" (28). Already investigating these propositions, Kimmerer explains that because Indigenous ways of knowing place humans as having the least experience on and with the earth (as opposed to a dominant Euro-Western hierarchy with humans at the top and plants near the bottom), we must look to "our teachers in other species for guidance" (*Braiding Sweetgrass* 9). For example, Kimmerer points out that plants know how to make medicine from light and water, which they then offer to others. Our listening can begin with paying attention to these processes by which other beings live, paying attention by way of a listening that does not require us to understand the other. This form of listening is not something that we are discovering through new material rhetorics, but something that has been in numerous Aboriginal and Indigenous cultures, many damaged in the modern project that Walter Mignolo describes as "the emergence of a structure of control and management of authority, economy, subjectivity, gender and sexual norms and relations that were driven by Western Europeans both in their internal conflicts and in their exploitation of labor and expropriation of land" (7). Listening otherwise could be part of a larger movement to attend to or reinstate material and rhetorical ways of knowing that have been ignored or dismissed throughout the installation of Western modernity, and therefore could be built into larger collaborative, decolonial approaches.

In suggesting that a material, rhetorical practice of listening otherwise, aligned with TEKs, could contribute to decoloniality, we want to again be cautious. This hesitance comes from the care we wish to take in suggesting that a practice of listening, theorized and applied in parallel to Indigenous practice and relationality, can actively rupture and challenge colonial assumptions, or what Godwin Agboka describes as "the political economy of knowledge production that accords certain privileges and legitimacy to certain forms of knowing while invalidating Indigenous knowledges or viewpoints of research participants" (302). If listening otherwise has the potential to disrupt or question coloniality, it must not do so in the same way that Euro-Western science has employed TEKs in the past. That is, it must not see TEKs as a "resource for the world's ecologists to tap into in their search for solutions to modern environmental and ecological problems" (Simpson 375). We do not seek a methodology for "listening to plants" that appropriates and repurposes Indigenous knowledges for scientific purposes, as did the researchers of the 1970s noted above, nor do we want to frame "listening otherwise" as a new materialist rhetoric legible only to Western scholars, but instead reject the assumptions of communication practices that position Indigenous knowledge as something coherent only once subsumed into the Western project. We think similarly as Jennifer Clary-Lemon does in her work on Indigenous new materialism—that because colonization and linguistic imperialist constructions frame nature as an object that is central to notions of Western science, a path toward decoloniality must reject such an appropriation ("Gifts"). This chapter, and our attempt to see these ideas through, may not be successful, but they are an approach to hypothesize a methodology that incorporates both Indigenous theories and land-based anti-colonial thought in the study of trees in general and the Elliott State Forest in particular.

Listening Otherwise

Euro-Western definitions of listening and communication are filled with ideas that encourage us to separate humans from nonhumans who seemingly lack verbal or overtly representational symbolic language. The saturation of Euro-Western knowledge schema and discourse about language makes it difficult to recognize the breadth of what counts as communicating. Of course, as communicators we recognize a variety of nonverbal forms of communication within our species and with other animals who also have apparent faces and more obvious forms of connection-making. Yet the possibility of nonverbal communication with something like a tree or plant may make more apparent our expectation for some sense of "verbal" connection-making. Here, we briefly explain common conceptions of communication and listening in order to problematize how the largely unconscious expectations of these practices often prevent us from communicating beyond language. We then further develop that listening otherwise can be employed as an anti-colonial activity within arboreal rhetoric.

How to define communication unsurprisingly depends on who you ask. It may be useful to start with one well-known and oft-used model: Michael Reddy's "conduit metaphor" that explains language as a "conduit, transferring thoughts bodily from one person to another" (290). In this scenario, speakers insert their thoughts and feelings into words in order to convey them to others (290). Reddy goes so far as to explain listening via conduit transmission: "In listening or reading, people extract the thoughts and feelings once again from the words" (290). Reddy was not the first to define communication as a way of transmitting fully formed thoughts and feeling from one mind to another. Ferdinand de Saussure's early twentieth-century *Course in General Linguistics* similarly depicts communication with a circuit diagram moving between Person A and Person B. The dotted line goes from Person A's brain, out the mouth, into B's ear, and on to the brain. Of note, this "speech circuit" requires at least two individuals to be complete. From this conduit metaphor, studying rhetoric becomes the practice of studying "misunderstanding and its remedies," as I. A. Richards famously explained (qtd. in Hochmuth 9). This Western conduit model has certainly been troubled as social dimensions of communication were further explored (see Carey; Roberts and Bavelas), but many common rhetorical frameworks about communication stem from the notion of transmitting ideas from one being to another, ideally with the goal of greater understanding. Or, in the way John Stewart explains language and communication: "Languaging is the way humans 'do' understanding, and in the process collaboratively 'build,' 'remake,' or 'modify' worlds" ("Symbol" 41).

From this brief definition of communication, Person B in de Saussure's circuit diagram now requires us to ask: How does listening occur? What does the listener receive from the speaker? Listening, as differentiated from hearing, often connotes an act of interpretation or meaning-making, whereas hearing refers to the physiological act of perceiving sounds (Lipari 7). Listening requires that we take in, absorb, or understand something from the speaker, and in this process the listener does something with that information. But what does it mean to say that someone understands? Is the listener decoding the speaker's language or perhaps even translating it into their own understanding? In defining listening and understanding, Krista Ratcliffe's research remains a touchstone in rhetoric and composition. Ratcliffe defines rhetorical listening as "a trope for interpretive invention," which "signifies a stance of openness that a person may choose to assume in relation to any person, text or culture" (*Rhetorical Listening* 1). Ratcliffe identifies "rhetorical listening" as a tool of "cross-cultural conduct," both for recognizing and negotiating differences (1). Yet the idea of being able to "choose" a stance of openness means, of course, that the listener can also choose otherwise—not to be open to others, and not to negotiate differences. To assume that a logical, or even emotional choice takes place in our listening reifies a logos of individuality that Lipari helps us rethink. Ratcliffe and Lipari both approach understanding and misunderstanding with important differences. For Ratcliffe, the benefit of rhetorical listening lies in its capacity to create understanding. While she acknowledges that *understanding* is a contested term, Ratcliffe clarifies her definition by inverting the term *understanding* to mean "*standing under,* that is, consciously standing under discourses that surround us and others, while consciously acknowledging all our particular—and very fluid—standpoints" (*Rhetorical Listening* 28). In standing under our own and others' discourses, listening also entails "identifying" various discourses and then imagining their affects (28). Even in inverting the term, though, the goal of understanding assumes a conscious individual and a logos that can identify difference and then act ethically in accordance. In contrast, Lipari approaches understanding as something that leaves little room for others or for discovery because it requires some kind of agreement and can too easily subsume difference into what the listener is able to understand (140). In contrast to listening for understanding, practicing listening *otherwise* means that we consider the vulnerability of all beings and their relations without requiring that we can imagine or understand them.

We are certainly not the first to problematize understanding as listening's goal, nor are we the first to forward misunderstanding as a productive listening act (see Ballif; Ballif et al.; Ratcliffe, "Eavesdropping"). For Michelle Ballif, listening allows for the speaker and audience to "escape each other and the demand of the symbolic contract," whereas hearing, and understanding, demands an "*ending* point" (61). Ballif ultimately suggests a "con/fused listening" that asks, "What are the limits of my understanding of what is other? And, is there a possibility of just listening to those limits, rather than rushing in to hear?" (64). Lipari similarly privileges misunderstanding in order not to subsume or simplify the other into our understanding. At stake when we base our listening on understanding is how we defer to our preexisting knowledge schemas that organize what counts as language and communication, or even what counts as suffering. In a move akin to Ballif's claim that the other desires to remain other ("What is it?"; 64). Lipari defines listening otherwise as a "bearing witness" to alterity that requires a "loss of control" and disallows the listener to resort to what they already know, or have in common with the speaker (187). In this way, listening otherwise is not goal-oriented in terms of remedying misunderstanding or achieving consensus. Rather, Lipari explains the practice of listening otherwise as giving presence to something when we "*listen others to speech*" (200). Listening others to speech cannot have a predetermined goal, given that such a goal would subsume the other beneath what our listening has in mind. In this definition, Lipari explains a dialectical tension between "compassion (which emphasizes sharing) and alterity (which emphasizes difference)" (179). The tension shows up in the difficulty between understanding and expressing compassion without trying to subsume the other into one's own framework. Excesses of alterity exceed our knowledge and understanding, and so to base an ethical response on what we can identify with or understand (e.g., putting oneself in the other's shoes) will be a limited ethics prone to ideological leaning, and prone to Euro-Western assumptions of logos. As Jade Davis reminds us, "to be in the shoes of an Other still leaves you with your own feet"—feet that can step out of imagining the other's position and remain unchanged. Similarly, if our listening practice is based on the conduit method of communication, we reify what counts as communicating in terms of language and understanding. Yet Lipari explains that alterity prompts us to recognize that our ways of seeing are always partial ways of seeing, and that our reality is not reality (182). It is here where listening otherwise can be of use in decolonial tactics; it refuses to "understand" others into a Western ontology and refuses to validate the deep-seated assumptions of communication in a modern paradigm. Further, listening otherwise can be aligned with, or placed in service of, existing listening practices, in order to support the material conditions those practices require.

This form of listening without understanding can be productively compared with what Donal Carbaugh explains in his description of how the Blackfeet perform a place-based listening. For the Blackfeet, listening is a form of communication that is enacted in a specific way, and as Two Bears, a pseudonym for a participant in Carbaugh's conversations, describes, functions as "a carrier of cultural content, a historical way of being that invokes that history in the present" (261). This enactment of listening is similar to that which Lipari describes, in that it avoids preconceptions, a sense of control, or a goal of understanding, but also allows for bearing witness and learning as a material, place-based knowledge construction. Carbaugh explains Two Bears's perspective on listening:

> "You can come out here . . . sit down and listen, . . . sit and listen patiently"; "you have to listen. Be quiet. Be patient"; you can "think"; "you might hear." "Listening" this way can involve the listener in an intense, efficacious, and

> complex set of communicative acts in which one is not speaking, discussing, or disclosing, but sitting quietly, watching, and feeling-the-place, through all the senses. Presumed for the acts is an active co-presence with the natural and historical place in which, and to which one listens. The belief is that one can—at some times more than others—eventually "hear" and learn from it. (259)

Unlike "listening otherwise," Two Bears's sense of Blackfeet listening is dependent upon identifying specific locations where this listening can take place, and engaging in historical, cultural forms of communication that simply are not open to everyone. While this listening might also "*listen others to speech*" (Lipari 200), according to Carbaugh, Blackfeet listening "invites a cultural form of action," where listening, culture, and place are intimately entwined (257). Blackfeet listening is more closely aligned with a TEK than above descriptions of "listening otherwise," yet both are forms of listening that avoid imposing expectation, categorization, or agreement and instead are open to what Ratcliffe calls "interpretive invention" (*Rhetorical Listening* 1).

To begin from a practice of listening otherwise means that misunderstanding grounds our communicative acts; it is not something to overcome but something to embrace and sit with. As we suggest below, in an arboreal rhetorics, we "listen others to speech" from a position that does not require human language or understanding but rather approaches alterity as an aspect of being in relationship with other creatures. Better listening can lead to mutual reciprocity, a relational openness that we give ourselves to and in which we seek out that which is not only bound by dominant modes of Euro-Western expectation. Arguably, the difficult, and perhaps even painful, requirement of listening otherwise means that we must open ourselves to change, allow ourselves to transform and revise our ideas, and accept the realization that understanding is sustained by change. Similarly, our knowledge is also sustained by change, and so we approach listening otherwise as a temporarily stable practice from which to ethically respond to our relations.

Though it can be challenging to understand this form of listening as both a material and anti-colonial activity, this practice of listening otherwise is aligned with TEK and Indigenous listening practices—but carefully aligned with, not subsuming and not speaking for these same actions. Listening otherwise attempts to reject a Euro-Western environmental rhetorics that separates humans and nature into distinct spheres of ontology and does not offer an understanding or assume that listening is predicated on an attempt to locate what is being heard. Listening otherwise is thus a relational, inventive openness to the material interactions that cannot be disclosed by historical, Western ontological assumptions. Hopefully, an arboreal rhetorics describes a sympathetic openness to what Two Bears and others have articulated, but to which so many Western listeners have been unable to accept: We think with trees.

Arboreal Relations

Before introducing the practice of "listening otherwise," Lipari claims "we unthinkingly think with trees" (177). And in case the reader glossed over her point, or thought it merely subconscious possibility, she emphasizes her statement: "That bears repeating. *We think with trees*" (177). Lipari argues that listening to other humans already stretches our ethical listening practices since we "live in the ordinary realm of the social" where listening to trees, for most of us, remains "a bit beyond the pale" (177). Metaphorically though, Lipari lays out the range of ways trees undergird our thinking processes: from the branching patterns of Mandelbrot's "binary fractal trees," to Plato's idea that "the first prophetic utterance came from an oak tree," to ancient tree references in the Upanishads and Zen koans (177). So, while Western plant communication scholars have been identifying some unique intra-tree relations (as mentioned above), human listening to, with, and through trees might remain somewhat ineffable given our differences in language, growth, movement, and lifespan. Those differences have not stopped similarly ineffable explorations of tree-human relations from taking hold in popular culture, like current excitement over the Japanese concept of *Shinrin-yoku,* or "forest bathing," as a mindful practice and means of preventative medicine. Recent attention to time spent in nature, or what some studies term a "nature experience," is now prompting a wave of scientific research seeking to measure the effects of forested, natural environments on human health. One recent experiment measured cortisol and alpha-amylase in human saliva before participants took a "nature pill" of at least ten minutes (Hunter et al.). As unusual as this experiment may seem, the scientific community has been determined to calculate the impacts of human-arboreal relations, with the larger goal of identifying how these relations function.

Reflecting on studies of human-forest relations, Robin Wall Kimmerer notes that these scientific experiments are in fact a kind of conversation with plants. It is therefore overly deterministic to claim that plants cannot communicate simply because they do not speak like animals. Instead, Kimmerer shows that "plants answer questions by the way they live, by their responses to change" (*Braiding Sweetgrass* 158). This line of thought puts responsibility on the listener; we have to learn to ask in the language of the speaker. The question then becomes how to listen to that which is wholly other from oneself without doing away with difference. Learning from TEKs could help allow for additional nuance in these listening endeavors—especially for endeavors that move beyond alleviating human-experienced stress levels. While some TEK efforts have been intentionally and aggressively suppressed through colonial violence and replaced with Euro-Western scientific practices, the loss of these knowledge practices "has often had very serious negative consequences for the well-being of local and Indigenous communities, and for forests, associated ecosystems, their biodiversity, and capacity to produce environmental goods and services on a sustainable basis" (Parrotta et al. 2). Parotta et al. explain that recent interdisciplinary research that works alongside TEKs, especially in issues of forest management and biodiversity sustainability, have had a positive impact in policy making. They note the advancement of the Intergovernmental Science-Policy Platform on Biodiversity and Ecosystem Services and explain how the 2016 Thematic Assessment on Pollinators, Pollination and Food Production has been the result of such listening.

Another equally impactful method of listening comes from recent studies in anthropology like those of Eduardo Kohn. Mirroring Kimmerer's thoughts on human-tree relations, Kohn has asked, "How should we think with forests? How should we allow the thoughts in and of the nonhuman world to liberate our thinking?" (21). Kohn answers these questions by stating, as clearly as Kimmerer, that "forests are good to think because they themselves think. Forests think. I want to take this seriously, and I want to ask, What are the implications of this claim for our understandings of what it means to be human in a world that extends beyond us?" (21–22). Kohn's book builds from his ethnographic work with the Runa of the Upper Amazon and insights from semiotic theory. In Kohn's words, his book "aims to free our thinking of that excess conceptual baggage that has accumulated as a result of our exclusive attention—to the neglect of everything else—to that which makes us humans exceptional" (22). He focuses on the ethnographic project of thinking beyond the human, by way of understanding symbol systems as existing outside of human alphanumeric or representational traditions. Kohn's work aligns with other attempts to disrupt the Euro-Western, logos-driven conduit model of communication and understanding explained above. By listening to how forests think, Kohn argues, we might "understand how we might better live in a world we share with other kinds of lives" (22).

While Kohn sees this process as potentially resulting in new conceptual tools, his method is also another name for listening otherwise, attending to the things beyond the human that we do not hope to understand or contain, but instead cultivate and grow with. His work echoes Lipari's claims that there is no understanding without misunderstanding and that such misunderstanding is fundamental to being in relationships with trees. Others likewise make the argument that we are imperfect conduits for any human-tree relations that we might be present for or bear witness to.

In *Planting the Anthropocene,* Jennifer Clary-Lemon's study of Canadian tree planters shows that we can better listen to and speak for trees, and though such listening is difficult to articulate in representative symbols, we can make it visible through a combination of ethnographic and new materialist rhetorical methods. Canadian tree planters are communicative bodies in the midst of many other agencies and voices, from the saplings they plant, the rain that pours on their backs, the moose and grizzlies they encounter, and the dreams of continuous tree-planting that inhabit their sleep. Clary-Lemon argues that

> humans are constantly working through particular tensions—troubles—that come from contradictions in distinguishing between self and other. Between nature and culture, between human and nonhuman, between rational and non-rational. . . . [I]t is necessary to see ourselves as inconsistent creatures who make meaning with ambient, persuasive surrounds filled with underivable rhetoricity with other beings. (*Planting* 169)

In order to make sense of these numerous relations, we should, Clary-Lemon asserts, be willing to listen to the chora—the voices that speak to and through us, or as Thomas Rickert has offered, the voices of those that surround us, most often articulated in rhetorical scholarship as the polis, the stakeholder, or the audience (255). Unlike directed forms of written or oral communication, this chora is different; it allows "the generative potential of specific geographies to bubble up, to arise . . . pushing us to listen to the network or constellation rather than the grid, pushing us to listen to the human as only ever one player in a complex linkage of biotic and a-biotic assemblages" (*Planting* 169). We may only ever have access to partial, fleeting, or decomposing versions of these voices, and full understandings are likely outside of Euro-Western logos and its oversimplified ecosystems of attention, but new materialist listening practices can give rise to new articulations of these complex networks of voices.

Long-Term Ecological Reflections

For Clary-Lemon, these complex, affective entanglements can "allow glimpses of what it might look like to argue nature's other as ourselves, to grieve the un-grievable, to imagine trees and other bodies as beings beyond resource capital, and to imagine ourselves as part of how the forest thinks" (*Planting* 106). In order to apply such practices of listening otherwise, we also need a location to which our attentions can be cohered, hence our hypothetical use for the Elliott State Forest that began this chapter. Amidst ongoing plans for the forest, including recreation, public access, conservation, research, and tribal partnerships, if purchased by Oregon State University, the forest could be integrated into what is known as the Long-Term Ecological Reflections (LTEReflections) project. LTEReflections is a program meant to mirror the international Long-Term Ecological Research Network (LTER), an initiative of the National Science Foundation that focuses on providing stable spaces for controlled ecosystem experiments. These (currently twenty-eight) sites generate large open data sets with five common goals, including observation, large-scale experimentation, modeling, synthesis science, and outreach partnerships. One LTER site is the Oregon State University–controlled H. J. Andrews Experimental Forest in Blue River, Oregon, traditional home to the Kalapuya and Mollala, where numerous studies are ongoing, including vegetation surveys, ecosystem informatics, bird census research, and a unique log decomposition study meant to last 200 years (Cascade Center). Also meant to last for 200 years, the LTEReflections "brings together writers, humanists, and scientists to create a living, growing record of how we understand the forest and the relation of people to the forest, as that understanding and that forest both change over time" (Oregon State University, "Spring"). Like the LTER, the LTEReflections gathers thoughts, beliefs, experiences, and ideas over time, "assembling a long-term record of changing creative responses to an ever-changing landscape."

LTEReflections is hosted by Oregon State University's Spring Creek Project, an organization that sponsors writers' residencies, outreach events, readings, lectures, conversations, and symposia on ecological and environmental topics of critical importance to the health of humans and nature. Spring Creek's stated mission is to "bring together the practical wisdom of the environmental sciences, the clarity of philosophical analysis, and the creative, expressive power of the written word to find new ways to understand and re-imagine our relation(s) to the natural world" (Oregon State University, "Spring"). The human-nature relations demonstrated by the residencies might offer different ways of listening and new interactions. Along with the possibility to offer land reparations to Indigenous groups, and set aside forest for carbon sequestration efforts, an Elliott State Forest–based LTEReflections project could be an excellent location to launch additional rhetorical listening projects, in part because the fundamental beliefs of the project echo the ways of listening otherwise described in this chapter. LTEReflections adheres to the idea that we "should pay close attention to a particular place—to the mountains, rivers, people and the forests" (Oregon State University, "Long-Term"). LTEReflections projects are also meant to occur over many generations and emphasize that storytelling can sit alongside observation and experimentation, that interdisciplinarity is key to understanding complex places, and that "there is wisdom to be gained—that the more we know about the natural world and the place of humans in the world, the greater our insight into how we ought to live our lives" (Oregon State University, "Long-Term"). The opportunities for residencies, outreach, conversations, and more in the Elliott forest are deeply compelling, and could provide more instances for listening otherwise to the many relations within a forest.

Perhaps unsurprisingly, the first writer in residence in the LTEReflections project at the Andrews Forest was Robin Wall Kimmerer, and the result of her time at Andrews provides an exceptional example of how to listen otherwise to a forest and an ecosystem—and it offers a tentative version of arboreal rhetorics. Kimmerer's work for the *Andrews Forest Log* is entitled "Interview with a Watershed," and it narrates her time with researchers collecting data. She notes that the poet and physician Lewis Thomas explains how humans have several kinds of language, including chit-chat, conversation, and math. Kimmerer then goes on to detail the kinds of mathematical data that we can gather from scientific analyses of forest life, but also cautions us that data alone is not enough. She writes:

> There is danger in thinking that we do understand. We cannot say to the forest "Did you suffer terribly when the trees were all gone?" But we can measure the hemorrhage of nitrate washed away. We might want to ask about forgiveness, but instead we measure the increasing clarity and oxygen of the stream, and hope that it will suffice. Data alone do not bring understanding. (Kimmerer, "Interview")

The fourth form of language, Kimmerer explains, is the unspoken body language, not of people, but of material locations, of places. She argues that data alone does not reveal this language, and that deeper understanding comes from being in a place in what we might call listening otherwise. She asks, "Can you really understand a place without kneeling in the humus or standing quietly to watch the alder leaves drift down the stream? Being there, doing the field work is for me a way of becoming intimate with the place, really listening to the land. It makes for better science, because the land will suggest new questions" (Kimmerer, "Interview"). In *Braiding Sweetgrass,* Kimmerer provides a thoughtful meditation on what this kind of reflection might look like, specifically by considering our relationships with trees. Thinking about the Northeast, she asks, what would it mean to declare citizenship in Maple Nation, and then answers in multiple ways, explaining that maples provide shelter, fuel, heat, sugar, jobs, and purpose, among other things. Yet, Kimmerer suggests, they also

> create habitat for songbirds, and wildlife cover, golden leaves to shuffle through, tree forts and branches for swings. Centuries of their falling leaves have built this soil, now farmed for strawberries, apples, sweet corn, and hay. How much of the oxygen in our valley comes from our maples? How much carbon is taken from the atmosphere and stored away? These processes are what ecological scientists term ecosystem services, the structures and functions of the natural world that make life possible. We can assign an economic value to maple timber, or gallons of syrup, but ecosystem services are far more precious. And yet these services go unaccounted for in the human economy. As with the services of local government, we don't think about them unless they are missing. There is no official tax system to pay for these services, as we pay for snowplowing and schoolbooks. We get them for free, donated continually by maples. They do their share for us. The question is: How well do we do by them? (*Braiding Sweetgrass* 169–70)

What we have tentatively named here as an arboreal rhetoric is informed by Indigenous relationality and practices of listening otherwise. To engage in arboreal rhetorics suggests a way of relating in our human-tree interactions that does not require understanding but nonetheless holds humans responsible to our relations with the nonhuman world. In such a practice, communicating with trees might look like observations conducted over generations, allowing our scientific and humanistic inquiries to be guided by the land's questions and by the relations the land produces. Kohn explains that it is difficult not to simply project our own language systems and ways of relating onto forests due to the fact that "we are colonized by certain ways of thinking about relationality" (21). When human language structures the ways we can imagine thoughts, desires, and communication being expressed, then we can easily ignore what does not register as such. Yet we are suggesting that an arboreal rhetoric allows us to listen beyond a Euro-Western communication system predicated on human language and reason. Without framing trees solely within human expectations, listening otherwise occupies a position of not knowing that resists overly anthropomorphizing as a means to disclose understanding. Along with our tentativeness regarding arboreal rhetoric, we also hold listening otherwise lightly, and with an open palm. If we are to really practice ethical listening, then we are continually open to and sustained by change. And so, in sharing these ideas and listening otherwise, these very practices will transform in how they are taken up and heard. In this way, an arboreal rhetoric is one continually developing possibility for relationality with and beyond the human. Engaging an arboreal rhetoric allows for humans to be the students of nature rather than its masters; as Kimmerer reminds us, "the very best scientists are humble enough to listen" (*Braiding Sweetgrass* 333).

Works Cited

Agboka, Godwin Y. "Decolonial Methodologies: Social Justice Perspectives in Intercultural Technical Communication Research." *Journal of Technical Writing and Communication,* vol. 44, no. 3, 2014, pp. 297–327. https://doi.org/10.2190/TW.44.3.e.

Alpi, Amadeo, et al. "Plant Neurobiology: No Brain, No Gain?" *Trends in Plant Science,* vol. 12, no. 4, 2007, pp. 135–36. https://doi.org/10.1016/j.tplants.2007.03.002.

Backster, Cleve. "Evidence of a Primary Perception in Plant Life." *International Journal of Parapsychology,* vol. 10, no. 4, 1968, pp. 329–48.

Ballif, Michelle. "What Is It That the Audience Wants? Or, Notes toward a Listening with a Transgendered Ear for (Mis)Understanding." *JAC,* vol. 19, no. 1, 1999, pp. 51–70. https://www.jstor.org/stable/20866221.

Ballif, Michelle, et al. "Negotiating the Differend: A Feminist Trilogue." *JAC,* vol. 20, no. 3, 2000, pp. 583–625. https://www.jstor.org/stable/20866350.

Brenner, Eric D., et al. "Plant Neurobiology: An Integrated View of Plant Signaling." *Trends in Plant Science,* vol. 11, no. 8, 2006, pp. 413–19. https://doi.org/10.1016/j.tplants.2006.06.009.

Carey, James. *Communication as Culture: Essays on Media and Society.* Unwin Hyman, 1989.

Carbaugh, Donal. "'Just Listen': 'Listening' and Landscape among the Blackfeet." *Western Journal of Communication,* vol. 63, no. 3, 1999, pp. 250–70. https://doi.org/10.1080/10570319909374641.

Cascade Center for Ecosystem Management. "Dead Wood, Bugs, Fungi, and New Forests: The Log Decomposition Study." *AndrewsForest.org,* https://web.archive.org/web/20160303232211/http://andrewsforest.oregonstate.edu/research/related/ccem/pdf/decomp.pdf.

Clary-Lemon, Jennifer. "Gifts, Ancestors, and Relations: Notes toward an Indigenous New Materialism." *enculturation,* no. 30, 2019, http://enculturation.net/gifts_ancestors_and_relations.

———. *Planting the Anthropocene: Rhetorics of Natureculture.* Utah State UP, 2019.

Cooper, Marilyn M. "Listening to Strange Strangers, Modifying Dreams." *Rhetoric, through Everyday Things,* edited by Scot Barnett and Casey Boyle, U of Alabama P, 2016, pp. 17–29.

Cordova, V. F. *How It Is: The Native American Philosophy of V. F. Cordova.* U of Arizona P, 2007.

Davis, Jade. "Draft of Empathy Manifesto #1: Emerging Technologies (VR) or Technically Feeling." *Jade E. Davis, PhD,* https://jadedid.com/blog/2018/05/21/draft-of-empathy-manifesto-1-emerging-technologies-vr-or-technically-feeling/.

Deloria, Vine, Jr. *The Vine Deloria Jr., Reader.* Edited by Barbara Deloria et al., Fulcrum, 1999.

de Saussure, Ferdinand. *Course in General Linguistics.* Open Court Classics, 1998.

Druschke, Caroline Gottschalk. "Agonistic Methodology: A Rhetorical Case Study in Agricultural Stewardship." *Field Rhetoric: Ethnography, Ecology, and Engagement in the Places of*

Persuasion, edited by Candice Rai and Caroline Gottschalk Druschke, U of Alabama P, 2018, pp. 22–42.

Four Directions Council. *Forests, Indigenous Peoples and Biodiversity: Contribution of the Four Directions Council.* Submission to the Secretariat for the Convention on Biological Diversity, Lethbridge, Canada, Four Directions Council, 1996.

"From Tree to Shining Tree." *RadioLab*, 30 July 2016, https://www.wnycstudios.org/story/from-tree-to-shining-tree.

Gagliano, Monica. "The Mind of Plants: Thinking the Unthinkable." *Communicative & Integrative Biology*, vol. 10, no. 2, 2016. https://doi.org/10.1080/19420889.2017.1288333.

———. *Thus Spoke the Plant: A Remarkable Journey of Groundbreaking Scientific Discoveries and Personal Encounters with Plants.* North Atlantic Books, 2018.

Haas, Angela. "Race, Rhetoric, and Technology: A Case Study of Decolonial Technical Communication Theory, Methodology, and Pedagogy." *Journal of Business and Technical Communication*, vol. 26, no. 3, 2012, pp. 277–310. https://doi.org/10.1177/1050651912439539.

Haraway, Donna Jeanne. *The Companion Species Manifesto: Dogs, People, and Significant Otherness.* Prickly Paradigm, 2003.

Hochmuth, Marie. "I. A. Richards and the 'New Rhetoric.'" *The Quarterly Journal of Speech*, vol. 44, no. 1, 1958, pp. 1–16. https://www.jstor.org/stable/465482.

Hunter, MaryCarol R., et al. "Urban Nature Experiences Reduce Stress in the Context of Daily Life Based on Salivary Biomarkers." *Frontiers in Psychology*, vol. 10, 2019. https://doi.org/10.3389/fpsyg.2019.00722.

Itchuaqiyaq, Uluak Cana, and Breeanne Matheson. "Decolonizing Decoloniality: Considering the (Mis)use of Decolonial Frameworks in TPC Scholarship." *Communication Design Quarterly*, Online First, 2021. https://doi.org/10.1145/3437000.3437002.

Johnson, Martha. Introduction. *Lore: Capturing Traditional Environmental Knowledge*, edited by Martha Johnson, Dene Cultural Institute and the International Development Research Centre, 1992, pp. 3–22.

Kennedy, George A. "A Hoot in the Dark: The Evolution of General Rhetoric." *Philosophy & Rhetoric*, vol. 25, no. 1, 1992, pp. 1–21. https://www.jstor.org/stable/40238276.

Kimmerer, Robin Wall. *Braiding Sweetgrass: Indigenous Wisdom, Scientific Knowledge, and the Teachings of Plants.* Milkweed Editions, 2013.

———. "Interview with a Watershed." *Andrews Forest Log*, 2004, http://andrewsforestlog.org/residencies/brf/interview-with-a-watershed/.

———. "Native Knowledge for Native Ecosystems." *Journal of Forestry*, vol. 98, no. 8, 2000, pp. 6–7. https://doi.org/10.1093/jof/98.8.4.

Kohn, Eduardo. *How Forests Think: Toward an Anthropology beyond the Human.* U of California P, 2013.

Lipari, Lisbeth. *Listening, Thinking, Being: Toward an Ethics of Attunement.* Penn State UP, 2014.

Loehr, Franklin. *The Power of Prayer on Plants.* Doubleday, 1959.

Lyons, Scott. *X-Marks: Native Signatures of Assent.* U of Minnesota P, 2010.

Macfarlane, Robert. "The Secrets of the Wood Wide Web." *The New Yorker*, 7 Aug. 2016, https://www.newyorker.com/tech/annals-of-technology/the-secrets-of-the-wood-wide-w.

Mancuso, Stefano. *The Revolutionary Genius of Plants: A New Understanding of Plant Intelligence and Behavior.* Atria Books, 2018.

Mancuso, Stefano, and Allessandra Viola. *Brilliant Green: The Surprising History and Science of Plant Intelligence.* Island Press, 2015.

Mckoy, Temptaous. *Y'all Call It Technical and Professional Communication, We Call It #ForThe Culture: The Use of Amplification Rhetorics in Black Communities and Their Implications for Technical and Professional Communication Studies.* PhD dissertation, East Carolina University, 2019.

Mignolo, Walter D. *The Darker Side of Western Modernity: Global Futures, Decolonial Options.* Duke UP, 2012.

Muckelbauer, John. "Implicit Paradigms of Rhetoric: Aristotelian, Cultural, and Heliotropic." *Rhetoric, through Everyday Things,* edited by Scot Barnett and Casey Boyle, U of Alabama P, 2016, pp. 30–41.

Oregon Consensus. "Elliott State Forest: Next Step Considerations for Decoupling from Oregon's Common School Fund." October 2018, https://www.oregon.gov/dsl/Land/Documents/OregonConsensusElliottStateForestReportOctober2018.pdf.

Oregon State University. "Long-Term Ecological Reflections." https://liberalarts.oregonstate.edu/centers-and-initiatives/spring-creek-project/programs-and-residencies/long-term-ecological-reflections. Accessed 12 Aug. 2019.

———. "Spring Creek Project." https://liberalarts.oregonstate.edu/centers-and-initiatives/spring-creek-project. Accessed 12 Aug. 2019.

Parrotta, John, et al. "Traditional Knowledge for Sustainable Forest Management and Provision of Ecosystem Services." *International Journal of Biodiversity Science, Ecosystem Services & Management,* vol. 12, no. 1–2, 2016, pp. 1–4. https://doi.org/10.1080/21513732.2016.1169580.

Pollan, Michael. "The Intelligent Plant." *The New Yorker,* 15 Dec. 2013, http://www.newyorker.com/magazine/2013/12/23/the-intelligent-plant.

Portland Audubon. "Elliott State Forest." https://audubonportland.org/our-work/protect/habitat and-wildlife/forests/state-forests/elliott-state-forest/.

Public Lands Interpretive Association. "Oregon: Elliott State Forest." http://publiclands.org/Get-Books-and-Maps.php?plicstate=OR.

Ratcliffe, Krista. "Eavesdropping on Others." *JAC,* vol. 20, no. 4, 2000, pp. 908–19. https://www.jstor.org/stable/20866372.

———. *Rhetorical Listening: Identification, Gender, and Whiteness.* Southern Illinois UP, 2005.

Reddekop, Jarrad. *Thinking across Worlds: Indigenous Thought, Relational Ontology, and the Politics of Nature; Or, If Only Nietzsche Could Meet a Yachaj.* PhD dissertation, Western University, 2014.

Reddy, Michael J. "The Conduit Metaphor: A Case of Frame Conflict in Our Language about Language." *Metaphor and Thought,* edited by Andrew Ortony, Cambridge UP, 1979, pp. 284–310.

Retallack, Dorothy. *The Sound of Music and Plants.* DeVorss and Co., 1973.

Ribley, Anthony. "Rock or Bach an Issue to Plants, Singer Says." *The New York Times,* 21 Feb. 1971, p. 64. https://www.nytimes.com/1971/02/21/archives/rock-or-bach-an-issue-to-plants-singer-says.html.

Rickert, Thomas. "Towards the Chora: Kristeva, Derrida, and Ulmer on Emplaced Invention." *Philosophy and Rhetoric,* vol. 40, no. 3, 2007, pp. 251–73. https://www.jstor.org/stable/25655276.

Ríos, Gabriela Raquel. "Cultivating Land-Based Literacies." *Literacy in Composition Studies,* vol. 3, no. 1, 2015, pp. 60–70. https://doi.org/10.21623/1.3.1.5.

Roberts, Gillian L, and Janet Beavin Bavelas. "The Communicative Dictionary of Collaborative Meaning." *Beyond the Symbol Model,* edited by John Stewart, SUNY Press, 1996, pp. 136–60.

Rosiek, Jerry Lee, et al. "The New Materialisms and Indigenous Theories of Non-Human Agency: Making the Case for Respectful Anti-Colonial Engagement." *Qualitative Inquiry*, vol. 26, no. 3–4, 2019, pp. 331–46. https://doi.org/10.1177/1077800419830135.

Simard, Suzanne. "How Trees Talk to Each Other." *TED*, June 2016, https://www.ted.com/talks/suzanne_simard_how_trees_talk_to_each_other.

Simpson, Leanne R. "Anticolonial Strategies for the Recovery and Maintenance of Indigenous Knowledge." *American Indian Quarterly*, vol. 28, no. 3/4, 2004, pp. 373–84. https://www.jstor.org/stable/4138923.

Stewart, John. "The Symbol Model vs. Language." *Beyond the Symbol Model*, edited by John Stewart, SUNY Press, 1996, pp. 9–68.

Todd, Zoe. "An Indigenous Feminist's Take on the Ontological Turn: 'Ontology' Is Just Another Word for Colonialism." *Journal of Historical Sociology*, vol. 29, no. 1, 2016, pp. 4–22. https://doi.org/10.1111/johs.12124.

Tompkins, Peter, and Christopher Bird. *The Secret Life of Plants: A Fascinating Account of the Physical, Emotional and Spiritual Relations between Plants and Man*. Harper & Row, 1973.

Trewavas, Anthony. "Aspects of Plant Intelligence." *Annals of Botany* vol. 92, no. 1, 2003, pp. 1–20. https://doi.org/10.1093/aob/mcg101.

Tuck, Eve. "Breaking Up with Deleuze: Desire and Valuing the Irreconcilable." *International Journal of Qualitative Studies in Education*, vol. 23, no. 5, 2010, pp. 635–50. https://doi.org/10.1080/09518398.2010.500633.

Tuck, Eve, and K. Wayne Yang. "Decolonization Is Not a Metaphor." *Decolonization: Indigeneity, Education & Society* vol. 1, no. 1, 2012, pp. 1–40. https://jps.library.utoronto.ca/index.php/des/article/view/18630.

Watts, Vanessa. "Indigenous Place-Thought & Agency amongst Humans and Non-Humans (First Woman and Sky Woman Go on a European World Tour!)." *Decolonization: Indigeneity, Education & Society*, vol. 2, no. 1, 2013, pp. 20–34. https://jps.library.utoronto.ca/index.php/des/article/view/19145.

Wohlleben, Peter. *The Hidden Life of Trees: What They Feel, How They Communicate*. Translated by Jane Billinghurst, Greystone Books Ltd., 2015.

CHAPTER 4

Smoke and Mirrors

Re-Creating Material Relation(ship)s through Mexica Story

CHRISTINA V. CEDILLO

As I compose this essay, people everywhere are demanding that governments mobilize against impending climate catastrophe.[1] Without minimizing such efforts, I must remind readers that this struggle has proven ongoing for Indigenous peoples since the arrival of European settlers until now. From Canada's Idle No More movement to the Waorani tribe's court battles in Ecuador, Native peoples seek to protect Earth's ecosystems by seeking public platforms to remind politicians, the media, and whitestream activists that the dominant culture ignores Indigenous ecological wisdom to its own detriment. Such wisdom transcends the current moment of threat. Even before 500 years of colonial exploitation, Indigenous stories forewarned of the damage that unchecked human recklessness could wreak. The intimate relationship between people and Earth goes both ways; environmental devastation brings with it the threat of human extinction. Thus, these stories emphasize that people must recognize Earth as our relative and part of our very makeup. Yet Euro-Western science and philosophy have often discounted these stories as proof of primitive naiveté.

Currently, humanity's problematic relationship with the world around us has informed a new materialist turn in the academy, a turn that foregrounds the material world's influence on the human. New materialisms aim

1. This essay was written on the historic homelands of the Karankawa and Akokisa peoples.

to expose how human subjectivity and agency rely on complex networks of inter-animation. Thus, by "returning to the most fundamental questions about the nature of matter and the place of embodied humans within the material world" (Coole and Frost 3–4), new materialisms provide crucial insights as we contemplate humanity's future. However, from an Indigenous perspective, recognition of the material world's vitality comes rather late. Native stories articulated this understanding millennia ago, along with humanity's need to be a good relative. One such story is that of the Mexica trickster figure Tezcatlipoca, Quetzalcoatl's twin and a co-creator of our current age.

Here, I present the Nahua story of Tezcatlipoca as a framework for knowing our relational place in the world. This framework runs counter to Euro-Western thinking that stresses division and disidentification. Detachment undergirds even the conscientious thinking encouraged by new materialisms, which emphasize interconnectedness. Using Tezcatlipoca's story, I consider the case of a petrochemical plant explosion in Deer Park, Texas, and its construal as an event from both colonial and relational perspectives. As humanity confronts cataclysmic climate change, we must understand how humanness and agency are often constructed at the expense of the nonhuman to instead acknowledge that we are (part) of the world.

Smoke and Mirrors: A Story

Before recalling/retelling this story, I wish to note that this is the version of the Nahua creation story that I learned as I was growing up and seeking to learn more about my own cultural background, which was excluded from the standard curriculum even in a city that is over 95 percent Latinx.[2] Later, I would become reacquainted with this story while forming community with other members of my cultural background while living in Tongva, Kizh, and Chumash territory.[3] However, it must be stressed that this is by no means the "original" version, if such a version existed, but one filtered through centuries of written tradition established by Christian priests seeking to pin down Mesoamerican beliefs, and then interpreted by Mexican and Xicanx scholars for nationalist ends. As Richard Haly explains, while European clergy tried to "make sense" of colonized peoples by setting down Indigenous stories as though they represented a conclusive, knowable history, such inscription practices ignore the "performative character of these tellings" and the "contin-

2. The border city of Laredo, Texas, which is settled on Coahuiltecan land.

3. That is, in different areas of the Los Angeles, California, metro area.

gency of agreement among those present when the act of telling took place" (304). As a Xicanx person whose roots on this continent are located in the lands of the Guachichil, Coahuiltecans, and Laguneros (now known as northern Mexico) rather than those of the Mexica, I deem it crucial to explain this complex narrative context to avoid a simplistic appropriation of these stories. Instead, I acknowledge my particular relationality to their wisdom within a colonial situation that, given rampant cultural genocide, obliges many of us to engage surviving Indigenous stories metonymically. For it is a failure to acknowledge our relationality to those around us, human and nonhuman, that I argue furthers harmful attitudes of entitlement rather than accountability and relationship. At the same time, as Andrea Riley Mukavetz reminds us, maintaining a relational scholarly practice means you must "develop a rich, deep, and reciprocal relationship to the land you dwell on and the Indigenous people of that land" and "carry those histories, cultures, and teachings with you in your writing, research, teaching, and everyday practice" (548). Thus, here I share with you this story as I learned it at home and as a visitor with the goal of being a good relative, one responsible to past and future relations.

At the beginning, Ometecuhtli and Omecihuatl, Father and Mother, fashioned the four directions, the Four Tezcatlipocas. Black Tezcatlipoca is Tezcatlipoca, ruler of the north, the night wind, cunning, sorcery, and sensuality. Blue Tezcatlipoca is Huitzilopochtli, who rules the south, the Sun, warfare, and sacrifice. White Tezcatlipoca is Quetzalcoatl, who rules the west, the sky, intellect, and agriculture. Red Tezcatlipoca is Xipe Totec, ruler of the east, affliction, fertility, and corn. He sacrificed his skin to provide food for humans, which is why corn kernels shed their coverings as they sprout to feed us. All four beings act as one [meaning together] and as One [meaning one unified power], as do Ometecuhtli and Omecihuatl, Father and Mother.

The Four Tezcatlipocas created the universe, including the Sun and Moon. There have been five Suns, meaning ages of time and the celestial bodies that ruled over them. The First Sun began when Tezcatlipoca sacrificed himself and ended when the original people, raucous giants, were destroyed by Tezcatlipoca's animals, jaguars. Quetzalcoatl ruled the Second Sun, but Tezcatlipoca dethroned him and the people who survived the destruction became monkeys. This is why monkeys and humans are so similar and why Tezcatlipoca and Quetzalcoatl are twins and enemies, light and dark, body and spirit, who act as one and as One. One cannot exist without the other. And to show this truth, that nothing is all good or bad, Quetzalcoatl destroyed the Third Sun, ruled by Tlaloc, the rain, and transformed people into animals. Tlaloc's wife, Chalchihuitlicue, ruled the

Fourth Sun, and during this time, human beings were made out of corn. Those of us living today are their descendants, which explains why we are vulnerable to temptation and disease but also driven by compassion and emotion. Corn is life. As Chalchihuitlicue is the river and lake, this age ended in flood.

The Fifth Sun began with an earthquake and will end this way, too, because Ollin, its symbol, means movement. Tezcatlipoca and his brothers created the Sun and Moon. The Sun—Nanahuatzin or Tonatiuh, depending on the story—was sickly and needed blood to burn in the sky. This explains why humanity is part of the earth and sky, our lives dependent on earth and sky for sustenance and survival. Our flesh and blood are of the earth, and when we die, we become the earth and corn that sustains others. We inhabit the Fifth Sun, which is ending or has ended. We don't know what follows but we know our fate is the same as that of the earth. This is because Tezcatlipoca and his twin Quetzalcoatl made the land by slaying the sea monster, Cipactli, who inhabited the world's waters through sacrifice. Tezcatlipoca stuck his leg out over the water and offered his foot to Cipactli as bait. Cipactli rose from the deep and seized Tezcatlipoca's foot, allowing Quetzalcoatl to seize the monster so that they could use her body to make the land. Tezcatlipoca replaced his foot with an obsidian mirror through which he sees all things and dispenses justice. This is why Tezcatlipoca is called "Smoking Mirror," and why, despite being a trickster, he is also one of humanity's patrons.

New/Old/Living Materialities

Typically, when people speak of smoke and mirrors, they refer to falsehoods that obscure truth. Here, smoke and mirrors evoke truth regarding our place in the universe. Humans are not at the center or the periphery of existence, but always in relation. Stories like Tezcatlipoca's reject divisions between human and nonhuman, Subject and object. What emerges through this story is an understanding that our humanity is both ecological and part of a much greater ecology. We are not agents contemplating other agents with which we share materiality; we are not Subjects recognizing that other (possible) Subjects make us who and what we are. Instead, we should understand ourselves as expressions of a shared subjectivity, matter contemplating itself from a location and perspective that deems itself human. It's important to understand that all other perspectives express that subjectivity through their respective forms—as water, as a rain forest, as an ocelot—for which reason humanity cannot claim subjectivity as its independent right in thought or action. In the story of Tezcatlipoca, we find antecedents to concepts central to new materialist perspectives, although these notions as expressed in new materialisms do not engage that sense of singularity in exactly the same way. Hence, I now briefly focus on three such concepts—*entanglement, vibrancy,* and *agency*—explaining how they appear first in Euro-Western theory and then in the story of Tezcatlipoca.

New materialisms emerge from conversations between fields of study including posthumanism, characterized by thinkers like N. Katherine Hayles and Cary Wolfe, and cyborg and techno theories, as articulated by critics like Donna Haraway and Judy Wajcman. These fields' concerns regarding inured boundaries separating the human from technology (including animals as tools) inform new materialism's focus on our ethical and material entanglements with the world. Haraway argues that much of what we are is determined by technology and social codes: "The cyborg is our ontology; it gives us our politics" (7). The cyborg proves a fusion of imaginary and material realities, with these factors determining human progress and forms of oppression. In setting out how we arrived at a historical juncture where cultural conditions render bodies and cybernetic technologies interchangeable, Hayles pushes back on associations of subjectivity with "disembodiment" and attempts to "put back into the picture the flesh that continues to be erased" (5). A decade later, Wolfe applies posthumanism to questions of biopower, ethics, and nonhuman animals, arguing that we must "attend to the specificity of the human . . . [by] acknowledging that it is fundamentally a prosthetic creature that has coevolved with various forms of technicity and materiality, forms that are radically 'not-human' and yet have nevertheless made the human what it is" (xxv). That is, humanity is defined according to the things that we, in turn, seek to define. Understanding how technologies inform the human is crucial, especially when social hierarchies and power imbalances decide who has access to legitimized technologies, and hence, a greater claim to full humanity. Thus, Wajcman examines how technologies "[express] the networks of social relations in which they are embedded" (108).

New materialisms hone our attention on the roles the material world plays in defining our humanity and subjectivity. The human (as individual and notion) is fundamentally entangled within networks and ecologies of matter and their management, raising questions regarding "vibrancy" and, consequently, agency. Jane Bennett argues that composing a "more ecological sensibility" attuned to these issues requires us "to *experience* the relationship between persons and other materialities more horizontally" (10). Human individuation must be problematized. We should understand ourselves as vital materiality whose disidentification from germs and nonhuman animals is predicated on a need to justify our exploitation of the world around us.

This insight holds for nonorganic matter that we use and abuse with a clear conscience, thinking the nonorganic is "nonliving." Bennett reminds us that humans are always already in community with other organisms and things. Human beings are not singular entities, but assemblages made up of microbes, organ systems, and so on. Thus, agency, or "the efficacy or effectivity to which that term has traditionally referred," must be understood as "distributed across an ontologically heterogeneous field, rather than being a capacity localized in a human body or in a collective produced (only) by human efforts" (23). Included in this heterogeneous field is nonorganic matter. The organic and nonorganic are "living," or "vibrant," due to this "thing-power" (6).

While these ideas complicate typical views of the relationship between the human and nonhuman, they do not go far enough in recognizing collective being, constitution, and power, given their basis in a not-fully-examined privileged epistemology. For example, in a much-cited passage, Bennett claims that "it is difficult . . . for a public convened by environmentalism to include animals, vegetables, or minerals as bona fide members, for nonhumans are already named as a passive environment or perhaps a recalcitrant context for human action. . . . If environmentalists are selves who live on earth, vital materialists are selves who live as earth" (111). This understanding of a public erases Indigenous perspectives that have always asserted the sentience, agency, and knowledge of all things. Furthermore, as the story of Tezcatlipoca shows us, we do not only "live as earth" or have it within us—we *are* earth. By appealing to the notion of entanglement across heterogeneous ontologies, theories like Bennett's articulate a vital interrelationship that can nonetheless privilege the human (and privileged humans at that) and simply catalyze action, rather than highlight intrarelationship within a unified subjectivity that requires responsible action toward the whole.

While Bennett focuses on the relationship between power, vitality, and agency, Karen Barad tackles the problem of subjectivity within such fields. Barad describes matter as "inexhaustible, exuberant, and prolific" and bodies as "intra-actively co-constituted" with their environments (170). Separability proves key, particularly when one attempts to observe objectively or what we may more popularly term "scientifically." The human forms part of the "apparatus" of understanding, so spatial separation is required for the purpose of perspective. She advances the notion of agential separability, or "*the agentially enacted material condition of exteriority-within-phenomena [that] provides the condition for the possibility of objectivity*" to resolve the indeterminacy of ontological separation within the apparatus (175). Barad seeks a new methodology "attentive to, and responsive/responsible to, the specificity of material entanglements in their agential becoming" (91). She eschews a subjectivity that posits the human as separate from its environment, and an objectivity that views things neutrally from a distance, in favor of an objectivity that takes our entanglements into account; the apparatus as a tool for understanding objectivity is always situated. This arrangement has significant consequences for the notion of agency, since the agency necessary to observation and/as action is distributed along the apparatus.

Barad's theories more closely resonate with the perspective suggested by the Tezcatlipoca story, although the notion of agential separation nonetheless poses a problem. Agential separability provides a means to contend with perspective and/as action, which all things may have regardless of ontology. However, such separation implies the possibility of an individuation that this story would ask we define with great caution. We are always knowing and acting from within the whole; indeed, seeing subjectivity and agency as anything but collective is what has led to our current catastrophic moment due to coloniality's privileging of (certain) humans above the rest of the material world. This is not to quibble with Barad's choice of words but to stress that the apparatus might instead highlight the relations/relationships we bring with us when we observe, because that "objectivity" necessarily has ramifications far beyond ourselves. How we perceive and act affects everyone and everything because we are all materially and ethically conjoined. Whereas new materialism in the vein of Barad or Haraway seeks to reconcile an ingrained perception based on duality that distinguishes between subjects and objects or nature and culture, stories like Tezcatlipoca's remind us that such distinctions prove false. Nature is culture when one lives with the land rather than on it. The spaces we inhabit "are made recursively through specific, material practices rooted in specific land bases, through the cultural practices linked to that place, and through the accompanying theoretical practices that arise from that place" (Powell 388). We express subjectivity only in relation to all our relations.

For someone of my cultural background, the story of Tezcatlipoca reminds us that all things and concepts are not just entangled but part of a whole. As Davíd Carrasco explains, "Tezcatlipoca was sometimes cast as the supernatural antagonist of Quetzalcoatl, the deity associated with cultural creativity, urban order, and priestly wisdom." Representative of the "darker" aspects of the world, Tezcatlipoca is easily typecast as a mono-dimensional villain. However, the world is not characterized by dichotomies as a Euro-Western perspective suggests. Even practitioners of what might now be considered the dark arts served Quetzalcoatl, and Tezcatlipoca himself provided humankind with corn, which he simultaneously created and embodied (Olivier 61, 73). This story evokes much later work by philosophers, semioticians, and rhetoricians who argue that all language and phenomena cohere and are made coherent by the ecologies they inhabit.

Historian Guilhem Olivier suggests this much about the Divine Twins, saying that "if we consider the structure of the names of Quetzalcoatl and Tezcatlipoca, we see that both are composed of two elements: one that is basically celestial (quetzal and smoke), and one that is terrestrial (the serpent and the mirror)" (78). If we privilege binaries, the twins represent duality, since the figures are both celestial and terrestrial. From a perspective that sees all things as related, however, their connection proves more complicated. In a bit of rhetorical chiasmus, the quetzal bird and the snake are both celestial and terrestrial: The quetzal inhabits both the land and the sky, nesting in the trees; the serpent crawls along the earth and also climbs into the trees, meaning it is not bound to one space. Thus, Quetzalcoatl's name, "Feathered Serpent," can represent the celestial, the terrestrial, and a mix that is simultaneously both and something altogether different. Likewise, the smoke and mirror are of the earth and sky: As smoke, the resin that once rose into the heavens as part of a tree is transformed and travels upward again, bearing prayers into the sky; the mirror, made of volcanic obsidian that came from deep inside the earth, is a scrying tool through which humanity receives celestial knowledge. Hence, Tezcatlipoca's name, "Smoking Mirror," also indicates the celestial, the terrestrial, and a mix that is simultaneously both and something altogether different.

In addition, the quetzal, serpent, smoke, and mirror are all objects associated with knowledge as well as entities of the everyday world. All of them are celestial and terrestrial and confound those categories. For now, I want to highlight those closely associated with Tezcatlipoca's figure. His obsidian looking glass, through which he observes the world—which he simultaneously inhabits in various guises—is a "circular disk with a shaft through it and two curling forms representing smoke attached to the edges [and] this emblem of the smoking mirror was intimately associated with the divine power of the Aztec tlatoani (king)" (Carrasco). The mirror itself smokes, since obsidian is the result of cooled molten rock, but also because its paradoxical im/material state exemplifies the inseparability of body and spirit, matter and mind. It explains why humans and the earth and the sky are connected. This seemingly simple story transcends those entanglements Euro-Western philosophy now aims to center; this story conveys, illustrates, and instantiates a belief where there is no -is and -is not, but rather, includes a both and sometimes either, both and sometimes neither, because everything is the Everything.

As a result, the world including the organic and nonorganic is vibrant and has agency, each entity in its own way without recourse to ontological taxonomies. They merit more than respect but an ethical responsibility, not only because they allow us to be human and express who we are but because they are our relations. This concept of relations is not bolstered by the idea of independent or distinct ontologies, an idea that inevitably falls back on relationships as axiology, but connectedness. The vital connection that is relationship and the vital connections that are relations resist the "objectivity" that grounds colonial perspectives through dualistic and ethical gradation. Explaining this in (colonial) language and thought alone proves difficult; relationship and relations must be felt and lived. Stories like that of Tezcatlipoca account for and enact relations/relationship. These stories are not just words but "take place" (Powell 391), rendering spaces habitable or inhabitable for humans and nonhumans through the ethical, rhetorical, political, affective, historical, and material enmeshments they illustrate and enact.

In "Beyond the Life/Not Life Binary: A Feminist-Indigenous Reading of Cryopreservation, Interspecies Thinking and the New Materialisms," Kim TallBear shares an important example.. Speaking to the importance of pipestone and pipestone quarries to Indigenous peoplehood, TallBear explains that without them, "prayers would be grounded, human social relations impaired, and everyday lives of quarriers and carvers depleted of the meaning they derive from working with stone" (195). Story explains the significance of the cannupa ok'e, the quarry, to Indigenous peoples and why humans and the land are relations. However, TallBear reminds us that the Indigenous peoples connected to the quarries and pipestone still struggle for sovereignty and recognition, and contend with Euro-Western thinking that posits history and the present, and the material and immaterial, as antithetical. In debates over the commercial sale of pipestone objects at the quarries, much of the discourse revolves around the notion of the "sacred," which can only be attended by a notion of the "profane." She writes, "This stance is potentially at odds with a view of relationality that would acknowledge that indigenous peoples and the stone have long existed in more intimate and complex sets of relations than the notions of 'sacred' and 'profane' can represent" (196). TallBear states that academic conversations would "benefit from indigenous standpoints that never forgot the interrelatedness of all things" (180), because forgetting this knowledge entails epistemological, corporeal, and material violence. Indigenous knowledges can inform fields like new materialisms by showing that notions of entanglement, vibrancy, and agency are not new and may actually be more productively considered from perspectives that have not only entertained these ideas but exceeded them.

Indigenous knowledges can also inform how we tackle the issue of the apparatus, that is, how we may make sense of the world while being in and of the world. To deal with this question, Bennett raises the Deleuzian notion of adsorption, a "kind of part-whole relationship" that gathers elements "in a way that both forms a coalition and yet preserves something of the agential impetus of each element" (35). Barad goes further, saying, "Making knowledge is not simply about making facts but about making worlds, or rather, it is about making specific worldly configurations—not in the sense of making them up ex nihilo, or out of language, beliefs, or ideas, but in the sense of materially engaging as part of the world in giving it specific material form" (91). Again, these two lines of thought have a familiar ring to them, given that the "part-whole relationship" denoted by adsorption evokes the fundamental relationship among all things while simultaneously understanding them as existing and acting independently and together.

Yet, as the story of Tezcatlipoca(s) shows us, we have long known that things act as one (that is, as ostensibly distinct entities) and as One (as a whole). And, understanding that making knowledge is about "making worlds" in turn evokes the long-held Indigenous belief that in the one world many might be found. Indeed, in the EZLN's 1996 "Cuarta declaración de la selva Lacandona," they declare, "El mundo que queremos es uno donde quepan muchos mundos / We want a world where many worlds fit." Arturo Escobar tells us that this statement partially informs the notion of the pluriverse, which refers to "a vision of the world that echoes the autopoietic dynamics and creativity of the Earth and the indubitable fact that no living being exists independently of the Earth" (14). It is no coincidence that the notion of the pluriverse is explicitly political when addressing the climate crisis, if by "political" we mean organized attempts to translate belief into action. In Escobar's work, a pluriversal approach informs how thinkers take on "the steady worsening of planetary ecological and social life conditions and of the inability of established policy and knowledge institutions to imagine ways out of such crisis conditions" by accounting for situatedness and material conditions (13).

For this reason, I share with you a counter-framework based in the story of Tezcatlipoca and analyze the petrochemical plant explosion to explain what going beyond entanglement, vibrancy, and agency may look like through one Indigenous lens and what the results of such analysis means for us with/in the world. Colonization tries to silence such stories to promote the dominionism that threatens Earth. Sanctioned by Euro-Western religion and the "common sense" inspired by it, dominionism suggests that human life stands apart from and over the material world and outside of its time frame. Nature signifies an untamed past, humanity a cultured futurity. Such an outlook "den[ies] the complex ecology that goes into [our own] identity" (Arola 218), and necessarily elides our ethical responsibilities to all life, including the earth, water, air, and sky. But this attitude has also been sanctioned by scientists and philosophers, so much so that academics now seek new ways to appreciate the nonhuman and the material, even if that means reducing humans to mere objects. Given all this, I argue that a not-new approach that centers Indigenous knowledge-making proves necessary, one that recognizes stories as embodied epistemologies and temporality as material. Such stories must be stressed and practiced, because Euro-Western thought can orient our observation toward detachment even while seeking to highlight interconnectedness.

Rhetorical Dis/Separation: A Trickster Framework

In *New Materialisms: Ontology, Agency, and Politics,* Diana Coole and Samantha Frost argue that matter is political (7). Unless we acknowledge this dimension of materiality, we risk ignoring our responsibilities to the nonhuman world. In response to this point, here I want to add to conversations about entanglements by thinking about the role that rhetoric assumes in enabling, maintaining, and breaking vital relationships. Dominant culture onto-rhetorical taxonomies justify connections based on domination. Only by deconstructing—and decolonizing—a presumed ontological divide between humanity and "Nature" can prevailing structures of exploitation be overturned, replaced not with a paternalistic take on stewardship but a relationality informed by respect and reciprocity (see Wilson). By "decolonizing," I refer to what Waziyatawin and Michael Yellow Bird describe as undoing the intellectual and spiritual harm imposed by colonization and (re)learning to "think consciously and critically about the meaning of terms from within their own cultural framework" (*Minds Only* 4). They stress that "decolonization . . . is not about tweaking the existing structure to make it more Indigenous-friendly or a little less oppressive," but recognizing that the "existing system is fundamentally and irreparably flawed" (*Eyes Only* 4).[4] In other words, there can be no mistaking what decolonization entails: recognizing the sovereignty and land rights of Indigenous peoples and the rights to language and culture that have been forcibly, violently suppressed, as well as centering Native epistemologies, traditions, and culturally specific rhetorics that transmit knowledges necessary to everyday life and liberation. Recognition and relationship are vital acts for Native peoples. In contrast, mere appropriation of Native thinking or modification of settler technologies serve as mechanisms of colonization, iterations of dominance under the guise of self-actualization.

4. Waziyatawin and Yellow Bird explicitly state that they have written the two handbooks I cite here only for Indigenous readers especially as they begin the painstaking work of decolonizing and reclaiming their cultural knowledges. They ask settler audiences to refrain from reading these works. Therefore, I quote only from the introductions to these handbooks and remind non-Indigenous readers to please respect the authors' request.

Notably, the figure of Tezcatlipoca represents the matter that makes us human, as well as agency, subjectivity, and relationality-as-responsibility due to his sacrifice. Tezcatlipoca is a trickster, and tricksters are maligned as deceivers in binary belief systems. However, tricksters teach us valuable lessons in understanding the world. Tezcatlipoca's story shows us that rhetoric is not a representation of reality but a crucial aspect of reality with a significant place in the network of existence. Reality and representation may be experienced differently, but both are active parts of knowing. Therefore, we must respect all beings (organic and nonorganic) with our words and/as actions because the world's cohesion depends on ethically maintaining our part of the whole and understanding the world via our place with/in and as the world. To this end, I suggest two terms that, like Tezcatlipoca, signify and embody what they mean: *teotl* and *nepantla.*

Teotl is the "one thing" that exists. According to James Maffie, this "continually dynamic, vivifying, self-generating and self-regenerating sacred power, force, or energy" is "identical with reality" and "identical with everything that exists" as well as "the basic stuff of reality" (*Aztec* 21–22). This power-in-motion is "fully copresent and coextensional with the cosmos," being "as concrete and immediate as the water we drink, air we breathe, and food we eat" (29). Teotl is the unifying energy that ties the universe together and *is* the universe, a concept that renders even entanglement too dissociative a notion. Teotl exists in a constant process of making and unmaking, illustrated by the fact that reality is always in flux; this idea runs contrary to the desire for stability and fixity evinced in Euro-Western thought.

Nepantla, theorized most notably by Gloria Anzaldúa, is a one aspect of teotl's "motion-change" that unites "inamic partners in agonistic tension" so that both remain but also create something new through their back-and-forth action (Maffie, *Aztec* 355). For example, the mineral lime breaks down corn but together they make tortillas in which both lime and corn are yet present. Nepantla is often misconstrued as a liminal condition (if one privileges polarities), but liminality and nepantla posit contradictory understandings of the world. While liminality "occurs only temporarily in interstitial transitions from one established state of being or permanent structure to another," nepantla is "neither temporary nor exceptional but rather the permanent condition of the cosmos, human existence, and indeed reality itself" because everything is always in the process of becoming and therefore ontologically unfixed (*Aztec* 363). Maffie writes, "Nepantla-processes suspend things within a dynamic, unstable, and destabilizing *ontological zone* between conventional categories: a zone in which things become ill-defined ambiguous, and anomalous; a zone in which things disappear into the interstices between conventional categories; and finally, a zone from which emerges a novel [third thing]" ("Pre-Columbian" 14). We find teotl and nepantla at play in the story of Tezcatlipoca since he/they act as one and as One, struggling and causing chaos that is actually a type of order. These seemingly oppositional states, like the Tezcatlipocas, are not just working in sync but expressions of the same. All things are vibrant and agential as they enact relationship and transformation, a point evocative of Barad's notion of diffraction (73).

Teotl and nepantla reveal that divisions exist only conceptually. Everything is always what it was and what it will be, and we simply catch glimpses at particular moments before things are once more transformed. Thus, the apparatus must not only capture the "from where" of observation but the "from when," even while apprehending these as expedient distinctions. As I note above, Tezcatlipoca is a trickster, and tricksters barter in illusions to reveal basic truths. He has associations with religious and political rhetorics (De Sahagun; Smith) that are not always savory. And yet, diminishing his indispensable position in Nahua life vis-à-vis a culturally dislocated lens entails ignoring how he resists dichotomies like good and evil, spiritual and carnal, light and dark. Such thinking denies the complexity of reality—and the violence wrought when such oppositions are imposed on the material world.

Anzaldúa's theorization of nepantla familiarizes us to these ever-present rhetorical dimensions of analysis that cannot be discounted if we are to understand these distinctions as conceptual rather than ontological. Because of teotl, nepantla has psychological, geographical, and material dimensions:

> The Mexican immigrant at the moment of crossing the barbed wired fence into a hostile "paradise" of el norte, the U.S., is caught in a state of nepantla. Others who find themselves in this bewildering transitional space may be the straight person coming out as lesbian, gay, bi, or [trans], or a person from working-class origins crossing into middle-classness and privilege.

Disorientation is the interruption of a particular orientation, therefore an awareness that our ingrained orientations are constructed. In another story of Tezcatlipoca and Quetzalcoatl, Tezcatlipoca tricks his brother into committing various transgressions. Quetzalcoatl is surprised by his own misdeeds, realizing only afterward that even he, the wisest of all, can fall to wrongdoing. Ostensible opposites, knowledge and foolishness, are inseparable in the process of transformation. Like the story of Tezcatlipoca and his brother, nepantla signifies an unstable "ontological zone" only if we accept the notion of discrete ontologies.

Anzaldúa describes nepantla as a place of uncertainty and "identity breakdowns" as people move between spaces, identities, and worlds. Like teotl, nepantla gives rise to "third things." However, as Eve Tuck and Marcia McKenzie note, nepantla must be understood in real, material terms. Borders are sites of "psychic, physical, and emotional conflict" (41). Borders and border crossing are not metaphors, a trope that mystifies the violence affecting people who inhabit and traverse borderlands. Borderlands exist vis-à-vis histories of "domination, dispossession, and appropriation" that separate Earth and bodies ontologically, politically, and materially (41). Having grown up on the border, I want to stress that the border may be a rhetorical performance, but it has material heft, and through its concrete, steel, and customs agents, it is very much "alive." Rhetorics encapsulate, enliven, and sustain the networks of which they are part, so we must be critical of how, where, and when power, agency, and meaning are distributed because this constellation informs definitions of ontology. Furthermore, particular distributions give rise to temporalities that undergird coloniality through myths of progress and modernity. These myths posit a teleological center at the expense of a lesser, externally construed environment. Perspectives informed by Indigenous knowledges instead apprehend things (events and entities) as materially and spatiotemporally conjoined.

Accordingly, Tezcatlipoca's story renders an onto-rhetorical analytical apparatus that allows us to contend with our relational situatedness. Teotl asks us to consider the relationality among elements in a rhetorical event, how they are dis/separate (act as one and as One), and the reciprocity between them, that is, how they constitute one another over time. Nepantla asks us to consider not just the kairos of a situation but its chronos of becoming (from an Indigenous perspective), meaning the deep histories informing the event and beyond. Thus, reciprocity must be considered across this temporal ecology; we must understand the stories connected to these elements, and how they enact dis/separation among elements across notions of time. In sum, I posit teotl as the what-ness/how-ness and nepantla as the where-ness/when-ness of a rhetorical event, and this apparatus constrains our rhetorics to specific ideological and material contexts. I hope the why-ness is apparent: Our world is on the brink of climate cataclysm. Except that, for Indigenous peoples and their descendants, cataclysm has been ongoing during the centuries that capitalist colonialism has ravaged Earth for profit. Thus, I provide an example of how humans act and are acted upon within networks of vitality, agency, and meaning from one Indigenous perspective to hopefully clarify something of what settler epistemology has obfuscated and to highlight what Native peoples have been saying all along.

The Smoke of Chemical Fire(s): One Story / Many Stories

On March 17, 2019, an Intercontinental Terminals Company (ITC) petrochemical storage facility caught fire in Deer Park, Texas, located about eighteen miles east of downtown Houston. In total, eleven storage units containing hazardous chemicals like xylene, naptha, and pyrolysis gasoline were destroyed. For four days, the fire burned, and after the plant's "make-shift dike" broke, it released these toxins into the air, Tucker Bayou, and Galveston Bay (Vera). Due to the smoke and changing weather conditions, school districts in Pasadena, Channelview, Sheldon, and Galena Park closed and canceled after-school activities. Darran Simon, Madison Park, and Rebekah Riess of *CNN News* reported that "as the fire burned, sending towering black clouds and a fireball into the sky late Tuesday, neighbors were worried about the heavy, dark smoke." Yet, local authorities assured the local communities that the air quality held in the good-to-moderate range.

On March 22, a flare-up at the ITC facility sparked a second fire, destroying additional storage units. The second fire was contained that day, and Harris County officials notified citizens via social media that no shelter-in-place order had been issued (Chavez and Alsup). In April, the Harris County District Attorney's Office filed charges against the ITC plant. A press release issued by Harris County DA Kim Ogg noted that "water pollution was at criminal levels between March 17 and 21" due to the disaster (Vera). As a result, ITC faced up to $100,000 for each of five charges filed by the DA's Office.

This is where the story of the Deer Park fire(s) becomes part of mine and not mine, where I felt what it means to act as one and as One. I had the privilege to flee this hazard, knowing that other members of my community did not, but also knowing that evading this threat proved impossible because the contaminants compelling my escape would now be intimate acquaintances to us all. After the second flare-up, I drove up Interstate 45, which bisects the Houston metroplex, leaving town to avoid the toxicity. From downtown Houston, I watched the giant plume of smoke rise into the sky about sixteen miles away, turning the clouds an eerie gray. That week, many of my students were out due to the previous fire. Some remained indoors, unable to get to work or school; others had left their homes without clothes or textbooks. Students emailed to let me know that they were going to the doctor or had visited urgent care due to headaches and painful sinuses, the primary signs of xylene and naptha exposure. Many do not have insurance. Some came to school to catch a breath of fresh air because, while the smoke was visible from Clear Lake, there were no fumes. Located about twelve miles away from Deer Park, Clear Lake is an affluent neighborhood, unlike the communities forced into lockdown.

On TV and social media, people derived a sense of gravity from images of roiling flame and dense smoke. Yet "on the ground," disaster looked different. We often speak about catastrophe and its effects without understanding that the effects are the catastrophe; they cannot be separated unless you are watching from outside. From a dominant culture perspective, the notion of an *effect* meaning a result allows an ontological disconnect between the event phenomenon and the protracted, mundane injuries that compose it. What is affected and how (teotl) depends on the where and when (nepantla) of people's lives. An event passes, but recognizing the relationships expressed by the "event" abstraction entails recognizing the "small-scale" implications along with the "large-scale" ones. As the story of Tezcatlipoca shows through its concatenation of Earth and human (we are corn, Cipactli, Tezcatlipoca), our bodies inevitably epitomize what happens to the land and other humans and nonhumans.

From an external perspective, such as that enacted by the media, this disaster proved costly in terms of corporate losses: as repairs, cleanup costs, fines, and community outreach. Such losses are known abstractly, as crunched numbers and brief actions intended to leave the event behind. In contrast, those intimately affected by the disaster—local denizens, plant workers, and the environment—experience it as an assemblage of visceral, material, affective, and rhetorical repercussions. That "event" lives on as the symptoms of chemical poisoning; as missed classes and work shifts, doctor's visits, and environmental toxicity; as the persistent threat that the same kind of disaster will surely happen again; and as the knowledge that all of this misery has been and will be erased by fiscal concerns due to the class, ethnoracial identities, and nonhuman status of those most harmed. Humans and nonhumans embody disaster.

In an interview on PBS's *Amanpour and Company*, nineteen-year-old climate activist Xiuhtezcatl Martinez (Indigenous Mexican, US) explains, "We're seeing projections of everything from $600 trillion of damages from climate destruction in the next 80 years to a billion people being displaced . . . [but] there are people that are already suffering every single day. . . . We are seeing massive amounts of destruction and pain already" ("Xiuhtezcatl Martinez"). Disasters are instantiations of colonial calamity, not effects. "Effect" privileges those with epistemic room to view rising sea levels or a toxic chemical cloud as they approach in some possible future subjunctive time (see Massumi), not as an everyday reality. Vulnerable humans and nonhumans are affected in the ever-present. Broadcasts discussed chemical toxicity in terms of human physiology, warning that xylene and naptha cause "eye, nose, throat and skin irritation," even death if inhaled (Vera), but we heard little about their effects on water or air, or the entities that inhabit either. Instead, the ever-present marked by contamination was—is—usurped by the future subjunctive time of privileged humans and nonhumans like the economy and petrochemicals. But there is no separation of past, present, and potential future for the Earth and peoples who already know what it means for colonization to poison everything and kill for profit and power (see Gross). In the Tezcatlipoca story, the raucous giants were destroyed because they ruined everything in their midst, but the entire cosmos paid the price. Likewise, even as vast corporations dispute the veracity of climate change to protect their interests, all of the world, including their corporate constituents, must suffer the consequences.

The fire(s) exist(s) also within a smaller, but no less significant, kairotic continuum. The day before the first Deer Park Fire, an ExxonMobil refinery in Baytown, Texas, eleven miles from Deer Park, caught fire. Although the fire was extinguished within hours, a report to the Texas Commission on Environmental Quality noted that the refinery continued to release 5,500 pounds of toxic nitrogen oxides (4,000 over the allowed limit), thirty-five pounds of hydrogen sulfide (twice the allowed limit), and 484 pounds of benzene through March 24. The damage was so significant, even by statistical standards, that in April, Harris County Pollution Control filed a civil suit against ExxonMobil for violations of the US Clean Air Act to force the company to comply with safety regulations. Harris County had already sued ExxonMobil in 2006, "for a spill that coated a nearby public housing project with oil"; in 2011, "for releasing more than 50 tons of propylene, the petrochemical and ozone precursor," and emitting a hydrogen-sulfide-like odor from the Baytown refinery; and in 2017, "for releasing 10 million pounds of pollutants into the air over eight years" (Trevizo). The severity of the 2019 fire brought public awareness back to these previous violations even though entire communities had been living the material impacts of these "forgotten" offenses for over a decade. The where/when of their lives, determined by the what/how of their class and ethnoracial status, ensured that their stories did not matter.

Two weeks later, another chemical plant fire at the KMCO facility, in Crosby, Texas, sixteen miles from Baytown, killed one person and critically injured several others after a transfer wire ignited an isobutylene tank. Residents within a one-mile radius of the plant were advised to stay indoors and four school districts serving about 30,000 students went into lockdown. One plant worker disclosed that the alarms had not sounded; employees were unaware anything had happened until the fire swept through the plant, sending people scrambling over the fence because the plant gates were locked ("1 Dead"). In 2015, the Environmental Protection Agency had cited KMCO for failing to ensure the plant complied with risk-management regulations. In

2016, the plant faced federal sanctions after it was discovered that, between 2008 and 2012, employees had falsified air testing logs submitted to Texas and US environmental authorities. Between 2018 and 2019, the plant received three notices of clean-air violations. Furthermore, Crosby had seen chemical fires before. In 2017, another plant caught fire after floods from Hurricane Harvey cut the power that kept organic peroxides refrigerated. In 2018, the Harris County DA indicted the plant's company, chemicals manufacturer Arkema North America, and its manager and chief executive, Richard Rowe, for their roles in the chemical release. Evacuations in the area displaced 200-plus people for over a week, with twenty-one needing treatment for chemical exposure. The company decried the charges as "outrageous" and "unprecedented" since the hurricane was an unforeseeable "act of God" (Mele).

I belabor the facts in this secondary chronology to show that the Deer Park disaster inhabits a human-land relationship that transcends the bounds of its own history. Like the others, this petrochemical plant explosion was shaped by where/when of race and class, and the what/how of coloniality. According to the US Census Bureau, Deer Park is 63 percent white, 2 percent African American, and 32 percent Latinx; Baytown is 35 percent white, 16 percent African American, and 46 percent Latinx; and Crosby is 40 percent white, 4 percent African American, and 56 percent Latinx. (In contrast, Clear Lake is approximately 90 percent white, less than 1 percent African American, and 6 percent Latinxs of any race.) Four of the top five employers in Deer Park are chemical companies: Shell Refinery and Chemical Plant (3,200 employees), Universal Plant Services (1,353), Lubrizol Specialty Chemicals (1,360), and Dow Chemical (1,330) (City of Deer Park). The largest employer in Baytown is ExxonMobil (3,785 employees) (Baytown). Those exposed to chemical toxicity are those dependent on the plants for their livelihood, plants that exploit, exacerbate, and perpetuate human and nonhuman vulnerability to guarantee continuous profitability.

These numbers speak volumes regarding subjectivities erased under narratives of separation. For petrochemical executives damage control is disaster control—controlling the narratives and lives of humans and nonhumans without power. The same week as the Deer Park fire, executives from Chevron, ExxonMobil, and other chemical corporations held a conference in San Antonio, Texas, to address "the demonization of fossil fuels" (Luck). In a *Houston Chronicle* article, an executive claimed, "We know what we do is good. We're just miserable at communicating it to anyone else." That same article stressed that the petrochemical sector's safety ratings were "four times lower than the overall manufacturing industry," but that employees attended daily safety meetings. Meanwhile, a spokesperson for ITC issued a quasi-apology to the residents of Deer Park, where 30 percent of ITC employees live: "They're out there fighting this fire the best they can . . . [and] their family is of concern. So of course, ITC would apologize to any of them" (Simon et al.). Like threat, the apology exists in subjunctive time where disaster and its attendant obligations exist for the privileged. But stories like that of Tezcatlipoca tell us there is no recourse to another temporality because everything is connected. Notions of linear time are colonial constructs that decenter harmony and intrarelationship because they posit time as outside eventful space rather than bound to Earth's plight.

As Dustin Edwards argues, "understanding the practice of making and listening to stories . . . is never an apolitical or neutral activity" (63). Corporations know well the rhetorical power of stories in evading ethical responsibility. Although the ExxonMobil fire in Baytown released nitrogen oxides and hydrogen sulfide, and the plant had been cited multiple times for toxic pollution, it was overshadowed by the ITC fire(s) even though the ExxonMobil plant continued to spew chemicals for over a week. Writing for the *Houston Chronicle,* Perla Trevizo reports that ExxonMobil claimed these leaks had no "adverse impact" on the surrounding communities, declaring itself "a leader in safe, reliable and environmentally responsible operations . . . committed to operating in a manner that protects the safety and health of our personnel and our community." That community does not include the air, land, or water, or the working-class people whose bodies shield those who benefit from plant production. I am reminded of a story Zoe Todd shares in which she notes that Inuit climate change activist Sheila Watt-Cloutier had been nominated for the Nobel Peace Prize in 2007 alongside Al Gore, "only to be dropped before the prize was later awarded to Gore and the [Intergovernmental Panel on Climate Change]" (6). I remember reading her words and wondering why the award was awarded to members of the culture that caused the damage. Do members of the dominant culture not see themselves as a community or in community, but only as individuals? Is dissociation rather than dis/separation at the core of their identification? Do they not realize that the where/when of their modern world is built on what/how Othered humans and nonhumans suffer? Thus, I wonder how they can advance any notion of ontology when they cannot identify with each other, let alone nonhumans.

In addressing the United Nations, fifteen-year-old Autumn Peltier (Anishinaabe-kwe, Wikwemikong First Nation, Canada) declared, "Many people don't think water is alive or has a spirit. My people believe this to be true" (Kent). She argued that water's personhood must be acknowledged. When Indigenous peoples demand personhood for water, land, and nonhuman animals, whitestream audiences laugh, because something not human cannot be regarded as human, though this happens all the time. In a statement responding to a Harris County DA indictment, Arkema North America declared itself a victim of Hurricane Harvey (Mele), ostensibly rendering the indictment void. Todd speaks of climate theories that render the environment *aer nullius,* just as settlers declared the land *terra nullius* despite the presence of people. *Aer nullius*—"a blank commons to be populated by very Euro-Western theories of resilience, the Anthropocene, Actor Network Theory and other ideas that dominate the anthropological and climate change arenas of the moment" (8). This notion creates the problem to "solve" the problem and in the process erases matter and/as bodies—what I term *materia nullius,* a theoretical apparatus that "flattens, distorts and erases the embodied, legal-governance and spiritual aspects of Indigenous thinking" (Todd 9). Heeding Tezcatlipoca's wisdom, for me even the Anthropocene proves too limited in its view of human activity as the dominant force influencing the environment. This is not to say we can eschew our ethical responsibilities but that there is no "environment" external to humanity. Furthermore, nonhuman elements have agency; they, too, can destroy even without our intervention. In the story I shared, the different ages reveal what happens when humans or nonhumans are out of balance with the whole. This is not a myth but a warning. Only by being good relations can we determine when any of us needs healing, and the open-endedness of the story of the Five Suns invites us to cultivate that knowledge in order to keep the story-as-enacted-relationship going.

Conclusion

What all this suggests, to me at least, is a need to step away from naive construals of vibrancy and agency. As Tezcatlipoca's story shows, all things are "vibrant" or alive because they are parts of one whole; even his being is part of the earth and us by virtue of his lost foot. To deny agency, safety, and respect to nonhumans is to deny our own, no matter our claims to dominance, because there is no human outside of earthly relations/relationship. Hence, Native stories warn against this kind of hubris. New materialisms may account for ethics of power, but they also need to heed the lived knowledges inherent to Indigenous stories. Humanity cannot claim a privileged materiality made "vibrant" through its outright denial to the nonhuman world and justified through utilitarianism. For that reason, I invoke the figure of Tezcatlipoca here to stress acting as one and as One and to acknowledge the intimately ethical, experiential, and material dimensions of life long ignored by Euro-Western thinking. I do so to suggest that learning cannot be dislocated through the violence of abstract universality even if we are all related. Histories, like parallel universes, inhabit the same spaces where lived stories implicate them—of necessity, colonized peoples have long had to recognize and live with the implications of the pluriverse.

Separation can no longer prove a ruling architectonic if our relationships with/in Earth are to be healed. Instead, we must foreground communal kinship and ideo-material enmeshment in recognition of a more complex positionality. As Heather Alberro notes, "entanglement with nature exists in the Western world too. But the global socioeconomic systems birthed by this region were founded on the exploitation of the natural world for profit. Transforming these entrenched ways of working is no easy feat." This transformation includes changing how we see ourselves "entangled with Nature." I have used the term *Nature* here as a form of translation because we are not so much entangled with as part of the world. When we exploit nonhumans, we abuse ourselves. As rising temperatures and elemental contamination threaten to make life unlivable for all within a few decades, we must all choose intrarelationship over dominion.

Works Cited

"1 Dead and 2 Injured in Explosion at Texas Chemical Plant." *CBS News*, 2 Apr. 2019, https://www.cbsnews.com/news/crosby-texas-explosion-kmco-chemical-plant-today-2019-04-02-live-updates/. Accessed 22 Sept. 2019.

Alberro, Heather. "Humanity and Nature Are Not Separate—We Must See Them as One to Fix the Climate Crisis." *The Conversation*, 17 Sept. 2019, https://theconversation.com/humanity-and-nature-are-not-separate-we-must-see-them-as-one-to-fix-the-climate-crisis-122110. Accessed 20 Sept. 2019.

Anzaldúa, Gloria. "Chicana Artists: Exploring Nepantla, el lugar de la frontera." *NACLA Report on the Americas*, 25 Sept. 2007, https://nacla.org/article/chicana-artists-exploring-nepantla-el-lugar-de-la-frontera. Accessed 21 Jan. 2022.

Arola, Kristin L. "It's My Revolution: Learning to See the Mixedblood." *Composing(Media) = Composing(Embodiment)*, edited by Kristin L. Arola and Anne F. Wysocki, UP of Colorado, 2012, pp. 213–26.

Barad, Karen. *Meeting the Universe Halfway: Quantum Physics and the Entanglement of Matter and Meaning*. Duke UP, 2007.

Baytown. "Major Employers." *Baytown.org*, http://baytownedf.org/site-selection/major-employers. Accessed 29 Sept. 2019.

Bennett, Jane. *Vibrant Matter: A Political Ecology of Things*. Duke UP, 2010.

Carrasco, Davíd. "Tezcatlipoca." *Encyclopedia of Religion*, edited by Lindsay Jones, 2nd ed., vol. 13, Macmillan Reference USA, 2005, Gale eBooks.

Chavez, Nicole, and Dave Alsup. "Firefighters Contain Latest Flare Up at Deer Park, Texas, Chemical Plant," *CNN*, 22 Mar. 2019, https://www.cnn.com/2019/03/22/us/deer-park-chemical-fire/index.html. Accessed 17 Sept. 2019.

City of Deer Park Economic Development Department. "Community Overview." http://www.deerparktx.gov/315/Community-Overview. Accessed 29 Sept. 2019.

Coole, Diana, and Samantha Frost. "Introducing the New Materialisms." *New Materialisms: Ontology, Agency, and Politics*, edited by Diana Coole and Samantha Frost, Duke UP, 2010, pp. 1–43.

De Sahagun, Bernardino. *Florentine Codex: General History of the Things of New Spain*. Translated by Arthur J. O. Anderson and Charles E. Dibble, U of Utah P, 1969.

Edwards, Dustin. "Digital Rhetoric on a Damaged Planet: Storying Digital Damage as Incentive Response to the Anthropocene." *Rhetoric Review*, vol 39, no. 1, 2020, pp. 59–72.

Escobar, Arturo. "Transiciones: A Space for Research and Design for Transitions to the Pluriverse." *Design Philosophy Papers*, vol. 13, no. 1, 2015, pp. 13–23.

EZLN. "Cuarta declaración de la selva Lacandona." *Enlace Zapatista*, 1996, http://enlacezapatista.ezln.org.mx/1996/01/01/cuarta-declaracion-de-la-selva-lacandona/.

Gross, Lawrence William. *Anishinaabe Ways of Knowing and Being*. Ashgate, 2014.

Haly, Richard. "Bare Bones: Rethinking Mesoamerican Divinity." *History of Religions*, vol. 31, no. 3, 1992, pp. 269–304.

Haraway, Donna J. *Manifestly Haraway*. U of Minnesota P, 2016.

Hayles, N. Katherine. *How We Became Posthuman: Virtual Bodies in Cybernetics, Literature, and Informatics*. U of Chicago P, 1999.

Kent, Melissa. "Canadian Teen Tells UN 'Warrior Up' to Protect Water." *CBC News*, 22 Mar. 2018, https://www.cbc.ca/news/canada/autumn-peltier-un-water-activist-united-nations-1.4584871. Accessed 20 Sept. 2019.

Luck, Marissa. "Deer Park Fire a 'Blemish' for the Petrochemical Industry's Image." *Houston Chronicle*, 26 Mar. 2019, https://www.houstonchronicle.com/business/energy/article/Deer-Park-fire-a-blemish-for-the-image-of-13717661.php. Accessed 19 Sept. 2019.

Maffie, James. *Aztec Philosophy: Understanding a World in Motion*. UP of Colorado, 2014.

———. "Pre-Columbian Philosophies." *A Companion to Latin American Philosophy*, edited by Susana Nuccetelli et al., Wiley-Blackwell, 2010, pp 9–22.

Massumi, Brian. "The Future Birth of the Affective Fact: The Political Ontology of Threat." *The Affect Theory Reader*, edited by Melissa Gregg and Gregory J. Seigworth, Duke UP, 2010, pp. 52–70.

Mele, Christopher. "Chemical Maker and Its Chief Indicted for Explosions during Hurricane Harvey." *New York Times*, 3 Aug. 2018, https://www.nytimes.com/2018/08/03/business/arkema-chemical-plant-explosion-texas.html. Accessed 21 Sept. 2019.

Olivier, Guilhem. "Enemy Brothers or Divine Twins? A Comparative Approach between Tezcatlipoca and Quetzalcoatl, Two Major Deities from Ancient Mexico." *Tezcatlipoca: Trickster and Supreme Deity*, edited by Elizabeth Baquedano, UP of Colorado, 2015, pp. 59–82.

Powell, Malea. "2012 CCCC Chair's Address: Stories Take Place: A Performance in One Act." *College Composition and Communication*, vol. 71, no. 4, 2020, pp. 383–406.

Riley Mukavetz, Andrea. "Developing a Relational Scholarly Practice: Snakes, Dreams, and Grandmothers." *College Composition and Communication*, vol. 64, no. 2, 2012, pp. 545–65.

Simon, Darran, et al. "A Huge Fire at a Texas Chemical Plant Is Out, 4 Days after It Started." *CNN*, 20 Mar. 2019, https://www.cnn.com/2019/03/20/us/deer-park-itc-plant-fire-wednesday/index.html. Accessed 19 Sept. 2019.

Smith, Michael E. "The Archaeology of Tezcatlipoca." *Tezcatlipoca: Trickster and Supreme Deity,* edited by Elizabeth Baquedano, UP of Colorado, 2015, pp. 7–39.

TallBear, Kim. "Beyond the Life/Not Life Binary: A Feminist-Indigenous Reading of Cryopreservation, Interspecies Thinking and the New Materialisms." *Cryopolitics: Frozen Life in a Melting World,* edited by Joanna Radin and Emma Kowal, MIT P, 2017, pp. 179–202.

Todd, Zoe. "An Indigenous Feminist's Take on the Ontological Turn: 'Ontology' Is Just Another Word for Colonialism." *Journal of Historical Sociology,* vol. 29, no. 1, 2016, pp. 4–22.

Trevizo, Perla. "Harris County Sues Exxon Mobil over 'Illegal' Emissions Release after Baytown Refinery Fire." *Houston Chronicle,* 7 June 2019, https://www.houstonchronicle.com/news/houston-texas/houston/article/Harris-County-sues-Exxon-Mobil-over-illegal-13961152.php. Accessed 20 Sept. 2019.

Tuck, Eve, and Marcia McKenzie. *Place in Research: Theory, Methodology, and Methods.* Routledge, 2014.

US Census Bureau. "QuickFacts: Deer Park City, Texas; Harris County, Texas; United States." 2019, https://www.census.gov/quickfacts/fact/table/deerparkcitytexas,harriscountytexas,US/PST045218. Accessed 29 Sept. 2019.

Vera, Amir. "Texas District Attorney Files Charges against Chemical Plant for Its 4-Day Fire." *CNN,* 29 Apr. 2019, https://www.cnn.com/2019/04/29/us/deer-park-itc-plant-fire-charges/index.html. Accessed 24 Sept. 2019.

Wajcman, Judy. *Technofeminism.* Polity Press, 2004.

Waziyatawin and Michael Yellow Bird. *For Indigenous Eyes Only: A Decolonization Handbook.* School of American Research, 2005.

———. *For Indigenous Minds Only: A Decolonization Handbook.* School for Advanced Research, 2012.

Wilson, Shawn. *Research Is Ceremony: Indigenous Research Methods.* Fernwood, 2008.

Wolfe, Cary. *What Is Posthumanism?* U of Minnesota P, 2010.

"Xiuhtezcatl Martinez on the Global Climate Strike." *PBS,* 19 Sept. 2019, http://www.pbs.org/wnet/amanpour-and-company/video/xiuhtezcatl-martinez-on-the-global-climate-strike/. Accessed 20 Sept. 2019.

CHAPTER 5

Perpetual (In)securities

(Re)Birthing Border Imperialism as Understood through Facultades Serpentinas

A. I. RAMÍREZ

> A central concern would have been to highlight the materiality of the body as the ultimate object of technologies of fear, understood as apparatuses of power aimed at carving into the flesh habits, predispositions, and associated emotions—in particular, hatred—conducive to setting social boundaries, to erecting and preserving hierarchies, to the perpetuation of domination.
>
> —Brian Massumi, *The Politics of Everyday Fear*

The global border industrial complex (GBIC) is a contradictory, imperial specter—a sensitive, recursive, globalized network or matrix of border (in) securities. As a technology of fear, the GBIC creates and reproduces bordered landscapes and ideologies wherein refugee and migrant mothers, women, and transwomen exist in perpetual anxiety. Brian Massumi describes that "assemblages of power," such as the GBIC, are experts at piercing the flesh, emotions, and behaviors that shape, not only the individual, but potentially the social network—all to further nonconsensual domination. This perpetual insecurity negatively affects the nervous system and facilitates the internalization of fear, which gets passed through the womb or intergenerationally. Border wall murals, understood as rhetorical texts, can articulate the rhetorical sensations of the GBIC and the consequences of those sensations. Through murals, artists express themselves and create a visual representation of the phenomenological consequences of border imperialism.

As a first-generation graduate student navigating a predominantly white and Eurocentric institution and field, I was laughed at for suggesting serpents and dreams could teach us anything. As a queer Mexicana-Chicana having experienced homophobic comments about my theory of the phallic feminine throughout ancient and contemporary cultural practices, I wanted to give it all up. It was reminiscent of how my grandparents' Kikapú (English: "Kickapoo") knowledge was deemed witchcraft and *brujeria,* and how the undocumented migrant experiences of my parents were characterized as shameful within US social and educational systems. Although I had committed my graduate studies to investigating the marginalization of Indigenous experiences, theories, and knowledge, I instinctively hid the serpent in my writings at first, as if to protect it. These personal experiences influenced my investigations into how serpent methodologies inform analysis on how structures of power are embedded in institutions, and in the case of my scholarship, how these structures of power—like ideology, architecture, and international policy—are embedded in global borders. It was these personal experiences that led me to wonder about the palpability and stickiness of border trauma, as I understand it though the serpent.

In order to describe what the border wall feels like, I apply *facultades serpentinas,* a pluri-versatile theory informed by ancient Mexican/Mexica serpentine awareness, and Gloria Anzaldúa's theory of *la facultad,* which she describes as a psychic reality defined as "the ability to shift between attention and see through the surface of things and situations" (*Bridge* 547).[1] *Facultades serpentinas,* specifically through the birth sequence of a *lecho de serpientes* / nest of serpents, a symbolic trope throughout the ancient world, is thus a phenomenological approach to my analysis of the GBIC border murals. I utilize auto-ethnographic observation methods as I describe sensory data gathered through my field research experiences of borders that have been painted with murals, including the Berlin Wall installation and mural in Los Angeles, and murals on the US/Mexico border wall in Tijuana. Second, I juxtapose my experiential research with analysis of news reports, videos, sounds/audio, and images of family separation. In this chapter, I seek to explain how border murals, as visual media, transmit what a border feels like. In other words, I ask: Can border wall murals communicate how and what the border feels like? What does it mean to think and feel in decolonizing ways, as opposed to settler colonial ways?

The facultades serpentinas that allows for a rhetorically sensing research method involves experiences with explicit and latent, underlying, and invisible aspects, layers, or traces at the border walls, as a way to sense the border.[2] Similar to the serpent symbol, this project describes how murals or public arts and walls can be understood in this dichotomous, contradictory way,

---

1. For more on *la facultad,* as defined by Gloria Anzaldúa, see *Borderlands / La Frontera,* "Now Let Us Shift," *Light in the Dark / Luz en lo Oscuro, Interviews/Entrevistas,* and *The Gloria Anzaldúa Reader.*

2. From Jane Bennett's *Vibrant Matter* (2010), where she analyzes various materials and assemblages as having "vibrant" energy and the capacity to "manifest traces of independence or aliveness" (xvi).

while embracing plurality through a facultades serpentinas and a lecho de serpientes / nest of serpents heuristic. The lecho de serpientes (or nest of serpents) heuristic looks at the movement of intersecting phenomena, such as the history of national borders, as well as the traces left behind, both materially and affectively by border walls and border wall murals. The layers of paint, the sounds along the borderlands, the emotional residue, all form part of my research data.

These sensorial and sensual methodologies, such as the facultades serpentinas, and the heuristic of lecho de serpientes, are helpful to inspect murals and national barriers for their affective capacity. The "touches" that happen with and through the senses—sensual things—is the link between the feeling, sensing, and knowing body. In this way, art has the potential to transform at the level of the episteme. In my description of rhetorical sensations (below) as a method of analysis, I will go further to explain how I go about gathering sensory data, and in my description of the lecho de serpientes heuristic as method, I draw links between the sensorial, rhetorical, and transnational. In defining the methodology, facultades serpentinas, as a theory and method for reading and understanding the cosmos and sociopolitical phenomena, I look to theories of affect and decolonization.

What I am sensing for and with the facultades serpentinas methodology is a deeper understanding of where or how creative consciousness is felt or born.[3] In her *sentipensante* (sensing/thinking) methodology, contemplative studies scholar and educator Laura Rendón describes a pedagogy infused with critical care as emerging from the solar plexus.[4] This internal, embodied, and deep knowledge can also be thought of through Patrisia Gonzales's writings of the *ombligo* or belly button in her book *Red Medicine*. Kikapú, Comanche, and Macehual scholar of Indigenous epistemologies and medicine Patrisia Gonzales describes the *ombligo* as "the seat and regulator of the spirit" (144). This umbilicus, the "*centro cósmico,* a cosmic center," also moves like a snake (149). In *Red Medicine,* Gonzales analyzes the Vaticanus B 39 codices and identifies how the birth guardian, Izquimili, is present to cut the umbilical cord that links the human to the cosmos. Gonzales writes: "In the *Ritual of the Bacabs,* the word *cantippte* evokes a snake pulsing in the stomach" (144). The lecho de serpientes methods that emerge from the facultades serpentinas as a methodology thus are a felt knowledge, informed by the body. This *ombligo,* or umbilicus, reference is important to remember, as it is in and through the belly that humans and serpents alike feel the world. Moreover, community

3. For more on rhetorical listening in the field of rhetoric and composition, see Sean M. Conrey's film *Listening for Phoné* (2016) and *Silence and Listening as Rhetorical Arts* (2011), edited by Cheryl Glenn and Krista Ratcliffe.

4. See Rendón, *Sentipensante.*

engaged Chicana scholar and muralist Judy Baca writes: "A mural's compositional lines draw the body of the unsuspecting passer by into the painting by the solar plexus"—the solar plexus, the pit of the stomach (155). This is where art is felt in the body, through the body.

Throughout this ongoing project, I take up a serpentine research method, theory, and practice of writing. Facultades serpentinas is not only a theory and method of research and writing, it is also a method of reading. I braid together several strands, several serpents. An illustrated stone slab titled "Lápida de serpientes," or "serpent tablet," housed at the Museo Nacional de Antropología in Mexico City depicts seven snakes braided together. Similarly, *La Lápida de Aparicio,* found in the state of Veracruz in Mexico, is a stone-carved depiction of a sitting anthropo-figure with seven linear serpents, braided, seemingly emerging from the neck area. The *Aparicio* figure's serpent heads face out and away, as if in a sudden burst from the body, like a gush of blood. It seems as though the seven serpents were braided or in the process of making a braid as they emerged from the body. Indeed, where the head should be are snakes and blood in the form of snakes, braided together. Similar to these stone tablet depictions from Mexico, I weave back and forth between disciplines, traversing land, time, and dreamscapes, with my "forked tongue" (Anzaldúa, "Now Let Us Shift"). My plurisensory, transdisciplinary, transborder approach is often dizzying, overwhelming, and nonlinear, much like the GBIC. The complexities of complexes such as a nest of serpents and the GBIC are best understood with a similarly complex, maybe even a chaotic, system of analysis and research methods.

In this introductory section/strand/serpent, I've explained how facultades serpentinas, as both decolonial theory and method, are an ancient knowledge system that serves to understand affective and emotive rhetorics. In the following section/strand/serpent of this essay, I introduce the archive, the site of analysis, the case study, for this chapter: a section of the Berlin Wall in Los Angeles, California. I return to the murals again as the essay develops; much like braiding hair, a rope, or a basket, one returns over and over to a previous strand to make the hold strong.

There are many strands, many serpents, indeed a nest of serpents. They can be difficult to follow, even scary, traumatizing, much like an unnatural, national border.

The Wall Along Wilshire

The case study in this essay is a Berlin Wall, Cold War museum installation, and its murals. On November 8, 2009, to commemorate the twentieth anniversary of the fall of the Berlin Wall, the Wende Cold War Museum of Los Angeles held an evening ceremony that concluded with a reveal of the permanent installation of ten segments of the Berlin Wall, titled *The Wall Along Wilshire,* on Wilshire Boulevard across from the Los Angeles County Museum of Art (LACMA). The ceremony served as a memorialization and reanimation of the Berlin Wall "event," where instead of the city of Berlin being split, Los Angeles was metaphorically divided between east and west. The Wende Museum's Berlin Wall installation is a series of concrete slabs from the original Berlin Wall that once divided East and West Berlin, and on each slab is a mural.

On the north side of the Berlin Wall installation, which faces toward the LACMA and Wilshire Boulevard, murals include a standing Nelson Mandela and close-up of John F. Kennedy's face. The south-facing facade of the installation includes a mural of a skeleton, or *calaca,* as Captain America, with the letter "D" on his helmet, and various symbols of neoliberalism: surveillance camera, fast food restaurants, and a construction crane. *Calaca* is a colloquial term for a skeleton with human qualities. It is both alive and dead. The *calaca* is associated with peoples who celebrated the time of the dead, or Día de Los Muertos, to signify the time of the year when the dead return to the realm of the living.

On another slab of the south face of the installation is a mural titled *goodcancomefrombadcancomefromgood* by the artists known as German Herakut. "Herakut" is a name for the artist pair Jasmin Siddiqui (Hera), who grew up in the West Block, and Falk Lehmann (Akut), who grew up in the East Block of Berlin, Germany. *goodcancomefrombad* depicts two pregnant women positioned in opposite or upside-down directions, with long hair, both bodies turned toward one another, and both faces looking out toward their viewers. The way the bodies are positioned can be described as contradictory to one another, but still sharing a common experience. Phenomenologically, this reminds me of the yin-yang symbol.[5] The Berlin Wall museum installation and the mural *goodcancomefrombad* are both reanimations of past border events and provide an opportunity to reflect critically on the corporeal traumatic effects/affects national borders have in/on reproductive and creative migrant bodies. Here "reproduction" is a reference to both parenthood or childbirth, the ability to reproduce offspring, but also to the ability to create and re-create, such as in creating works of art, architecture, and even war machines. The

5. *The Internet Encyclopedia of Philosophy: A Peer-Reviewed Academic Resource,* citing Zhuang Zhou, more commonly known as Zhuagzi (Chinese philosopher around the fourth century BCE): "'When the *qi* of *yin* and *yang* are not in harmony, and cold and heat come in untimely ways, all things will be harmed.' . . . On the other hand, 'when the two have successful intercourse and achieve harmony, all things will be produced'" (Coutinho).

cosmic law of creative chaos means that all things are part of the process of creative destruction.

The cyclical and recursive undertones of *goodcancomefrombad* serve as sensational reminders of border imperialism against women, femmes, and children. The pregnant bodies in the border mural suggest that border imperialism not only traumatizes an individual, but does so intergenerationally through state hauntings—what Jasbir Puar calls "paranoid temporalities" and "anticipatory temporalities"—perpetual fear of the return of borders (*Terrorist* xx). Jaqueline Martínez points out that the recursivity and circulation of such oppressive mechanisms as the GBIC, within cultures and transnationally, means that such ideologies have rooted themselves in one's preconscious (xiii). The preconscious that Martínez identifies may be the place of felt/sensed imagination, images, and dreams—the psychic realm that precedes language (Anzaldúa, *Light in the Dark* 49). It is in this realm where artistic and animalistic sensibilities may be located. Perhaps it is where language is felt more than understood or intellectualized. Because art can be felt and be provocative, it may be able to provoke empathy and thereby humanize those affected by border violence.

In the following section I play with the many iterations of the word for *womb*—*matriz* (Spanish), *matrix* (English), *māter* (German)—particularly because of the implications that sexuality and maternity have in migration across borders for migrant women, children, and femmes. In this section, I delve deeper to explain how the womb, the birth sequence, and the nest of serpents form part of the facultades serpentinas. The womb, I argue, can be a trope to understand where artistic sensibilities arouse. Building from the work of Gonzales, Baca, and Rendón, I argue that deep belly thinking through the body, with the body, can sense deeper *vibraciónes*/vibrations (*víboras*/snakes).

Murals can be described as rhetorically sensational (as relating to the senses as a source of knowledge in order to make meaning) because they often depict state-sanctioned human rights abuses, futurity, pleasure and joy, feelings, and images that incite powerful emotional responses (also understood as a mural's affect). Both rhetoric and decolonization are concepts that require an intimate link with sensation/sensorium and the solar plexus. Visceral responses manifest like a pulse from within, a provocation, a sensed knowledge—and both rhetoric and decolonization are a part of a larger collective imagination. The embodiment of theory is opposed to the suppression of the sensing body (such as in the colonizing epistemes that dichotomize natural experiences such as in the separation of mind and body). Thinking/sensing or embodied knowledge is an important feature of decolonial, feminist, and Indigenous thinking. For me, this "solar plexus," this gut feeling, can also happen thinking through the womb, thinking with the womb, thinking about the womb. A womb of a serpent: a sensing/thinking creature.

The Wall Along Wilshire *strand is meant to introduce my sites of analysis and link the theoretical components of facultades serpentinas to an understanding of the GBIC. Each strand, each border, a part of a whole. Each serpent/strand dynamic, each contradictory. I carry the dueling, contradictory concepts of creation and destruction throughout the rest of the essay. In the following section, I braid in the concept of the womb as both a social cavity as well as a network within which ideas, social constructs, and concrete infrastructure (for example) are created. Not even the womb, the* matriz/matrix/māter, *are free of this cosmic contradiction: destructive and creative.*

Matriz/Matrix/Māter

> We tend to slip out of togetherness the way we slip out of the womb, bloody and messy and surprised to be alone. And clever—able to learn with our whole bodies the ways of this world.
>
> —adrienne maree brown, *Emergent Strategy: Shaping Change, Changing Worlds*

> I have seen three women give birth
> and with each contraction
> the mighty hips break and stretch,
> the leathery mouth of a snake
> I watched as they writhed
> inside the all-consuming pain, pure as God,
> fists clenched, wailing something
> not quite human, but animal enough
>
> —Tiana Clark, "Cottonmouth," *I Can't Talk about the Trees without the Blood*

adrienne maree brown's metaphor of birth and womb similarly describe the affect of how one might encounter borders and art. We are freshly born, sensitive, learning through our bodies, never having encountered fear, but the shock of border violence shatters one's innocence. The GBIC's systemic violence has more than just material or tangible consequences. It has a matrix, and womb, of emotional, affective, and intergenerational traumatic effects, particularly on the bodies of migrant communities and families. The systemic violences that many migrants face in the US and around the world are physical, psychological, and economical. Crossing the border is not the only treacherous part of migration. This also includes exploitations of labor, deadly labor conditions, xenophobic attacks, anxiety of deportation or detention (and poor conditions therein), family and loved ones separation, and lack of law enforcement protection (such as in crime protection). Therefore, pursuing a description of listening and affect is not purely theoretical, nor simply a discursive analysis. Indeed, investigating border wall art is a political, ethical, and cultural imperative that is done by walking next to the border, touching it, sensing it, looking at it up close, listening in between its microscopic layers, and tasting its air.

The *matriz,* the Spanish word for *womb,* is also the term for *matrix.* The *matriz* of the GBIC is made up of interdependent, dark, messy, bloody umbilical cords in perpetual motion. The root word of *matrix* is the word *māter* (*mādər*), or *matter,* the beginning and end of all things at once. The GBIC and the wall murals are a similarly pluralistic and multidirectional framework: the framework of the serpentine matrix, a nest of serpents. The nest of snakes is a guiding metaphor to describe the phenomenology of border wall murals. Border phenomena or the process of "bordering" can also be understood as complex and contradictory because it is the right of a sovereign nation to delineate its boundaries in order to avoid external, and potentially oppressive, governing systems.

Serpents and humans are highly sensitive and susceptible to their surroundings and the lived experience of their mother: their creatrix. Like humans, some serpents, such as the anaconda, give birth (*dar a luz*) to live babies. A nest, a womb, a matrix.

The GBIC can similarly be understood as this nest of serpents, un lecho de serpientes, from which both good and bad have been born. Facultades serpentinas, through a lecho de serpientes heuristic, can be utilized to describe both the GBIC, its affects on and in the body, as well as how to critically sense border wall murals in order to understand that palpable "emotional residue" Gloria E. Anzaldúa claims sticks to the border (*Borderlands* 25). Similarly, the border as una "herida abierta," an "open wound" . . . an open womb . . . that Anzaldúa refers to, can be understood through the lecho de serpientes (nest of serpents), as a sexual, sensual-political border, oozing, infected by US patriarchal imperialism. Harsh Walia, activist, writer, and popular educator, defines what is happening at transnational borders as *border imperialism.* In *Undoing Border Imperialism,* Walia presents four processes of border imperialism: displacements, criminalization of migration, racialized hierarchies of national and imperial identity (belonging), and state-mediated exploitation of migrant labor (37–78). Border phenomena can be politically weaponized and used as a tactic of colonization. For example, Wendy Brown in *Walled States, Waning Sovereignty* describes the case of the Israel/Palestine wall as a "bid for sovereignty" on behalf of the Israeli nation-state as it forcefully occupies Palestinian territory (46).

Migration is often thought of as the promise of a better life, but it is all too often met with violence and exploitation, especially for the most vulnerable, and sometimes the end of life. Women, femmes, and children in particular are at risk. For example, in *Captivity beyond Prisons: Criminalization Experiences of Latina (Im)Migrants,* scholar of incarceration and racialized and gendered state violence Martha D. Escobar examines how the US enacts its matrix of ideological and military and carceral powers on and against (im)migrant women's bodies (11). Grace Chang, scholar in human trafficking, globalization, and migration, similarly reminds us that women and pregnant women are particularly targeted for their production and reproduction, as their labor is exploited, and simultaneously discriminated against for their childbearing capacity because they are "seen as responsible for reproduction and consumption, as they are blamed for the strains thought to be imposed by immigrants on public resources" (5).[6] Interdisciplinary Chicana feminist scholar in sociology and community studies Michelle Téllez details how multinational corporations exploit women's labor in Mexico and around the world at the border through the globalized maquiladora phenomena. Téllez notes that maquiladora managers have required women to take pregnancy tests or show their underwear to prove they are menstruating. The state targets vulnerable populations, particularly women and femmes, as they are seen to be most capable of production/reproduction, thus capable of challenging state power in numbers and knowledge. Téllez further argues that the borderlands are also a transformational place, where a politicized transfronteriza identity can emerge.

This ongoing project considers the sensitive vulnerability of migration, but specifically how migrant displacements, criminalization, racialization, and exploitation of labor affects children, women, and femmes over time and how the skin and womb, or *matriz,* of the border wall reveals humanizing narratives that governments try to silence and obscure. In *Community Literacy and the Rhetoric of Public Engagement,* Linda Flower quotes Elenore Long to describe one of five formative elements of community literacies as "the guiding metaphor" in which a space might be imagined as "a womb" (18). The GBIC is complex and it is transnational. It is a network of architectural and ideological systems, serving to separate and demoralize. However, in the same

6. See also Eithne Luibhéid and Lionel Cantú Jr.'s *Queer Migrations: Sexuality, US Citizenship, and Border Crossings* (2005) and Eithne Luibhéid's *Entry Denied: Controlling Sexuality at the Border* (2002).

way, that network or matrix, although powerful, if understood differently, can be a space of transformation and rebirth.

In mathematics and computer science, matrices are used widely for simulation and constructing things like computer graphics and QR codes.[7] Technologically speaking, they are utilized to construct simulated representations and experiences. The #, hashtag, or octothorpe, functions in a similar multidirectional way as the symbol is used to link similar virtual experiences or topics. A grid or spreadsheet, such as in virtual reality spaces and video games that are dependent on mathematical or digital matrices, also function this way.[8] If a video game may be described as an assemblage or arrangement of fantasy and sensory experiences, the definition of *assemblage* might also explain the phenomenology of border wall murals. Such an assemblage attends to the initial womb or social cavity, as well as what is birthed: mediated sensory experiences, with sometimes real deadly consequences. Since the serpent has contradictory qualities, the serpentine assemblage can describe the pluralistic interconnectedness of GBIC as well as what is at stake for children, women, and femmes.

The embodied and tentacular assemblage to the material and affective capacity of the GBIC and border wall murals is a chaotic, sensitive, and pluralistic assemblage of serpents: the nest of serpents. Similar to intersectional theory, which recognizes the politics of intersecting identities and lived experiences, according to Jasbir Puar, an assemblage overlaps, is unstable, and is always in motion, as exemplified in her concept of a homeland as

> cohered through sensation, vibrations, echoes, speed, feedback loops, recursive folds and feelings . . . spatial rather than locational or place based phenomena, coalescing through corporealities, affectivities, and, I would add, multiple and contingent temporalities, as much as it is memory of place, networks (of travel, communication, and informational exchange), the myth of the imminent return to origin, and the progressive telos of origin to diaspora. (*Terrorist* 171)

Puar's pluralistic definition of *homeland* is parallel to the serpentine matriz/matrix/māter. The womb is a "home" where one grows up, and where

---

7. Artist and doctoral candidate Lizbeth De La Cruz Santana blends border mural arts and QR code technology: "A US Veteran, Mothers of Kids Born in America: Interactive Border Wall Mural Honors the Deported," *USA Today*, 11 Aug. 2019, https://www.usatoday.com/story/news/nation/2019/08/11/tijuana-border-interactive-mural-honors-deported-immigrants/1981435001/.

8. According to AIE, the function of a matrix "can be reused for other cool applications like reflection (if the model needs to be reflected over water or a mirror), scaling (making a bigger/smaller version of a model) or for calculating things like drift and orbit."

one grows up is contingent on space, bodies, affect, time, and relationality. Archaeologist Sara Ladrón de Guevara describes the serpent imagery she studied in El Tajin Mexico as a "vital movement, cycle without beginning nor end, and the beginning and the end" (59; translation mine). The recursive serpent symbol of the ouroboros, eating its own tail, speaks to the transformation process of serpents, time, and space—such as when a serpent sheds its delicate, shell-like skin. Instead of the ouroboros, a nest of snakes attends to the plurality of a social womb, particularly the feeling or affectivity of that recursivity (as in the return of borders and border (in)securities). The serpent is highly sensitive, and senses with all of its body. Like humans, like nature, the serpent is contradictory: both "good" and "bad," not all "good" and not all "bad." That is, both/and, and, neither/nor.

To sense the "skin" of a border wall might be understood as a method in new materialisms within academia, but there is nothing "new" about feeling for an object's "embodiments, affects, and relationalities" (Morrissey). Embodied knowledge, learning through the skin, through the body, is an ancient or traditional knowledge that has long been ignored and made invisible by Western modernity's logics of domination and territoriality. Moreover, Indigenous ontologies have long been demonized by colonization, Eurocentrism, and Christian doctrines. The consciousness that "things" have power, what Jane Bennett describes as "thing power," emerges through an awareness of relationality between all things—an awareness that has existed thousands of years before Western science evolved. For Indigenous peoples around the world, writes Kikapú, Comanche, and Macehual scholar and promotora Patrisia Gonzales, the awareness of this relationality and "thing power" was understood through multiple dimensions of knowledge, including what we now call embodied or experiential knowledge. Blackfoot scholar Leroy Little Bear argues that "the Native American paradigm is comprised of and includes ideas of constant motion and flux . . . the constant flux notion results from a 'spider web' network of relationships. In other words, everything is interrelated" (x). Everything is related and everything has spirit. Everything is everything, as Lauryn Hill sings, and it emerges from the same matter—matriz/matrix/māter. Better yet, everything is everything's everything.

Blackfoot scholar Leroy Little Bear looks to the spider web to illustrate the cosmic law of interdependence. For me, working from my own traditions as a Mexicana-Chicana, queer scholar, with Kikapú ancestry, Little Bear's spider web image appears as a nest of snakes. Like a spider web, the nest of serpents and the cosmos are in motion; they're sensitive and chaotic, creative and destructive.

Indigenous queer, Chican@, and feminist scholars, artists, and activists have long made arguments for a more embodied, sensual research praxis within and beyond academia. The purpose of my approach to rhetorically sensing border wall murals is to contribute to what community development and environmental sustainability scholar Sarah Marie Wiebe defines as "sensing policy," which seeks to examine and describe how people are affected by governing policies, in this case border policy and the tentacular GBIC. I ask: What does the nest of snakes (GBIC) look like, what does it smell, sound, taste, and feel like? Moreover, what are the political consequences of those sensations and the consequences of the affect of the global border phenomena or GBIC? What is the role of border wall mural affect?

Wiebe begins to address these questions in her book *Sensing Policy: Engaging Affected Communities at the Intersections of Environmental Justice and Decolonial Futures* when she describes a sensual policy as a relationally engaged praxis that can elicit a more public engagement in issues of public policy, within and outside of academia. A sensual policy validates the embodied experiences of peoples who live in harmful and oppressive situations, such as environmental hotspots and the borderlands.[9] Sensing policy, as in feeling policy, is a way of listening to the embodied experiences of people and how they feel the affects of current policy in order to transform those conditions/policies. Perhaps empathy, for a political purpose, is a better way of describing this listening or sensing process.

Empathy requires one to see the "both/and" relationship, even in the most violent circumstances. It is, for example, to see a serpent lunge and penetrate its target with its poisonous fangs, and also to see that the serpent is sensitive, practically defenseless, and perhaps fighting for its life. In *Staying with the Trouble: Making Kin in the Chthulucene,* Donna Haraway makes the argument for interspecies relationality, or interspecies empathy, not for the purpose of recuperation or a return to some pure or idyllic past (as in some critiques of decolonization), but instead to "stay with the trouble" of contradictions among all things and learn to co-create with all things, even death, even borders, imperialism, and colonization. Natalie Diaz, Mojave and Latinx poet, contemplates the contradiction of the postcolonial condition in her poem "Postcolonial Love Poem," wherein she describes how one might struggle with being both colonized and colonizer:

9. An environmental hotspot is defined as a biogeographic location threatened by human habitation, such as by industry, pollution, resources extraction, deforestation, illegal hunting, and so on. Environmental racism is often related to hotspots as many of these harmful projects exist in predominantly poor, Black, Indigenous, and Of Color communities. See Sarah Marie Wiebe's work in the bibliography for more on how Indigenous communities are affected by environmental hotspots.

those [wars] which started me,
which I lost and won—these ever-blooming wounds.
I was built by wage, and so I waged love and worse— (1)

Even in war there is light and life. *Colonization,* a word meaning "to grow" or "to cultivate," a life-giving force, is also a deadly word. A mother can also be deadly. A mother can be a monster.[10] As such, to "stay with the trouble" of contradictions is to understand something as having light-giving qualities, as well as darkness.

For Wiebe, the process in developing the theory of "sensing policy" arises from being in conversation and relation with the Aamjiwnaang First Nation peoples and the chemical plants polluting the land near Ontario, Canada. This pollution, Wiebe finds, is detrimental to the Aamjiwnaang peoples' health, intergenerationally, as well as their cultural expression Wiebe's sensing policy interrogates how the senses are also receptors of state policies and challenges legislation or rather legislators to feel and to sense in their own bodies oppressive policies, perhaps in order to prevent them from being further enforced. If Wiebe's sensing policy is indeed effective in touching audiences—their hearts, guts, senses—then it is possible that aesthetic or artificial bordered sites (murals and art installations) have not only the rhetorical capacity and vitality, or "thing power," to animate+reanimate colonizing architecture, but also the potential or potency to decolonize the "borderlands" at an epistemic level through the senses. In *Vibrant Matter: A Political Ecology of Things,* Jane Bennett explains the reason why and how "things" are provocative, as they "affect other bodies, enhancing or weakening their power" (3). The affective capacity of art can arouse empathy, relatability, and the power of the erotic. Audre Lorde defines the erotic in her essay/chapter "Uses of the Erotic: The Erotic as Power" in *Sister Outsider* as a sensual awareness and satisfaction, related to a critical feminine, spiritual knowledge, arrived at by sharing creative endeavors with others (53–59).

Murals as sensual and sensational rhetorics generate the capacity to confront the dominant narrative and material realities caused by the GBIC, specifically upon children, mothers, and femmes, but they can also reanimate those very traumas in the body. Similarly, the facultades serpentinas concentrates on the power of the sensual, the senses, sensations, in order to analyze critical transnational systems. For me, the place where I process sensation is deep in my belly. As a mother, I can speak about it as a womb. I understand it as the place where voice is born, from where all things are born.

10. See Ocean Vuong, *On Earth We Are Briefly Gorgeous.*

Although murals and border art alone will not solve the problems of borders, they do disrupt dominant narratives of borderlands, even if only for a short period of time. Analyzing borders through rhetorical listening and decolonial sensing methods can foster a critical consciousness about the GBIC. The Transnational Decolonial Institute's decolonial aesthetics as a practice of "identities-*in*-politics" that inspire "planetary revolution in knowledge and sensibility" and Juana María Rodríguez's definitions of "discursive spaces" in *Queer Latinidad* inform my contextualization of decolonial, especially Rodríguez's connections between bodies, landscapes, and discourse that highlight "the discursive effect of figures and shadows, stasis and movement, strategy and risk" (31). Art—murals in this case—creates openings or imaginative cracks in the wall that academics, activists, and residents can explore and exploit for change.

Given the proliferation of the intergenerational tragedies directly correlated with the GBIC, an embodied description—or sensual theory—of what a border wall "feels" like, sounds like, tastes like is just one approach to understanding the phenomenology of borderlands.[11] Listening with and to the body helps to arrive at an understanding of what lies below the skin, in the body, in the heart: listening to others, and listening to all things nonhuman, such as the environment, such as concrete walls.[12] In other words, when analyzing rhetorics of border murals by way of listening with the body, I am talking about experiencing border murals as affectual.[13] Listening for sensation, in order to trace border phenomenology is, as Jaqueline M. Martínez explains, an attempt to "articulate the essential existential structures of what is present in the immediate lived experience of a person" (x). Moreover, a phenomeno-

11. For my project, I draw from two descriptions of phenomenology. One is from Sara Ahmed's *Queer Phenomenology,* wherein Ahmed concentrates on "the significance of nearness or what is ready-to-hand, and the role of repeated and habitual actions in shaping bodies and worlds" (2). My understanding of phenomenology also depends on Michelle M. Wright's description of "epiphenomenal time" in *Physics of Blackness,* as many temporalities at once in the "now": "imagined through individual perceptions in various ways depending on the context" (4). And finally, Jaqueline M. Martínez in *Phenomenology of Chicana Experience & Identity* describes the limits of a phenomenological methodology, concluding that "phenomenological research always remains open ended" and "is therefore bound to its own interrelation with other and the world" (xi).

12. What I mean by "rhetorical listening" is less about human-to-human communication, though that kind of listening is similarly vital. Rhetorical listening in this project is about "listening" (as in becoming attuned to and in (dis)harmony or (im)balance with reality) with more than ears, but with our bodies.

13. This understanding of rhetorical sensations, which builds on "rhetorical listening," is informed by Shelly Streeby's book *Radical Sensations: World Movements, Violence, and Visual Culture,* wherein she writes that artists can provoke audiences to act through sentimental and sensational images. My theorizing on sensing the border is also grounded in the literal listening described in *Silence and Listening as Rhetorical Arts,* edited by Cheryl Glenn and Krista Ratcliffe.

logical experiential approach, such as tracing the sensations within a nest of serpents, might attend to the social, emotional, personal, and global transformations occurring, while also possibly bringing about transformations of oppressive conditions. The serpent birth sequence and subsequent nest of snakes can offer a kind of thinking/feeling, sensing or rhetorical listening to the slippery political work necessary to both understanding and transformation. It also helps to imagine a juxtaposition between sensual experience and border imperialism. As a rhetorical text, the Berlin Wall installation and its murals (including the *goodcancomefrombad* mural by the artists Herakut) makes a serpentine claim, that good can come from bad and that bad can come from good. This confusing and chaotic border phenomenon impacts both the physical body as well as the mind and emotion.

I have braided together the theory of facultades serpentinas, the archive: Berlin Wall section, and the womb/matriz metaphor. Each thread carries similar characteristics: (1) the pluralistic affect and emotions as knowledge producers in the body, that both the serpent and humans (particularly mothers in this section) feel through the belly; (2) contradiction, and learning to be satisfied with contraction as "goodcancomefrombadcancomefromgood"; and (3) a recursive nest of serpents, as illustrated by the Berlin Wall as the GBIC. In the following strand, I will contextualize the embodied and affective consequences as well as the intergenerational traumas of migration on femmes, women, and children in relation to the border and the GBIC.

Rebirthing Border Terrorisms

Soon as you have your baby, I am going to kill you.

—Rep. Sheila Jackson Lee, recounting a refugee mother's narrative on *Democracy Now!* ("Caged Children")

I am driving with my own children, listening to the audio recorded by Propublica *of migrant children crying after being separated from their parents and confined to cages. We are silent as we hear the children's wails. I listen to my body as their voices vibrate throughout the car speakers—the voices and sentiments,* sentimientos, *that had been missing from the US/Mexico border debate. My children and I are quiet and still as we look each other in the eyes. We hear the voice of the male guard, mocking the children's cries, calling their laments "an orchestra"—a cacophony of terror. As Rep. Sheila Jackson comes on to retell the story of a pregnant migrant mother, my body suddenly feels cold as I empathize with the mother's fear and as I visualize children crying in cages. I feel a deep sorrow and want to cry. I remember, my body remembers, the moment, the voices.*

The monstrous border "event" at the US/Mexico border, with its global reach, produces an assemblage of recursive intensities of violence; so too have other borders, across time and across the world. These traumas—embodied memories of violence—are recorded on and in the human body, as well as the land. They may disappear and reappear, such as the Berlin Wall did as an art installation.

The Berlin Wall is no longer a "death strip" but is now a piece of disaster art that can provoke the return of the trauma from a past border event. When explaining how a nation-state weaponizes sexuality and racialized terrorism, and how that violence is embodied specifically by Sikhs, Muslims, and Arabs, Jasbir Puar writes that "tactile [or haptic] knowledges install normativizing traces of danger, fear, and melancholia into the bodies of racialized terrorist look-alikes" (*Terrorist* 194). Moreover, "memory (of trauma) is dislodged as the primary arbiter of remembering (and forgetting)" (195). Traces and memorials of violence are thus the curse, the symptom, and the cure.

Although museums and muralists have the capacity to decolonize a borderland space, they also can reanimate borderlands by shedding light on the problem without critique and reviving border traumas without understanding the root of such trauma. The GBIC is manifested in Los Angeles through the Wende Museum installation, and the Berlin Wall persists in provoking physical, lived, and material consequences. The emotional pain, palpable fear, and intergenerational traumas are borders that continue to emerge from the GBIC.

Informed by the *goodcancomefrombad* mural on the Berlin Wall installation in Los Angeles, I connect the metaphor of the womb to the birth sequence of the anaconda and the theory of facultades serpentinas as the embodied knowledge that drives the serpentine trialectic in my writing, and explain how it can serve what Chela Sandoval calls "oppositional consciousness"—what Sara Ladrón de Guevara calls la "coincidentia oppositorum (oposición de contrarios)" (59)—to Western colonizing ontologies. Thinking and feeling through the facultades serpentinas may allow one to experience borderlands in similar ways as the serpent: sensitive, attuned to subtle rhythms, contradictory, recursive, and defensive. I came to learn about sensual theory first through the serpent, though I would not have called it that then. I remember several childhood dreams of a serpent. I was both frightened and seduced by dreams of it and the concrete carvings and murals from Mexíco that I only saw in travel magazines and commercials. Serpents became my muse and my guide. As I moved through readings within and beyond graduate courses, the sensational or sensual knowledge of the serpent was made more real. I gave it words, a political purpose, and related it to the work of Chican@, Black, Indigenous, and Of Color theorists, activists, and artists.

I rely on images of the ouroboros, a nest of serpents, and an anaconda birth sequence to help describe the politics of sensation, phenomenology, and the GBIC—in a kind of contradictory, pluralistic, recoiling, serpentine dance, intertwined and messy. I see the return of the Berlin Wall as recursive intensifications that reemerge throughout history and throughout the world.[14] That is to say, history and events do not merely repeat themselves but are re-created and repurposed, and they affect the world around them to different intensifications. This is what typically remains unseen with the figure of the ouroboros: the life that remains after it has devoured itself.

A border wall, a real death trap for anyone who tries to trespass it, devours itself too, injures the "mindbodyspiritplacetime" of the borderlands: the space that gives it life, to the point of self-destruction. What life is there after the wall comes down, after it devours itself, again? The anaconda who eats its stillborn babies does so for the purpose of self-preservation. Nature is like this: destructive and creative. Humans are like this.

I consider the womb as a social cavity from which border insecurities emerge and link the metaphorical womb to the embodied trauma produced by the expansive global bordering phenomena, which primarily terrorizes women, children, and femmes. I concentrate on the womb metaphor, with an understanding that it is not synonymous with reproduction, motherhood/parenthood, or cisgender women. Using the sensory experiences of listening to children who have been detained by US Customs and Border Patrol, narratives of migrant women, children, and femmes as presented through news reports, and a play on the etymology of the word *womb,* which includes the terms *matrix* and *māter,* I argue that the womb is a metaphorical creative space, where "goodcancomefrombad . . ." and "badcancomefromgood. . . ." The womb in this chapter is a birth cavern, as well as the matrix or framework within which the GBIC evolves. One can sense that framework and its consequences through an embodied and sensorial approach, such as the facultades serpentinas, the ability to sense in the same way a serpent might.

With attention on the sensuality of border wall murals, through embodied, serpentine, knowledge ways, I seek to answer how border imperialism and border wall murals provoke sensations in one's body, in memories, or on the skin (as goosebumps, chills, etc.): What does the border feel like? What does it mean to listen to the skin of the border wall? How is our own skin implicated and touched, how does it react to borders and border wall murals? Further underneath—under the skin, in the body—what does it feel like to

14. Jasbir Puar defines "recursive intensities" through the serpentine turban wrapping Sikh men wear, and writes that each ceremonial turban wrap is similar and different, each turban moves in different speeds, each ages differently (*Terrorist,* 171–92).

know fear of bordering, or the spark from art, *desde las entrañas*, from the gut, from the womb? Through a serpentine trialectic informed by ancient theories, dreams, arts, and my own embodied experience (i.e., experiential knowledge), I address the border walls and their murals' themes through a threefold approach to the facultades serpentinas. I perform this trialectic (or polylectic) dance with the concepts of birth, time, place, and contradiction: (1) lecho de serpientes, or nest of serpents, as a pluri-sensory field research process; (2) serpentine contradictions, focusing on border murals as signaled by the *goodcancomefrombad* mural; and (3) serpentine time as recursive intensifications in the reappearance of a border in the Berlin Wall installation.

Encounters with borders and border wall murals, described as rhetorical sensations, is a process in describing embodied understanding, reading, listening, thinking, and feeling. Like phenomenology, the facultades serpentinas engages in an analysis of first-person sensory experiences. According to Anzaldúa, *facultad* is a deep, felt, critical awareness of phenomenological sensory experiences. A facultades serpentinas helped me to focus on, to be entranced by, the serpent birth sequence and nest of serpents, as both theory and methodology. The birth and nest of serpents teaches me as a philosopher, researcher, and writer to feel deeply about how a freshly born snake might feel, experience, sense, or touch the world with each and every register of its senses. This facultades serpentinas is cyclical and pluralistic, like the ouroboros that eternally devours itself, and the lecho de serpientes in constant, chaotic, sensual movement. It is through the complex and contradictory facultades serpentinas that I seek to describe what the border wall feels like, and to gather a "feeling of a place" (Kuhn).

The encounter with a border wall, to be "in touch" with the GBIC, means to be willing to feel the border wall but also to feel what another human being might feel, to be sensitive and open to one another's vulnerability. Perhaps this is a call for more radical empathy, that is, to feel another's trauma in order to be provoked to action. Border mural art, taken as affective, rhetorical objects, helps to answer the consequences of such feeling or sensation of border phenomena.

Border art and art installations, as embodied meaning-making systems, can reveal the affective capacity of the GBIC, and how the GBIC and its affects are continuously reanimated and re-created throughout different times in history and in different parts of the world. That art can reveal as much as it can conceal may be explained as a birth sequence. Much like the serpent shedding its skin to become, or be born anew, a human is born, it is pushed toward light. Indigenous or Traditional knowledge that I refer to here is an embodied cosmology, it is not the same as the phenomenology of Western, European thinking about consciousness and experience. The "light" is associated with knowledge in Western knowledge systems. In Spanish, the phrase "to give birth" is *dar a luz*; translated, it means "to give light." In many ways, birth is knowledge.

Dar a luz is the act of "giving light" or coming into light and is used to describe the moment of birth as the child emerges from its mother's womb. A birth sequence can also be considered a critical consciousness (*conscientização*) as one comes into the world, sensitive. *Dar a luz* is often painful and bloody, and encapsulates life and death, as not even the birth of new life is spared from the presence of death and darkness. My mother thought I would die when she gave birth to me, *cuando me dio a luz*, as I was born blue in the face, not breathing, with the umbilical cord (the life cord) wrapped twice around my neck. Giving light and coming into light are creative and destructive processes, capacities that border wall murals also have. Part of the decolonization process is to think about the artistic process, and the art itself, as theory. Border wall murals, through the muralists, reveal what might not be otherwise made evident by popular or circulating communication media. For example, Judy Baca writes about her community muralism process:

> Murals sing gospel from our streets and preach to us about who we can be,
> What we fear, and to what we can aspire.
> In their highest moments, murals can reveal to us what is hidden,
> Challenge the prevailing dialogues,
> Transform people's lives.
> Murals exercise our most important rights of free speech
> And can indeed be the catalysts for change in difficult times.
> Times such as these . . . (156)

Despite the potential for contradiction of border murals, it is more apparent that art sheds light onto political issues. In this way, mural art can be an epistemologically liberating and possibly decolonizing tool.

Understanding border art as a powerful experience that happens in the body and on the skin can provoke a spark of awareness of the interconnected ideological and geopolitical assemblage of power that is the GBIC. My serpentine analysis of the border wall murals and why they return is an embodied, meaning-making approach: It is an analysis of both "skin" and "body." My definitions of embodied meaning-making are informed by Phil Bratta and Malea Powell, who explain that "*all* rhetoric is a product of cultural systems and that *all* cultures are rhetorical (i.e., they have meaning-making systems that are meaningful and that can be traced synchronically, diachronically, and a-chronically), understanding the specificity of the bodies *and* subjectivities engaged in those practices must be central." My language, my birth sequence, and giving birth to my children, as well as the ancient stories I was told about birth and serpents, all inform this theorizing. I introduce this cultural rhetoric as the theory and method to understanding the affect of borders.

Death and rebirth are contradictory, they are chaotic, they challenge the "good/bad" dichotomy and accept a "both/and" and *"neither/nor" framework of such social systems. The serpent teaches this, and so can border wall murals. In this final strand, I return to the beginning, to an earlier strand. Similarly, the title of the mural* goodcancomefrombadcancomefromgood *elicits a recursive, nauseating affect, signaling both the return of a border, a return or rebirth of a border, and also, as is its contradictory nature, a signal of a promise of good things to come.*

goodcancomefrombadcancomefromgood

The Wende Museum, as part of their commemoration of the fall of the Berlin Wall, commissioned artists, both local and transnational, to revive past Berlin Wall murals already on the concrete wall and to paint new murals. Also, as part of the evening events, the organizers erected a false *Wall Across Wilshire.* The museum curator stated the impetus for the installation was to "replicate the Berlin Wall's function as a site for political and personal expression." "To mark the occasion, The Wende brought ten original Berlin Wall segments to Los Angeles, installed them at 5900 Wilshire Boulevard, one of the key East-West streets in the city, and invited established and emerging artists to reflect upon history and paint five of the ten segments" (Wende Museum). In addition to the *Wall Along Wilshire,* which is the permanent installation, *The Wall Project Documentary* documents the process that the Wende Museum took to erect a temporary pseudo-border wall, a temporary border wall or museum installation titled *Wall Across Wilshire*. The Berlin Wall is reborn and transformed yet again. It is not recast; rather it is another spectral figure. The empty shells left behind by a serpent, a lingering and fragile memory of what it once was.

The *Wall Across Wilshire* was constructed of permeable materials made to resemble or mimic a border wall and was painted by commissioned, local, and well-known artists. The *Wall Across Wilshire* was symbolically broken down by the participating audience members present as part of the evening's events on November 8, 2009. (I recommend that the reader take a moment now to watch the accompanying documentary, *The Wall Project Documentary* [Davis, 2010], as it is a performative act that the reader can experience along with my theoretical analysis).

By ceremoniously tearing down the *Wall Across Wilshire* and installing the *Wall Along Wilshire*, the Wende Museum performed the material impermanence of national borders, illustrating that they are indeed porous, portable, penetrable, and permeable. The documentary does not detail whether or not the ceremony addressed the cyclical temporality or present consequences of global border politics, ideologies, or technologies.

The performative act of knocking down a wall and Berlin Wall museum installation falls within the definition of Western aesthetics that seek visual beauty for the sake of pleasure only. The two installations are thus symbolic of the recursivity of borders, border wall murals, and embodied border violence. They are evidence that borders move across time and space like serpents, devouring and reproducing themselves. Gabriele Hayes, a former Berlin resident interviewed for *The Wall Project Documentary* and who also spoke at the 2009 ceremony, hauntingly describes how she "got chills" from seeing the original Berlin Wall slabs in Los Angeles, where she lives now. She stated in her speech at the ceremony: "Your whole life comes back in your mind . . . things you did, things you couldn't do. . . . [T]his will give people a glimpse of how we lived in East Germany. . . . I'm very honored to be here tonight, and to be able to say 'I am free.'"[15] These statements by Hayes demonstrate both the capacity of mural art forms and art curation or installation to incite nostalgia, trauma, and feelings of freedom in the mindbodyspiritplacetime. As Hayes stated, one's "whole life" is impacted. One's skin, body, worldview, and future—indeed, our genetic makeup—are "touched." Nagy Youssef et al. found that DNA methylation occurs during trauma (DNA methylation has been linked to depression and suicide). Their research suggested that, indeed, "trauma-induced methylation changes in humans" may be passed on intergenerationally, such as from mother to child. Intergenerational consequences of violence can be both physical and psychological. *Susto* is a term to describe the reaction to a traumatic event. *Susto* can be understood as a feeling of reliving past trauma to the point of entering a state of shock or possibly paralysis at the "flashback" of the traumatic event or events. *Susto* also defines a moment of trauma, or a trauma-inducing experience, as "soul loss," where

15. See Davis (2010).

the traumatic event (regardless of the length of such an event) causes one's soul to leave the body.[16] The Berlin Wall once split people's past and future in Germany; it split East and West Berlin, and was now splitting East and West Los Angeles. Ironically, not far from the wall's ceremonial location was the actively militarized division between the US and Mexico, between friends, families, neighborhoods, and loved ones. Like the serpent, *The Wall Along Wilshire* obscured a border's power, buying the state time to further its anti-immigration agenda. This performance, installation, and murals, intended to raise awareness about the consequences of borders, simultaneously hid the current consequences of the US/Mexico border.

The event and the installation of the Berlin Wall itself was a sensed reminder, eliciting memories and "sinking feelings," perhaps drowning feelings, flashbacks, of border violence in Europe that reveal how the architecture and rhetoric of borders are weaponized to extend the power of the state beyond its territory. Perhaps because of this Eurocentric view of the affect of borders, neither Hayes nor the people interviewed in the documentary made any mention of the militarized borders around the world that function much like the Berlin Wall did, like the current borders of India/Pakistan (c. 1988), Spain/Morocco (c. 2001), North/South Korea (c. 1953), Saudi/Yemen (c. 2004), Israel/Gaza and Israel/Palestine–West Bank, or Israel/Egypt. Furthermore, there was little mention of the "active" US/Mexico border just over 100 miles south of the event.

Of the many murals on the Berlin Wall installation, the mural *goodcancomefrombadcancomefromgood* hints at the nature of state-sanctioned violence, in that it is gendered, recursive, and dizzying. This particular mural and installation reveal evolving intensification of border violence inherent to the GBIC and the intergenerational anxiety and insecurities induced by that violence. A border creates an in-between place, a transitional place (e.g., liminal space, or Anzaldúa's *nepantla* theory), and the installation serves as both a memorial and an art piece; it both serves as a reminder (a process of remembering) and also obscures parts of the violent border history of East and West Berlin.

Mural art and museums can be both "good" and "bad." On the one hand, projects like *The Wall Along Wilshire* and arts institutions like the Wende Museum remind audiences that border walls are penetrable and destructible, and that borders can be recycled into seemingly innocuous art. On the other hand, mural arts and museums can reanimate border walls, rebirth them or

16. See Patrisia Gonzales's *Red Medicine* for more on *susto*.

bring them back to a zombie-like state, like the *calaca,* and obscure the realities of border imperialism for the sake of aesthetics. Herakut's *goodcancomefrombad* hints toward the recursive, reproducing border imperialism, and also the affect of that phenomena on children, women, and femmes.

The memorialization and reanimation of the Berlin Wall was an impulse or desire to return the wall to its original function as a nation-state territory marker and technology of war. According to the curator, the installation was intended to remind audiences of the Berlin Wall's brutal past so that the US and the world would not allow that past to be repeated—the installation/memorial, curated to "assist in remembering" and "preserve in memory" ("Memorialization"). However, this preservation of memory also serves the state as it freezes audiences in a perpetual cycle of retraumatization that overshadows the contributing policies and politics. José Quiroga defines memorialization as a condition within which the state can "buy time" to manage society's history and current narrative and, as such, shape its future (4). "Buying time," or memorialization, works by slowing down awareness of the present, by preserving objects or people in metal or rock, or both, while simultaneously constructing a narrative around said commemorative event/person.

Repetition and memorialization is a powerful rhetorical strategy and one used repeatedly throughout recorded history. Memorialization happens, for example, every year on September 11 (9/11) as audiences worldwide are called by mass media to remember the tragic events of that day in 2001. News coverage begins weeks before and escalates to nonstop coverage of commemorative events. The memorialization of 9/11 every year repeats retraumatization as audiences are "assisted in remembering" by rewatching the traumatic event through broad media coverage. In the case of 9/11, memorialization comes by way of images and commentary throughout almost all media platforms, including images of the US flag, images of the twin Trade Center buildings as they once stood, video of the planes crashing into them, and video of the buildings falling. Audiences are "assisted in remembering" so that they may "never forget." "Never forget," Mark Lilla writes, was once assigned to the Jewish Holocaust, but has since been reassigned to the events of 9/11. It is a rhetorical tool used to cause remembrance and nationalist cohesiveness, while at the same time "forgetting" or obscuring by using tragedy to overshadow state corruption. Since then, and in 2020, with the COVID-19 pandemic, it is likely that "never forget" will be reimagined as a nationalist narrative to reconvene the nation and its citizens, and again obscure state violence. Even decades after the original event, the US public, and audiences around the world, receive these reminders to "never forget" the violence that much of the world witnessed. "Never forget," politicians and media outlets will say again and again. "Never forget" that those were "terrorist," "terrorism," and "terror" attacks. Each year, the "War on Terror" is validated as an honorable quest for security and justice. People are reminded of the tragedy and retraumatized, and also told the narrative of the innocence as a country, the collective resilience of US citizens (as opposed to noncitizens), and the duties of military leaders (including presidents). The US continues to exploit 9/11 (a memorable name) as justification to its audiences of military presence, deadly violence, and perpetual wars. The repeated threat of "terrorist attacks" and justified retaliation keeps the public in a perpetual state of fear, practically immobilized in shock, as they develop an apathy toward current state-sanctioned violence such as family separation, migrant death, and other human rights abuses at borders. When the state imparts violence and murder, however, the logic of exceptionalism and rhetorics of law enforcement, terms like *national security,* and criminalized subjectivities preserve a nation-state's right to maim (see Puar, *Maim*).

The reemergence of the Berlin Wall as a museum installation in Los Angeles similarly serves as an example of the recursive rebirth of border imperialism, regenerating effects on and in the femme and maternal body and their young unborn children's minds. The border wall and the murals, the violence and border breakdown can be sensed years later, and may stick to material and ephemeral objects, things. The Wende Museum succeeded in memorializing the Berlin Wall by reactivating it, provoking a felt memory of violent, imperialist territoriality. And the event was a rhetorical failure. The Berlin Wall was reborn half dead, half alive. It failed to stop or curb state-sanctioned border violence, and it contributed to the cyclical rebirth of monstrous borders. Perhaps inadvertently, the Wende Museum was complicit in rebirthing border imperialism. It was both "good" and "bad" and served as a reminder that border walls and state violence cross time and space, and that border imperialism can return to affect the mindbodyspiritplacetime similarly and with a different intensity. The state made itself known again through the art and art installation. Through the re-erection of the fallen Berlin Wall, regarded as part of the distant past, their repressed and unresolved border violence was made felt in the minds and bodies of audiences who suffered because of the Berlin Wall, or who are suffering now because of similar technologies of territoriality.

Avery Gordon, in *Ghostly Matters: Haunting and the Sociological Imagination,* defines "haunting" as exemplified by the phenomena occurring at the moment of encounter with the Berlin Wall in Los Angeles, and is worth citing in its completeness:

> Haunting is one way in which abusive systems of power make themselves known and their impacts felt in everyday life, especially when they are supposedly over and done with (slavery, for instance) or when their oppressive nature is denied (as in free labor or national security). Haunting is not the same as being exploited, traumatized, or oppressed although it usually involves these experiences or is produced by them. What's distinctive about haunting is that it is an animated state in which a repressed or unresolved social violence is making itself known, sometimes very directly, sometimes more obliquely. I used the term haunting to describe those singular yet repetitive instances when home becomes unfamiliar, when your bearings on the world lose direction, when the over-and-done-with comes alive, when what's been in your blind spot comes into view. (xvi)

The Wende Museum performance and installation made audiences feel as though Los Angeles had "become unfamiliar." The site of the ceremony became reminiscent of Cold War Berlin, and audiences participated in a reanimation of the specter of the Berlin Wall. It is this zombie-like, experiential haunting, that sociology scholar Avery Gordon describes as the moments in which "abusive systems of power make themselves known (xvi)."[?] The ceremony, performance, installation, and mural fall short of intervening in state powers. As Gordon describes, abusive state power is not always explicit, and thus such a performance may be just one way that state-sanctioned border violence manifests itself indirectly. Murals further animate the wall, such as in the *goodcancomefrombad* mural. The mural sheds light on, *dar a luz,* border violence, and also on the contradiction of border walls. Border wall murals mostly amplify border violence, drawing attention to the problem, while also reanimating the border. The installation and performance breaks down one border while resurrecting another, and eliciting hope and fear in the same night.

The Wende Museum, in an effort to "shed light," enlighten, *dar a luz,* to border issues, also further obscures the phenomenology of borders. It brings back the darkness, bad memories, fear, from the past and into the present. A decolonial aesthetic reading, one that seeks to liberate the senses of border art, reveals what is at stake temporally, locally/globally, and for the material bodies that encounter the borders around the world—particularly for femmes, mothers, and children. Attentive to significations of state-sanctioned violence against migrant mothers in conjunction with the comparative border murals, the installation also amplifies artistic attempts to resist the dehumanization of *los del otro lado* (the ones on the other side) at different points in history and bordered nations around the world. *goodcancomefrombad* is just one of many border wall murals in which the faces, names, and symbolism of humanity have been created. The inhumanity of border violence, particularly for women, mothers, children, and femmes, is unique as they have been historically marginalized around the world.

Violence and trauma induced by global bordering have proven to have intergenerational, long-lasting, and recurring effects for individuals as well as parents and their children—in some cases, not yet born—and include such maladies as separation anxiety, depression, and post-traumatic stress disorder (PTSD).[17] Evidence of mothers' and children's deadly journeys are captured in world news reports. The world again and again bears witness to border violence—babies washing up on shores, unaccompanied migrant minors pregnant as a result of rape, families separated, children attacked by the state, missing and separated family members, and many found murdered or left for dead.[18] Pregnant mothers and young migrant and refugee children make the journeys from their homes in Ecuador, Guatemala, El Salvador, Syria, Yemen, Tunisia, Uganda, Somalia, and other countries, all fleeing violence, only to encounter more violence at borders all over the world. While this is not an exhaustive list, the countries I've included here are countries that are currently experiencing prolonged and heightened unsafe conditions as a result of the global border phenomena or GBIC.

The people forced to migrate within such unsafe conditions may encounter more than one border, and that border may be a road, a bridge, an ocean, or a barbed wire steel fence. I describe only some instances of their migration and the borders they might encounter throughout this chapter. With the proliferation of borders, concern from (im)migrant advocates, activists, health clinicians, and academics grows with the numbers of hundreds of people who must heal and undo trauma from migration, diaspora, and refugeeism, a process that could take years.

How is it possible to see borders and borderlands of concrete and razor wire around the world as anything more than violent divisions? In the case

---

17. According to the American Psychological Association, "The Psychology of Immigration" (2019). See also "Garza V. Hargan: En Banc D.C. Circuit Upholds Order Requiring HHS [Health and Human Services] to Allow an Undocumented Minor to Have an Abortion" in *Harvard Law Review*, 10 Apr. 2018, https://harvardlawreview.org/2018/04/garza-v-hargan/.

18. The subtitle in the *Independent*'s news report in September 2015, which carried the image of a young child who washed ashore, reads: "The boy was part of a group of 11 Syrians who drowned off the coastal town of Bodrum in Turkey after an apparent failed attempt to flee the war-ravaged country." https://www.independent.co.uk/news/world/europe/if-these-extraordinarily-powerful-images-of-a-dead-syrian-child-washed-up-on-a-beach-don-t-change-10482757.html.

of border wall art and the idea of security, something "bad" comes from something good, and "good" can birth something bad. Filled with a sense of insecurity and fear, people turn to the state for protection from villainized, dehumanized, and false predators, such as migrants. In that state of perpetual fear, people willingly give up their civil rights to the state in exchange for safety. This is a process that Naomi Klein defines as "disaster capitalism," wherein the state capitalizes on crises (whether national or international) for political and economic gain. Insecurity can come from the false sense of "security" or a feeling that the state must serve to secure and reinstate safety. The recurring border event, the phenomena associated with rebirthing borders and border violence, are both rhetorical and material processes that induce fear and the remembrance of fear, a fear that is felt in the mindbodyspiritplacetime, as well as intergenerationally. Perhaps anxieties of property and territory are entangled with the idea of home and belonging through the politicized rhetorics of safety and security. In inducing fear in the people, the nation-state moves to a paternalistic role. However, there is life along the border. It is more than a deadly militarized zone; it is also a space of creative capacity. It is a contradictory place and moves across the landscape like a serpent.

A surface reading of a corporeal reaction can lead a keen observer to the causes of that external reaction, and possibly to a path of healing or of balance. The perpetual return of the GBIC ensures the world stays in a loop of (re)traumatization and perpetual fear. To elicit a perpetual insecurity, as a borderland rhetoric, is a discursive and material strategy of war and control. By listening critically, with one's whole body, to the skin of the border, and to feel and sense it by looking below its surface—its skin, its womb—it is possible to arrive at an understanding of the possibilities that border murals hold for a kind of liberation of thinking through art. Art, like the serpent, and like humans, can alter realities—it is neither all good nor all bad, and can be about darkness and light, *da a luz*.

Art has been used by governments and organizations to sell their products, ideas, and realities. The philosophers of the European Enlightenment brought about overcentralization of the objective empirical knowledge in Western thinking, and invisibilized the epistemological possibilities of non-Western peoples. Indeed, Western or Eurocentric philosophers, like Immanuel Kant, held an overreliance on "reason" that deemed encounters with Black and Indigenous philosophies as absent of reason. Jean-Jacques Rousseau, often touted as critical of Enlightenment-era philosophy, famously critiqued non-freedom in *The Social Contract* when he wrote: "Man is born free and he is everywhere in chains." Meant to be metaphorical, Rousseau's statement obscures European-owned slaves and the material chains that slaves are physically born into. In an attempt to reason, reason itself is twisted in that it too reveals and also obscures. It advances and also constrains, applied to a general will; it coils itself around the people, tightening reason's grip around voices that challenge linear and oppressive logics. Once understood as emancipatory, the Enlightenment brought about epistemological and ontological freedom for Western peoples, while simultaneously choking out other ways of being and thinking.

As artists interpret the realities of the borderlands, some explicitly challenge human rights violations in order to amplify the good that comes from the bad of the borderlands. Staying with the contradiction can perhaps bring about an understanding of a path toward balance. Embracing the contradiction can also help to see how the state uses this contradiction as political maneuvers, as in the case of weaponizing intimacy. In one instance, politicians claim compassion and sensuality, even relate to each other publicly with sexualized undertones, and on the other, they criminalize sexualities, separate families, and put children into cages.

It is difficult to see dangerous politicians and borderlands as capable of contributing to critical studies, though listening to their contradictions can lead to ways to destabilize tyranny. To some, it is practically unfathomable to imagine that a border can be anything more than a death strip, but it can be. It was impossible for me to imagine the serpent being anything more than a deadly beast, but it is.

Works Cited

Ahmed, Sara. *The Cultural Politics of Emotion.* 2nd ed., Edinburgh UP, 2014.

———. *Living a Feminist Life.* Duke UP, 2016.

———. *Queer Phenomenology: Orientations, Objects, Others.* Duke UP, 2006.

Ahmed, Sara, and Jackie Stacey. "Introduction: Dermographies." *Thinking through the Skin,* edited by Sara Ahmed and Jackie Stacey, Routledge, 2001, pp. 1–17.

AIE. "Video Game Math: Matrices." 20 Apr. 2019, aie.edu/video-game-math-matrices/

Alarcón, Norma. "Chicana Feminism: In the Tracks of 'the' Native Woman." *Cultural Studies,* vol. 4, no. 3, 2006, pp. 248–56.

Anzaldúa, Gloria E. *Borderlands / La Frontera: The New Mestiza.* Aunt Lute Books, 2007.

———. *The Gloria Anzaldúa Reader.* Duke UP, 2009.

———. *Interviews/Entrevistas: Gloria E. Anzaldúa.* Edited by AnaLouise Keating, Routledge, 2000.

———. *Light in the Dark / Luz en lo Oscuro: Rewriting Identity, Spirituality, Reality.* Edited by AnaLouise Keating, Duke UP, 2015.

———. "Now Let Us Shift . . . the Path of Conocimiento . . . Inner Work, Public Acts." *This Bridge We Call Home: Radical Visions for Transformation,* edited by Gloria Anzaldúa and AnaLouise Keating, Routledge, 2002, pp. 540–78.

Artnet. "Herakut: Artworks." https://www.artnet.com/artists/herakut/.

Baca, Judith F. "The Human Story at the Intersection of Ethics, Aesthetics, and Social Justice." *Journal of Moral Education,* vol. 34, no. 2, June 2005, pp. 153–69.

Badali, Joel John. "Migrants in the Closet: LGBT Migrants, Homonationalism, and the Right to Refuge in Serbia." *Journal of Gay & Lesbian Social Services,* vol. 31, no. 1, 2019, pp. 89–119.

Bennett, Jane. *Vibrant Matter: A Political Ecology of Things.* Duke UP, 2010.

Bratta, Phil, and Malea Powell. "Introduction to the Special Issue: Entering the Cultural Rhetorics Conversations." *enculturation: A Journal of Rhetoric, Writing, and Culture,* 20 Apr. 2016, http://enculturation.net/entering-the-cultural-rhetorics-conversations.

brown, adrienne maree. *Emergent Strategy: Shaping Change, Changing Worlds.* AK Press, 2017.

Brown, Wendy. *Walled States, Waning Sovereignty.* Zone Books; distributed by MIT P, 2010.

"Caged Children & Terrified Infants: Rep. Sheila Jackson Lee Describes 'Acts of Indecency' at Border." *Democracy Now!,* 19 June 2018, https://www.democracynow.org/2018/6/19/caged_children_terrified_infants_rep_sheila.

Campt, Tina M. "Imagine Otherwise: Tina Campt on Listening to Images." Hosted and created by Cathy Hannabach, *IOF: Ideas on Fire,* 2018. Podcast.

———. *Listening to Images.* Duke UP, 2017.

Chang, Grace. *Disposable Domestics: Immigrant Women Workers in the Global Economy.* Haymarket Books, 2016.

Chávez, Karma R. "The Body: An Abstract and Actual Rhetorical Concept." *Rhetoric Society Quarterly,* vol. 48, no. 3, 2018, pp. 242–50.

———. "Border (In)Securities: Normative and Differential Belonging in LGBTQ and Immigrant Rights Discourse." *Communication and Critical/Cultural Studies,* vol. 7, no. 2, 2010, pp 136–55.

Clark, Tiana. *I Can't Talk about the Trees without the Blood.* U of Pittsburgh P, 2018.

Coutinho, Steve. "Zhuangzi (Chuang-Tzu, 369–298 B.C.E.)." *The Internet Encyclopedia of Philosophy: A Peer-Reviewed Academic Resource,* https://iep.utm.edu, 21 Jan. 2022.

Davis, Brian. "The Wall Project." *The Wende Museum.* YouTube, 26 Apr. 2010, https://youtu.be/4df_QXdOvY.

de Bastion, Myles. "How a Deaf Musician Is Helping Others 'See with Sound.'" *Great Big Story,* 4 July 2017. YouTube, https://youtu.be/OdwXPZ4vu-c.

Decolonization: Indigeneity, Education & Society. "Submission Preparation Checklist." https://jps.library.utoronto.ca/index.php/des/about/submissions.

Diaz, Natalie. "Postcolonial Love Poem." *Postcolonial Love Poem,* Graywolf Press, 2020, p. 1.

Endres, Danielle, et al. "In Situ Rhetoric: Intersections between Qualitative Inquiry, Fieldwork, and Rhetoric." *Cultural Studies ↔ Critical Methodologies,* vol. 16, no. 6, Dec. 2016, pp. 511–24.

Escobar, Martha D. *Captivity Beyond Prisons: Criminalization Experiences of Latina (Im)Migrants.* U of Texas P, 2016.

Flower, Linda. *Community Literacy and the Rhetoric of Public Engagement.* Southern Illinois UP, 2008

Gonzales, Patrisia. *Red Medicine: Traditional Indigenous Rites of Birthing and Healing.* U of Arizona P, 2012.

Gordon, Avery F. *Ghostly Matters: Haunting and the Sociological Imagination.* U of Minnesota P, 2008.

Haraway, Donna. *Staying with the Trouble: Making Kin in the Chthulucene.* Duke UP, 2016.

Harvard Medical School. "Stress and the Sensitive Gut." *Harvard Health Publishing,* 21 Aug. 2019, https://www.health.harvard.edu/newsletter_article/stress-and-the-sensitive-gut. Accessed 5 May 2020.

Hill, Lauryn. "Everything Is Everything." *The Miseducation of Lauryn Hill.* Sony Legacy, 1998.

Investigación y primeras conclusiones de las desapariciones y homicidios de los normalistas de Ayotzinapa por Grupo Interdisciplinario de Expertos Independientes (GIEI). 2015.

Klein, Naomi. *The Shock Doctrine: The Rise of Disaster Capitalism.* Henry Holt and Company, 2010.

Kuhn, Jedediah. Personal conversation, 5 June 2020.

Lacy, Alberto Ruy Sánchez. "Los Sueños de la Serpiente." *Serpientes en el Arte Prehispánico: Artes de México,* 2002, pp. 6–7.

Ladrón de Guevara, Sara. "La Obsesión de la Serpiente." *Serpientes en el Arte Prehispánico: Artes de México,* 2002, pp. 56–59.

Lara, Irene. "Sensing the Serpent in the Mother, Dando a Luz a la Madre Serpiente: Chicana Spirituality, Sexuality, and Mamihood." *Fleshing the Spirit: Spirituality and Activism in Chicana, Latina, and Indigenous Women's Lives,* edited by Elisa Facio and Irene Lara, U of Arizona P, 2014, pp. 113–34.

Licona, Adela C. *Zines in Third Space: Radical Cooperation and Borderlands Rhetoric.* SUNY P, 2012.

Lilla, Mark. "Never Forget." *New York Magazine,* 26 Aug. 2011.

Little Bear, Leroy. *Naturalizing Indigenous Knowledge.* Canadian Council on Learning. U of Saskatchewan, 2009.

Lorde, Audre. *Sister Outsider: Essays and Speeches.* Crossing Press, 2007.

Luibhéid, Eithne. *Entry Denied: Controlling Sexuality at the Border.* U of Minnesota P, 2002.

Luibhéid, Eithne, and Lionel Cantú, Jr., editors. *Queer Migrations: Sexuality, US Citizenship, and Border Crossings.* U of Minnesota P, 2005.

Marks, Laura U. *The Skin of Film: Experimental Cinema and Intercultural Experience.* U of Rochester P, 1996.

———. *Touch: Sensuous Theory and Multisensory Media.* U of Minnesota P, 2002.

Martínez, Jacqueline M. *Phenomenology of Chicana Experience & Identity: Communication and Transformation in Praxis.* Rowman & Littlefield, 2000.

Massumi, Brian. *The Politics of Everyday Fear.* U of Minnesota P, 1993.

McKinnon, Sara L., et al. *Text + Field: Innovations in Rhetorical Method.* Pennsylvania State UP, 2016.

"Memorialization, n." *OED Online,* Oxford University Press, December 2021, www.oed.com/view/Entry/253417. Accessed 22 Jan. 2022.

Mezzadra, Sandro, and Brett Neilson. *Border as Method, or, the Multiplication of Labor.* Duke UP, 2013.

Middleton, Michael, et al. *Participatory Critical Rhetoric: Theoretical and Methodological Foundations for Studying Rhetoric in Situ,* Lexington Books, 2015.

Mignolo, Walter. *The Darker Side of the Renaissance: Literacy, Territoriality, and Colonization.* U of Michigan P, 1995.

———. *The Darker Side of Western Modernity: Global Futures, Decolonial Options.* Duke UP, 2011.

Miller, Todd. *More Than a Wall: Corporate Profiteering and the Militarization of US Borders,* edited by Nick Buxton, Transnational Institute, 2019. https://www.tni.org/en/morethanawall.

Morrissey, Megan Elizabeth. "Border Matters: A New Materialist Critique of Installation Art on the U.S.–Mexico Border." *Journal of International and Intercultural Communication,* vol. 14, no. 1, 2021, pp. 3–20.

Muñoz, José Esteban. *Cruising Utopia: The Then and There of Queer Futurity.* New York UP, 2009.

———. *Disidentifications: Queers of Color and the Performance of Politics.* U of Minnesota P, 1999.

———. "Ephemera as Evidence: Introductory Notes to Queer Acts." *Women & Performance: A Journal of Feminist Theory,* vol. 8, no. 2, 1996, pp. 5–16.

Neumaier, Diane. "Judy Baca: Our People Are the Internal Exiles." *Making Face, Making Soul / Haciendo Caras: Creative and Critical Perspectives by Feminist of Color,* edited by Gloria E. Anzaldúa, Aunt Lute Books, 1990, pp. 256–70.

Perez, Laura E. *Chicana Art: The Politics of Spiritual and Aesthetic Altarities.* Duke UP, 2007.

Pezzullo, Phaedra, and Catalina M. de Onís. "Rethinking Rhetorical Field Methods on a Precarious Planet." *Communication Monographs,* vol. 85, no. 1, Mar. 2018, pp. 103–22.

Probyn, Elspeth. "Eating Skin." *Thinking through the Skin,* edited by Sara Ahmed and Jackie Stacey, Routledge, 2001, pp. 87–103.

Puar, Jasbir K. *The Right to Maim: Debility, Capacity, Disability.* Duke UP, 2017.

———. *Terrorist Assemblages: Homonationalism in Queer Times.* Duke UP, 2007.

Quiroga, José. *Cuban Palimpsests.* U of Minnesota P, 2005.

Rai, Candice, and Caroline Gottschalk Druschke. *Field Rhetoric: Ethnography, Ecology, and Engagement in the Places of Persuasion.* U of Alabama P, 2018.

Rendón, Laura I. *Sentipensante (Sensing/Thinking) Pedagogy Educating for Wholeness, Social Justice, and Liberation.* Stylus, 2009.

Rodriguez, Juana María. *Queer Latinidad.* New York University Press, 2003.

———. *Sexual Features, Queer Gestures, and Other Latina Longings.* New York UP, 2014.

Rousseau, Jean-Jacques. *The Social Contract.* Philosophical Library / Open Road, 2016.

Sandoval, Chela. *Methodology of the Oppressed.* U of Minnesota P, 2000.

Serpientes en el Arte Prehispánico. *Artes de México.* No. 32, 2002.

Simpson, Leanne. "Land as Pedagogy: Nishnaabeg Intelligence and Rebellious Transformation." *Decolonization: Indigeneity, Education & Society,* vol. 3, no. 3, 2014, pp. 1–25.

———. "Pretending Fearless." *This Accident of Being Lost: Songs and Stories,* House of Anansi Press, 2017, pp. 95–97.

Soto, Sandra K. *Reading Chican@ Like a Queer: The De-Mastery of Desire.* U of Texas P, 2010.

Tamaira, A. M. "Walls of Empowerment: Reading Public Murals in a Kanaka Maoli Context." *The Contemporary Pacific,* vol. 29, no. 1, 2017, pp. 1–36.

Téllez, Michelle, and Alejandra I. Ramírez. "How Artists Can Shape Understanding of the US-Mexico Border." *Latino NPR,* 18 Jan. 2018, https://www.latinousa.org/2018/01/18/artists-can-shape-understanding-u-s-mexico-border/.

Walia, Harsha. *Undoing Border Imperialism.* AK Press, 2013.

The Wende Museum. "The Wall Project." http://www.wendemuseum.org/programs/wall-project.

Wiebe, Sarah Marie. "Sensing Policy: Engaging Affected Communities at the Intersections of Environmental Justice and Decolonial Futures." *Politics, Groups, and Identities,* vol. 8, no. 1, 2020, pp. 181–93.

Wright, Michelle M. *Physics of Blackness: Beyond the Middle Passage Epistemology.* U of Minnesota P, 2015.

Youssef, Nagy A., et al. "The Effects of Trauma, with or without PTSD, on the Transgenerational DNA Methylation Alterations in Human Offsprings." *Brain Sciences,* vol. 8, no. 5, 2018, article 83.

CHAPTER 6

Corn, Oil, and Cultivating Dissent through "Seeds of Resistance"

A Case Study on Rhetorics of Survivance and the Protest Assemblage

MATTHEW WHITAKER

On May 31, 2014, members of the Cowboy Indian Alliance convened at a small farm outside of Neligh, Nebraska, to plant sacred seeds of Ponka[1] corn in the projected path of the Keystone XL pipeline. Led by Mekasi Camp Horinek and Amos Hinton—citizens of the Ponca Tribe of Oklahoma—the Alliance gathered on a patch of recently tilled soil, spread a blanket, and laid out the items necessary for a spiritual cleansing of the land: a basket of Ponka red corn seeds, a jar of water from the Ogallala Aquifer, a sacred pipe, a sage bundle, and a braid of sweetgrass. Beneath gathering storm clouds, Hinton and Horinek lit the sage, saying a prayer to the four directions as the sweet-smelling smoke billowed around them. Horinek explained the significance of the ceremony to the group, saying, "Together our families will plant sacred red corn seed in our ancestral soil. As the corn grows it will stand strong for us, to help us protect and keep Mother Earth safe for our children, as we fight this battle against the Keystone XL pipeline" (Andrei). He then passed around the jar of water, inviting each member to drink from it. Art Tanderup—co-owner of the property and member of the Alliance—climbed atop his John Deere tractor and set a thirty-inch spacing for the crop rows. As he drove across the field, members of the Alliance fanned out behind him, using their hands,

1. The nineteenth-century spelling of the tribe—*Ponka*—is used in the official names of the heirloom corn varietals. In all other contexts *except* in reference to the corn, I use the current spelling, *Ponca.*

feet, and improvised sticks to sow seeds of resistance. They worked through intermittent rain and thunder, planting three and a half acres of corn over the course of two days.

Corn-planting may seem like an unusual form of advocacy, but as noted by Jonathan Alexander et al., "expanding the range and modalities of protest [is] a hallmark of activist work at the turn of the century" (11). As a decolonial entity, the Alliance exemplifies this shift toward more dramatic, embodied forms of protest—forms that do the work of politics in unruly, disruptive ways. In 2014, their members set up tipis in front of the White House and rode horses to the front steps of the US Capitol as part of the "Reject and Protect" campaign. The same year, they organized a benefit concert with Neil Young and Willie Nelson, converting a cornfield into a rock-and-roll venue and donating the proceeds to organizations opposing the pipeline. Led by a group of imaginative organizers, the Alliance pushes at the boundaries of what people typically recognize as advocacy by taking up activities that blur the line between performance and protest. Their efforts resist hegemonic configurations of land and lifeways, serving as an invited response to settler colonialism. Perhaps nowhere is this more evident than in the Seeds of Resistance ceremony.

The ceremony is a ritualistic reimagining of place, an event that blends prayer, oration, and performance into a single decolonial text. The ceremony originated in 2014 but continues to the present, as each spring the Alliance gathers with members of the public outside of Neligh to plant Ponka heirloom corn in the pathway of the Keystone XL. Performed at the juncture of the Ponca Trail of Tears and the projected pathway of the Keystone XL, the ceremony is a deeply rhetorical event that brings together plants, people, soil, and sky for the purpose of revising public perceptions about what the Keystone XL pipeline means. On the one hand, it strains against shallow notions of "progress" routinely put forth by pipeline advocates, refuting—in a visceral, embodied way—the idea that "growth" can be measured exclusively in economic terms. On the other hand, it also implicitly repudiates claims made by pipeline critics who often universalize the Keystone XL as a "climate issue" that "affects us all." The rhetoric of the ceremony intervenes in these constructions, "expanding discursive space," as Nancy Fraser puts it, and opening new ethical and political possibilities for debate (qtd. in Weisser 610).

For members of the Alliance and many Indigenous people generally (though not all), the Keystone XL is not only reckless and short-sighted; it represents the newest instantiation of colonial terrorism—a brazen attempt to exploit Indigenous lands for the benefit of dominant society. While the ceremony is undoubtedly a critique of neoliberal policies and the kind of environmentally destructive practices they engender, it is also an indictment of the racial discrimination that underlies such policies. Under the proposed route, the Keystone XL would threaten tribal lands in Montana, South Dakota, Nebraska, Kansas, and Oklahoma, violating treaty rights, disturbing sites of cultural and historical significance, and endangering vital water sources like the Ogallala Aquifer. In May of 2017, tribes north and south of the Canadian border—representing thousands of Indigenous people in North America—signed a joint declaration against the Keystone XL, highlighting existing treaty rights and signaling opposition to the practice of building on, or adjacent to, Native lands without tribal consent ("Indigenous Leaders"). In response, both the Canadian and US governments have largely turned a deaf ear. The exchange of lawsuits between tribal groups, TransCanada, and various governmental agencies has endured now for over a decade, and yet at the time of this writing, the project proceeds apace—TransCanada promising to begin construction as early as April 2020.

Throughout this essay, I will use the terms *decolonial* and *decolonizing* in reference to practices that—in the words of Juanita Sundberg—expose "the ontological violence authorized by Eurocentric epistemologies both in scholarship and everyday life" (34). The ceremony vividly exposes Indigenous presence through the figure of tribal corn in a landscape the colonial gaze has configured as "empty," underscoring how projects like the Keystone XL perpetuate violence by erasing and/or disrupting the plant compositions that sustain Indigenous societies. This is in keeping with an Indigenous framework that understands the landscape and its inhabitants—not as external "others"—but as relatives and sources of spiritual connection. Describing "Country"—a core tenet of Indigenous materialisms—Alison Ravenscroft says it "is living, it is energy, and it is Law" (356). The practice of the ceremony is an embodied practice of this idea; it illuminates and centers an Indigenous way of knowing and relating to the more-than-human world and, thus, decolonizes settler interpretations of the human/environment relationship. Here, plants and other nonhuman aspects of the environment are regarded as relatives who are vital to cultural continuance rather than "resources" to be exploited for short-term economic profits. When situated within the potential site of the pipeline—understood in this context as a representation of the cultural paradigms of settler colonialism—the practice takes on a decidedly critical resonance, inviting rebuke of settler colonialism through a contrastive rhetoric that juxtaposes corn against oil.

In the following essay, I trace the Seeds of Resistance ceremony as an ontological assemblage—as an attempt to speak *through* the normative conventions of public, political, and legal discourses by enacting an interspecies rhetoric of survivance that, in the words of Malea Powell, seeks to "reimagine and re-figure" Indigenous presences within colonial matrices of power (400). "Survivance" invokes both survival and resistance: a renouncing of oppressive ideologies and a commitment to the continuation of Indigenous stories (see Vizenor). Senate floors, courtrooms, and the spaces in front of television cameras are, by their very nature, exclusionary, demanding certain rhetorical styles, while filtering out those deemed "uncivil" or "irrational." These exclusionary structures work to stifle dissent, repressing the circulation of critical perspectives, particularly when those perspectives are expressed in ways that don't correspond with the paradigms of white, standard discourse. In a commitment to decolonial praxis, the Alliance takes up rhetorical strategies that destabilize Eurocentric conceptions about what "counts" as an effective argument, trading textuality for materiality and logocentrism for body-centrism. Eschewing the conventional characteristics of speaking and writing in the public sphere, the Alliance adopts a resistive, interspecies rhetoric, drawing on the liveliness of tribal corn to critique colonial attitudes and affirm Indigenous lifeways.

Guided by the works of Kim TallBear and Jane Bennett, I apply materialist perspectives to the study of social movements—a discourse that has long neglected the discursive power of plants. My goal is to problematize theories of protest rhetoric that fixate on human embodiment to the exclusion of other corporeal entities. By "materialist perspectives," I mean perspectives that critique nature/culture dualisms and assume agency in all life forms, not merely those that reflect human traits. TallBear approaches materiality from an Indigenous framework that grants spiritual significance to the nonhuman world, while Bennett invokes a vital materiality to describe the animacy of "things." In an effort to illuminate the assembled natures of social movements, I draw from both scholars, presenting an alliance of theory that reimagines protest as an ontological assemblage—a "bringing-together" of humans, places, objects, and plants for the purpose of civic action. Using the Seeds of Resistance ceremony as a case study, I explore the implications of planting Native heirloom corn as an argumentative strategy, positing that such interspecies collaborations open new pathways for the study, analysis, and interpretation of protest rhetoric.

The Power and Relatedness of All Things: A Theoretical Frame

In searching for a theoretical framework that might draw out the communicative possibilities of tribal corn, I find much to appreciate in the writings of Kim

TallBear, who critiques Western dualisms that deprive members of the nonhuman world their speaking power. "Indigenous peoples have never forgotten," she writes, "that nonhumans are agential beings engaged in social relations that profoundly shape human lives" ("Indigenous" 234). Even objects traditionally perceived as inanimate—stones, thunder, stars—"are known within [Indigenous] ontologies to be sentient and knowing persons" (234). As a way of transcending the animate/inanimate divide, TallBear proposes an "indigenous metaphysic" modeled after the insights of Charles Eastman and Vine Deloria, Jr. An Indigenous metaphysic, she writes, is "an understanding of the intimate knowing relatedness of all things," an attention to "the co-constitutive entanglements between the material and immaterial" ("Beyond" 191). This relational, interspecies perspective foregrounds the way organisms are mutually constituted through interaction, and it does from a decidedly nonsecular standpoint that is unafraid of "enfolding spirits or souls into descriptions of the beingness of nonhumans" (191).

TallBear's exploration of the material and spiritual significance of red pipestone is a potent example of how relational thinking can reroute traditional understandings of "things," inspiring new ethical and intellectual engagements with the nonhuman world. TallBear writes that red pipestone is the preferred construction material for pipes and other ceremonial objects in Dakota, Lakota, and Nakota cultures. Quarries in southeastern Minnesota have long been considered the primary source of the stone, and because of settler colonial encroachment into these areas, the US National Park Service created Pipestone National Monument, permitting only Native Americans and federally recognized tribes to quarry the stone. Through archival research, interviews, and participant observation, TallBear investigates how the pipestone is constructed in Indigenous, regulatory, and scientific narratives, tracing the living connections and "social relations that proliferate as the stone emerges from the earth, is carved into pipe, and is passed from hand to hand" ("Beyond" 195). Through a kind of archaeological "recovery," TallBear illuminates the cultural and epistemological significance of the pipestone, constructing it—not as a dead, inert object—but as a lively "spirit being" who materializes Indigenous lifeways.

TallBear's animation of the material world—as well as her commitment to dismantling nature/culture binaries—is concomitant with aspects of new materialist thought, and in the spirit of a "theoretical alliance," I wish to open a space where their connections might be further contemplated. I use the phrase "theoretical alliance" as a gesture toward coalition building and the kind of multiracial, interethnic movement that opponents of the Keystone XL have come to embody. My hope is not to overcome, or gloss over, difference through empty calls for unity, but to ally divergent perspectives and leverage their collective strength toward a decolonial agenda. To accomplish this, I seek to draw out theoretical strains from new materialist and Indigenous thought and apply them to the study of protest. How is this work "decolonial"? Because it works to problematize a Western interpretation of protest that habitually overlooks more-than-human bodies, and it does so in service of a movement that challenges "Big Oil" projects and other violent machinations of settler colonial ideology.

Alliances are not synonymous with harmony,[2] and therefore differences between these approaches should be recognized and understood. TallBear and others have critiqued the "new" in new materialisms as expressing a situated, European knowledge that fails to take seriously (or even much consider) the intellectual contributions of Indigenous people. Writers at least as far back as Eastman and Deloria have discussed the vibrance and constitutive power of nonhuman entities. Claims of "newness," then, are not only inaccurate, but perpetuate a colonial tradition of not seeing the perspectives of Indigenous scholars. Additionally, new materialisms frequently dispense with nonsecular theories, which blind them to the spiritual significance of the nonhuman world and implicitly reinforce a knowledge-making system guided by European norms.

At the same time, while acknowledging where new materialisms fall short, it strikes me as a lack of prescience to disregard their contributions altogether. Dismantling colonial configurations of the human/environment relationship is a project that will require action along multiple fronts. We would do well, then, to seek commonality where it exists—not merely for the sake of unity, but for the sake of redistributing power along more equitable lines and preserving the ecological integrity of the environmental commons. This collaborative spirit is what animates the anti-pipeline movement, and as a theoretical expression of that spirit, I propose an allyship between TallBear's "indigenous metaphysic" ("Beyond" 191) and Jane Bennett's "thing-power" (6). Though these theories derive from a different set of interpretive frameworks, I believe they can be partnered to yield more productive ways of thinking about the assembled "natures" of protest events.

Toward this end, I propose a model of interpretation that draws together TallBear's emphasis on the metaphysical aspects of nonhuman nature with Bennett's notion of the ontological assemblage. Ascribing "thing-power" to dead rats, plastic caps, even heaping piles of trash—Bennett taps into the

2. See Zoltán Grossman's *Unlikely Alliances: Native Nations and White Communities Join to Defend Rural Lands.*

spontaneous, somewhat mysterious ways in which seemingly disparate items cohere to form new cultural terrains. Thing-power denotes "the curious ability of inanimate things to animate, to act, to produce effects dramatic and subtle," arising "from bodies inorganic as well as organic" (6). Similar to TallBear, Bennett rejects hierarchical systems that elevate certain ontological categories, insisting that all body types exert cultural force. Drawing on the works of Bruno Latour and Gilles Deleuze, she theorizes the assemblage as a mix of material-discursive "things"—a natureculture, or hybridization of ontological types. Neither subject nor object, the assemblage constitutes "an intervener," which "by virtue of its location . . . makes things happen, becomes the decisive force catalyzing an event" (9).

Bennett's focus on material intervention and locationality is useful insofar as it illuminates the role of nonhuman life in spaces of rhetorical action, thus displacing human actors from a perceived position of privilege. Here, agency occurs in the betweenness of bodies rather than a single, immutable source, inviting a more holistic perspective that gives serious consideration to the objects and materials composing public life. Conceptualizing the "thing-power" of a nonhuman entity means wrestling with its situatedness; it means studying that entity with an eye to its "role" in a broader ecology of meanings and materials.

Bennett's insistence that political disruption is materialized through the interactions of human and nonhuman bodies offers a productive lens for studying protest events, and yet she adheres to a tradition of secularism that denies metaphysical significance to the nonhuman world. While honoring Bennett's commitment to opening new ethical and political possibilities for studying material affairs, we should question her embrace of a rational Self that seems to be defined in opposition to a supposedly primitive, premodern "Other" (Sundberg). Rejecting spirituality as anti-intellectualism precludes many Indigenous forms of worldmaking and positions Indigenous people as objects rather than producers of knowledge. It is this aspect of Bennett's work I wish to push back on by featuring her voice alongside that of TallBear, who is not only willing to grant spiritual significance to nonhuman entities, but who insists on a dynamic conceptual framework that includes the sacred as a legitimate way of experiencing and knowing the material world.

Perhaps my reader sees these differences as irreconcilable, but if my research into this subject has taught me anything, it's that alliances exist in unlikely places. If harmony is a requisite to political collaboration, then efforts to preserve the environmental commons will inevitably proceed in piecemeal fashion, with each respective group acting upon its own self-interest. Such a view—whether theoretical or practical in nature—would be devastating to the momentum and efficacy of the anti-pipeline movement, which has sustained itself on coalition-building and polymorphic resistance to the cultural and ecological abuses committed by transnational corporations. Bennett's theory of a vital materialism is not congruent at all angles with TallBear's Indigenous metaphysic. Differences can and should be understood. And yet the habits of mind these authors encourage—an epistemological openness to nonhuman lifeforms, a critical stance toward animacy hierarchies, a distributed interpretation of agency—share an outlook that troubles prevailing attitudes about what it means to do and study protest, and if these theories are wielded in a way that elevates and centers Indigenous perspectives, I believe they can deliver a forceful blow to exploitive industries and the colonial imaginaries that power them.

Thinking through the productive tensions between "thing-power" and "the knowing relatedness of all things" opens intellectual pathways that punctuate and pass through Cartesian-inspired dualisms. TallBear's unworking of the animate/inanimate divide through Indigenous relationality, coupled with Bennett's insistence on the vibrancy of material life, contributes much in the way of understanding tribal corn's "speaking power." As a rhetorical act, corn-planting necessitates interspecies collaboration, creating an ontological assemblage—or "natureculture" (Haraway 4)—where human bodies, plant bodies, objects, tools, and the landscape itself become collectively "operationalized" in political discourse. In the following section, I examine how notions of the ontological assemblage have shaped the scholarly conversation around protest events, arguing that while progress has been made in dismantling animacy hierarchies, an overreliance on European theories and theorists have prevented meaningful engagement with plants in protest movements.

Plant Matters / Plants Matter: Social Movement Rhetoric and the Protest Assemblage

I advocate for an understanding of protest informed by the idea of a "rhetorical becoming," where agency is distributed across spatial and temporal scales rather than "possessed" by any one person or entity. "Becoming" denotes a movement, a process whereby objects, places, people, and "things" come into contact through networks of collective encounter. Scholars like Jenny Edbauer point out that traditional models of the rhetorical situation assume a "bordered, fixed space-location," thus restricting analysis to specific contexts and instances of time. The notion of rhetorical becoming does away with these borders, opening the rhetorical situation to the flows of public life, "to the fluidity and circulation of rhetoric as it is embedded in 'the ongoing social flux' that constitutes society" (qtd. in Gries 79). In other words, a protest—when seen through the lens of becoming—exceeds the moment in which a leading figure steps to the podium to deliver his or her message. Far more encompassing, it entails all the assembled forces and trajectories that collectively constitute that moment. The bodies of protestors, the objects that make up the protest scene, the cameras and technological systems mediating public perception of the protest, the material environment where the protest is situated—agency is not "held" by any one of these entities, but emerges relationally from the interactions between them.

In the context of social movement studies, the notion of rhetorical becoming has translated to a greater focus on the assembled natures of nontextual communication, particularly as it relates to place, embodiment, and materiality. Robert Cox and Christina Foust contend that this shift in focus was precipitated by the ways "in which modernist approaches privileged rationality and propositional rhetorics at the expense of other ways of knowing and acting in the world" (613–14). Turning to performance studies, scholars sought "greater recognition of the extrasymbolic, material character of human expression and the embodied and fluid nature of identity," giving rise to a new set of interpretive theories for the study of protest events (614). Correspondingly, place underwent a dramatic revitalization from a site of rhetorical action to an agent in its own right. Danielle Endres and Samantha Senda-Cook ascribe "place-power" to the locations where social movements occur, writing that "place is a performer along with activists in making and unmaking the possibilities of protest" (258)—a statement that underscores the performative character of the built environment and its ability to impart meaning into political acts of dissent. Places exert affect, reflect cultural values, and communicate ideological commitments—shaping the flow and movement of discourse and becoming "part of the message of the movement" itself (259).

But places are collectives of material things, not monolithic constructions. A church may look and feel singular in its disposition, but in fact is deeply atomistic—a veritable assemblage of pews, stained-glass windows, organ pipes, and altars. Some scholars theorize that social protests are materialized—not exclusively through place, but through the objects protestors carry, repurpose, and deploy *in place*. Katy Soar and Paul-François Tremlett offer a compelling "counter-archaeological analysis" of such movements, arguing that performativity, as an interpretative framework, invites attention to the material culture of protest, prompting consideration of "how the physical and conceptual features of the landscape are drawn upon to create new meanings" (430). The tents of the Occupy Wall Street movement; the pots and pans of the *cacerolazo* protests in Quebec, Canada; the recycled trash and "rubber duckie" inner tubes sported by members of the Tute Bianche movement in Milan, Italy—from a performative perspective, these "things" take on communicative significance by virtue of their circulation in and through a place of protest. Drawing upon the writings of Levi Strauss, Soar and Tremlett project a kind of disobedient liveliness onto these objects, arguing that "pre-existing materials are re-packaged and reused for new ends and purposes" by protestors (428). Through this ad hoc recombination—where a variety of material things are "lifted" from their "original" contexts and deployed in another—social movements take on characteristics of the bricoleur, eliciting subversive, politically charged encounters between people, places, and things.

As rhetorical entities, then, place and materiality share a close relationship, mutually creating and (re)creating the possibilities of dissent. It may be tempting to think of this relationship as a dialectic, a communicative exchange issuing back and forth between the place of protest and the objects that compose and move within it. But like all complex systems, protests harbor a plurality of interlocking features—the whole greater than the sum of its parts. One could argue that embodiment knits together place and materiality, forming a fleshy, connective thread between them. The structures of any environment have a say in what bodies can, and cannot, do, constraining and guiding them, giving shape and direction to acts of counterpublicity. At the same time, bodies are unruly forces in and of themselves and resistive to passive constructions. Sometimes the whole point of a protest is to assemble bodies in places where they shouldn't ordinarily be—transit lines, for instance, and busy avenues of commerce. "Enmeshed in a turbulent stream of multiple and conflictual discourses that shape what they mean in particular contexts," DeLuca contends that bodies are both symbolic and *extra*symbolic, representing deliberative, strategic forms of argumentation, but also exceeding those forms through a kind of raw materiality that outstrips human sense-making (12).

Bodies, then, aren't subservient to places, but interactive with them, much in the same way that objects are interactive with bodies. The tents of the Occupy Wall Street movement were assembled and inhabited by human protestors; the pots and pans of the *cacerolazo* protests were deployed through physical performance. As is so often the case in these situations, political acts of dissent are realized through the collaborations between objects and bodies, emerging through relationality. In fact, the connection between embodiment and materiality is so close that discussing them separately risks obscuring their enmeshed qualities. Because of the degree to which our biological selves have coevolved with the instruments around us, some scholars have done away with the distinction altogether. Nigel Thrift calls the human body a "tool-being" (10), and Greg Dickinson and Giorgia Aiello point out that the human body is itself a material entity: "Made up of bone and sinew, activated by chemical reactions and electrical charges, nourished by food, air, and water that are processed by microbes and bacteria throughout our body, driven by activating energies, the human processes and produces suasion in and through this materiality" (1296).

Bodies, objects, and places materialize protest events through their interactions and what Karen Barad calls "*intra*-actions," operating synergistically to produce counterpublic movements (141). My intervention in this conversation is subtle, but important insofar as it illuminates the connection between humans and other organisms, opening the possibility for a truly interspecies account of protest rhetoric. The idea of the rhetorical becoming, spurred along by materialist perspectives, has done much in the way of leveling animacy hierarchies, but perhaps because so many of these studies rely on Western interpretive frameworks, they often neglect other life-forms—like plants—from rhetorical consideration. Discussions of embodied protest routinely focus on human protestors, which negates, implicitly, the presence of other embodied actants, enacting, conceptually, a kind of ecological erasure. This tendency is widespread but most visible, perhaps, in DeLuca's writing. In analyzing the claims-making practices of "radical" ecology groups, DeLuca draws attention to the embodied practice of tree-sitting as a form of protest:

> For analysis, let us look at a protestor sitting on a platform 100 feet up in a giant Douglas fir. . . . What is striking about [this] image is the utter vulnerability of these protestors as they intervene on behalf of nature. Quite clearly, the Earth First!ers are putting at risk their bodies, their lives for wilderness, for trees. . . . By placing themselves at risk, Earth First!ers . . . proffer the humble thought that other animals have a right to live and have intrinsic value. (13)

Note here the passive construction of organic life—how human protestors are said to "intervene on behalf of nature." Under this framework, persuasion flows exclusively from the embodied actions of protestors themselves, rendering the Douglas fir little more than a plastic "prop" in the performance. The assumption, of course, is that trees are arhetorical—powerless against the threat of human encroachment and therefore dependent upon other, more altruistic humans to advocate *for them*.

TallBear's theory of an Indigenous metaphysic presents a challenge to depictions of protest rhetoric that reinforce and stabilize notions of an autonomous human agent who affects change independently of the ecological systems in which he or she is emplaced. DeLuca argues that bodies are not "determined or limited by verbal frames," that they "exceed the protocols of deliberative reasoning" by producing argumentative a/effects (13). And yet he frequently brackets the human body apart from its environment and expels other embodied presences, like the Douglas fir, from consideration as rhetorical entities. The Native American Ethnobotany Database lists 184 entries for the Douglas fir, detailing its extensive usage among Indigenous communities. The birfucating move that DeLuca intimates would not be possible from an Indigenous standpoint, because the Douglas fir would be recognized as kin—a relative who imparts gifts, plays an active role in ceremonial life, and serves various medicinal purposes (*Native*). An Indigenous metaphysic transfigures protest rhetoric into a boundary-crossing event—a practice done not on behalf of other organisms, but with and through other organisms. Looking at photos of these tree-sitting protestors, I'm struck by how a relational perspective changes DeLuca's analytic. Vulnerability does seem like a salient part of the message, but it's how and where these protestors are situated in relation to the Douglas fir that activates the message. Dwarfed by the fir's immense branches, the protestors appear frail and exposed, overshadowed in both a literal and metaphorical sense. Assembled together in such a precarious position, tree body and human body become part of a corporeal conversation—a rhetoric that exceeds humanness by stretching across species boundaries.

Narratives of "saving nature" lean too heavily on passive constructions of the nonhuman world, and in this way, they reinforce a neoliberal outlook that sees materiality as so much dead, inert "stuff." They also preserve humans' place at the center of public life and enable a conceptual splitting that cleaves nature from culture (TallBear, "Indigenous" 235). Practices like tree-sitting and corn-planting exemplify how politically disruptive groups deploy aspects of the environment to frame their arguments, convey messages of dissent, and enact political disruption. Studying the meaning of these events requires a theoretical framework that is sensitive enough to detect animacy in all variety of "things," particularly plants, that have been misunderstood and maligned by Western science as communicatively deficient. Applying Indigenous materialisms to the study of protest will, I hope, counteract this long-running tendency and give voice to vegetational presences.

The Seeds of Resistance ceremony offers a conceptual touchstone on questions that deal with embodiment, affect, and the diverse "natures" of protest. Rather than humans acting on behalf of nonhuman nature, the ceremony shows humans acting in collaboration with nonhuman nature to author a decolonial rhetoric of survivance. In the following section, then, I present a narrative vignette of my experience at the Seeds of Resistance ceremony, focusing on the rhetorical vibrancy of tribal corn and its ability to unsettle hegemonic place meanings.

A Note on Methods

On June 8, 2019, I traveled from Lincoln to Neligh, Nebraska, to participate in the Alliance's sixth annual Seeds of Resistance ceremony. The event was open to the public and I attended as an activist-scholar. I hoped my presence would contribute meaningfully to the anti-pipeline movement, and in this respect, I took on the responsibilities of activist and ally. At the same time, I also wished to study the interrelationships between performance, plant, and place—or how protestors used material aspects of the environment to articulate a rhetoric of survivance. By stepping into these dual roles, I hoped to achieve what Michael Apple calls "repositioning," where researchers leverage their institutional privilege "against the ideological . . . processes and forms that reproduce oppressive conditions" (65). Of course, I was under no illusion that my participation would prompt the kind of swift, liberatory change that protestors deserved, but I hoped to lend material and symbolic support to their efforts.

To understand how the meaning of the ceremony is interwoven with material objects and processes, I employed a mixed-methods approach, blending rhetorical and discourse analysis with ethnography. While much of my research was carried out in online spheres as a way to understand how members of the Alliance narrated their rhetorical exigence and invoked tribal corn in discussions of the Keystone XL, the participant-observation components were direct and immersive. As a researcher—particularly as a white, European researcher—I sought an embodied encounter that would enable me to draw conclusions based on my own experience of the event. In this respect, I'm inclined to agree with Greg Dickinson and Giorgia Aiello: When it comes to studying the places of persuasion—"being through there matters." Attending the ceremony in person offered me a glimpse into the affective dimensions of the protest that would have been invisible to me otherwise, and it allowed for a proximity that made it easier to reflect on my own privilege as a white researcher from the academy. Whereas I could travel back to Lincoln to carry on my affairs in ignorant bliss of the Keystone XL's potential construction, this sense of safety and distance was not possible for other participants. For these community members, the threat of the Keystone XL was immediate and tangible, and it couldn't be escaped through a simple drive down the road. "Repositioning" myself to be in closer proximity to the ceremony helped me understand this at a deeper level.

In an effort to enact collaborative forms of research rooted in principles of compassion, accountability, and mutual respect, I pursued what Krista Ratcliffe calls "rhetorical listening" by "standing under" the discourses of colonialism and letting the voices of those affected wash over and pool around me (205). I listened as white farmers spoke passionately about how the Keystone XL disrupts their operations and undermines their ability to manage the land in a way they see fit. I listened to Native members of the Alliance talk with conviction about their ancestral ties to the Plains landscape and how the Keystone XL threatens to diminish those ties. In speeches throughout the ceremony and in casual conversations between those speeches, I took the opportunity *to hear.*

And yet I also sought to extend those same listening practices to nonhuman entities by taking stock in the ideas of Barbara McClintock, who encourages scholars to develop a more holistic, embodied approach for studying members of the nonhuman world (see Keller). Participating in the ceremony provided me a space in which I could examine the Ponka corn's shape and texture, its size and mass—the way the seeds rolled around the calluses of my palms, how they looked in sunlight, how they felt when pressed between forefinger and thumb. In this way, I could practice a kind of full-bodied attentiveness, listening not only with my ears, but with all my senses and sensibilities.

At the same time, I wish to be up front about how my own experiences have positioned me in relation to the Ponka corn. As Shawn Wilson writes, knowledge "is a relationship with all of creation. It is with the animals, with the plants, with the earth" (74). I cannot conduct my research faithfully, then, without acknowledging the distance between myself and this particular strain of corn. For while I found—throughout the ceremony—moments to connect with this species in an emotional and physical way, I lack a lifetime of experiences with it, and because my identity is that of a settler, not an Indigenous person, the corn means and feels something different to me. My reader should know full well, then, that my representations and knowledge of the corn stem from my own limited worldview. I have learned from Indigenous thinkers who do have an intimate, lifelong relationship with this plant, and I have tried to represent those perspectives faithfully in the writing of this essay, but as an outsider to the community, I cannot claim a deep, ancestral knowledge about the existence and meaning of Ponka corn.

What I can do, though, is help my reader feel what it was like to encounter this particular species, in this particular environment, from my particular vantage point, and I can be intentional about the forms of research I choose to practice and how I represent my findings. Over the course of this inquiry, I have opted for empathic listening over data collecting, self-reflexivity over scientific objectivity. And because the ceremony pushes participants beyond the boundaries of reason and logic, I sought an openness to sources of knowledge traditionally excluded from academic research, like emotion, intuition, and spirituality. All these sources are part of the co-constitutive fabric of the material and the immaterial and thus none can be discarded, even (especially?) if they pose a challenge to the guiding paradigms of Western knowledge. In this way, I hope to not only illuminate a rhetoric that destabilizes Eurocentric conceptions of argumentation, but also to research that rhetoric in a way that honors Indigenous values and perspectives.

Wilson argues that research is a ceremony and that ceremonies create "a raised state of consciousness," bringing "participants into a state of mind that will allow for the extraordinary to take place" (69). What I witnessed at the Seeds of Resistance ceremony *was* extraordinary and it *did* elevate my consciousness, and for that reason, I've chosen to represent my findings in narrative form. That way, my reader might have a similar experience—might feel the power of the ceremony even at a spatial and temporal remove. Of course, the power of the ceremony issues, in no small part, from the material itself, so language alone won't do the experience justice, but perhaps it will open a space where readers have enough freedom to project their own meanings onto the events of that day. "By getting away from abstractions and rules," Wilson writes, "stories allow listeners to draw their own conclusions . . . to see others' life experiences through our own eyes" (17). I do not claim a universal knowledge of Ponka corn, only a knowledge that stems from my relationship to the plant, to the other participants who attended that day, and to the Plains landscape that nourishes all our bodies—human and nonhuman, Native and nonnative alike. The landscape does not discriminate, but academic systems do, and they have a way of privileging European communication styles; I present my narrative, then, as a rebuttal to those systems and a gesture toward Indigenous authors—like Wilson—who paved the way for more inclusive, more just standards in academic research.

Sedimented Meanings: Discourses of Place and the Tanderup Farm

The Seeds of Resistance ceremony is performed on the same farm, in the same field, year after year. Art and Helen Tanderup grow corn, soy, and rye in northeast Nebraska, and every spring pipeline fighters from across the region migrate to their property. Tucked away at the end of a long gravel road, the place feels peaceable and removed, like a reprieve. Sunlit fields give way to fringes of wildflowers and cottonwood trees, and the only thing matching the vastness of the crop rows is the vastness of the sky. Nearly 200 miles from the closest major city center, the Tanderup farm is what most consider "flyover country," just an empty spot on a map. Not a true destination at all, but a temporary stopping point on the way to a destination. In lieu of busy intersections and towering government structures are rolling hills, pockets of grassland, and miles upon miles of intensively cultivated fields.

But the picturesque, idyllic qualities of the landscape belie the truly contested nature of the space, masking a darker underside. Arriving at the entrance to the farm, I was greeted by a steel-tube gate with a sign that reads, "This land protected by neighbors coming together to end eminent domain for private gain." It was the first indication that not all is how it seems. The Tanderup farm may feel insulated from the chaos of modern political life, but in reality, it's a place of fractiousness and strife, a "contact zone," in the words of Mary Louise Pratt, where "cultures meet, grapple, and clash" (34).

Shortly after the Tanderups retired to the farm in 2010 (the property has been in Helen's family for over 100 years), they were approached by a representative of TransCanada who arrived at their doorstep with paperwork in tow, asking that they sign off on documents that would allow the company to build a section of pipeline through their land. "We need to look into things," they told the representative (Nahigyan). In the weeks and months following, the Tanderups teamed up with other individuals and organizations opposing the pipeline, and in November 2013, their farm became the site of a spiritual camp, where Indigenous leaders met with local landowners to discuss strategies for protecting the land. Squatted inside a tipi with elders of various Plains tribes, the Tanderups explained how the Ponca Trail of Tears and the proposed Keystone pathway bisect their property. The group prayed, burned sage, shared stories, and eventually formed a collaborative partnership that we know of today as the Cowboy Indian Alliance (Andrei).

After the Tanderups failed to comply with TransCanada's requests, the company took action against them, invoking the powers of eminent domain and seeking to obtain legal rights to build on their property. The Tanderups responded with a joint lawsuit, suing the company for unconstitutionally circumventing the Nebraska Public Service Commission (Song). They were dealt an early victory when TransCanada withdrew from the lawsuit, but after Donald Trump took office and "revived" the Keystone project, TransCanada mounted a comeback offensive, sending out a second round of lawsuits against landowners living in the proposed pathway of the pipeline. Once more, the Tanderups found their farm in the crosshairs of development.

•

Landscape, according to human geographer Yi-Fu Tuan, takes on meaning "through the steady accretion of sentiment over the years" (33). The Tanderup property is a living testament to this notion—its contours complexly layered with memory, affect, and symbolism. Events large and small have left their markings on it, shaping the farm into what it is today: a place of resistance.

It is said that when the Ponca tribe marched from north Nebraska to Oklahoma in 1877, they left bloody footprints in the snow ("Ponca"). It was early May when they passed through what is now the Tanderup farm. The 600-mile journey had just begun, but an unseasonably cold, wet spring was already making travel difficult. Trudging through harsh weather, the Ponca arrived in Neligh on May 22, camping on the outskirts of town in the Elkhorn River Valley. It rained all that night and into the next morning, so much so that the Ponca and their military holders were forced to halt camp for a day. Perhaps it was a cold that transformed into pneumonia, or perhaps it was simply exposure; later that afternoon, White Buffalo Girl, daughter of Black Elk and Moon Hawk, died. She was eighteen months old. Her grief-stricken father went to the townspeople of Neligh requesting help from a local carpenter, who fashioned a wooden cross from two fence posts (Hansen). The next day, the Ponca ascended a large windswept hill to the Neligh cemetery. Accompanied by many of the townspeople, they buried White Buffalo Girl, staking the wooden cross over her grave. Black Elk delivered a speech that was translated graveside, and eventually, years later, when the wooden cross was replaced with a white marble monument, the speech was carved into its stone face. It reads: "I want the whites to respect the grave of my child just as they do the graves of their own dead. The Indians do not like to leave the graves of their ancestors, but we had to move and hope it will be for the best. I leave the grave in your care. I may never see it again. Care for it for me."

White Buffalo Girl's death marked the first casualty of the Ponca Trail of Tears, but it was far from the last. Historians estimate that in the months to follow, nearly one third of the Ponca tribe perished, most from disease or just sheer exhaustion (Hansen). The story is well-known in Neligh. In fact, one might say it defines Neligh. The townspeople who were present at the burial were so moved by Black Elk's speech that they wrote it down and passed it on to their next of kin, immortalizing the message, ensuring that it wouldn't be forgotten. To this day, the townspeople of Neligh care for the gravesite, cleaning it, repairing it, maintaining it, often leaving little gifts, particularly around Mother's Day—teddy bears, coins, various trinkets. When I came to that windswept hill on the morning of the ceremony, the monument was encircled by seven paving stones and adorned with feathers, flowers, and jewelry. I read Black Elk's message several times over, felt the wind on my face, the ground under my feet, then turned and walked back to where I was parked—no more than a hundred yards from the trail that brought the Ponca to that cemetery. Were it still a well-defined path, I could have left my car and walked the short distance to the Tanderup farm.

•

The significance of the protest space is difficult to overstate, steeped as it is in discourses of colonialism, developmentism, and decolonialism—each vying to configure the farm in different ways. Evidence of this struggle—this "cultural clash," as Pratt refers to it—is written into the landscape itself, expressed in a language of gravesites and trails and pipelines. Memories of Indigenous displacement, and the emotions evoked by those memories, permeate the space, so much so that even from a remove, several miles distant from the Neligh cemetery, White Buffalo Girl's presence can be felt. The US's hostile attitude toward Indigenous people hangs over the Tanderup farm, suffusing it with affective energy. In the same way that Neligh has become synonymous with removal policies, the Tanderup farm, too, has become imaginatively intertwined with colonial violence, to the extent that disassociating the two becomes a near-insurmountable feat, like pulling Auschwitz from the cloud of genocide.

And yet, despite these hegemonic discourses, one feels at the Tanderup farm a deep sense of counter-resurgence, born out by interethnic collaborations between Indigenous and non-Indigenous people. The spirit camps, the corn plantings, the gates bearing anti-Keystone signage—all these material aspects of the site take on powerful resonance precisely because of the colonial context in which they're situated. They defy and disrupt the sedimented meanings of the site, opening new cultural and political possibilities—creating a new experience of place. That landscapes accrue meaning over time makes them more stable, and therefore more resistant to change. A rut becomes a rut through repetition. A trail becomes a trail through successive footfalls. But even places with long histories of abuse can be reprised and recovered. All they need is for an intervener to come along.

Gifts, Spirit Beings, and the Multiple Meanings of Tribal Corn

In the discourse that surrounds, produces, and flows through the ceremony, tribal corn is much more than a food product or "decor." It is a powerful symbol of Native identity, constituting what TallBear might refer to as a "spirit being": an agent endowed with mystical powers that moves seamlessly between the material and immaterial world—between the physical and the *meta*physical ("Beyond" 192). Corn is viewed with deep reverence and respect—it is sometimes referred to as "Mother Corn" in oral histories—and there are few natural entities endowed with more cultural and spiritual cachet. Corn's vibrancy has earned it a central role in the religious rites, creation narratives, and cultural lifeways of plains-dwelling tribes. In *Corn among the Indians of the Upper Missouri,* George F. Will and George E. Hyde assert that Native heirlooms were "held to be more sacred than the Buffalo" and figured strongly in ceremonial events (199). George Grinnell comes to a similar conclusion, writing that in Pawnee mythologies,

> Much is told about the power of the Mother Corn . . . which cares for and protects [the Pawnee], which taught them much that they know, and which, symbolizing the earth, represents in material form something which they revere. . . . Various explanations are given of the term "Mother," which is applied to the corn. . . . The reference may be to the fact that the corn has always supported and nourished them, as the child is nourished and supported by its mother's milk, or, with a deeper meaning, it may be to the produce power of the earth, which each year brings forth its increase. (114–15)

Grinnel's writing underscores the potency of tribal corn as a spiritual entity. The metaphor of "mother's milk" imbues it with life-giving properties—corn as a source of sustenance. And this, in part, is where tribal corn earns its power—from an ability to shape-shift and drift across boundaries. It is of the ground, "symbolizing the earth," a feature and extension of the landscape, but it is also of the body, like "mother's milk," *becoming* the body through consumption, its starches and nutrients transforming to tendons and muscles. Spirit in the flesh. Spirit *of* the flesh.

Today, members of the Alliance often refer to the corn as "blessed" or invoke it as a "gift," regarding it more as a relative than a product. Amos Hinton, a leader in the group, explains that "in [the Ponca's] creation story the Creator gave us three original gifts: red corn, a dog, and a bow" (Andrei). The red corn "symbolizes one of the gifts our Creator gave to us to sustain our lives" (Leizens). The description supplants corn's "objectness" with the meanings of a "gift"—something given and received, something exchanged based on principles of respect and mutuality. "Gifts invite reciprocity," writes Robin Wall Kimmerer; they "help form relationships" (Tonino). The power of tribal corn flows from its sustaining force, from its ability to impart strength and vitality onto those who receive it. Its cultivation, harvest, and consumption generates enduring relationships between people and the land, breaking down the divisions that limit their interactions—rendering these divisions more porous, more permeable.

But Alliance members have also extended tribal corn's spiritual qualities into current debates about resource extraction, treaty rights, and sustainable development, endowing it with new powers. Jane Kleeb, a leading organizer with the Alliance, refers to the corn as "a cherished symbol of our collective resistance to tarsands," adapting the corn's "original" meaning to fit with a different context—one that is more overtly political. Here, tribal corn is not only a form of sustenance and nourishment, but also a means of enacting dissent. It is justice-oriented—a resource to be deployed in the struggle for the environmental commons. As a symbol, it stands diametrically opposed to tar-sands oil, representing the inverse of what some might call "petroculture"—that is, a self-destructive dependence on fossil fuels. Tribal corn communicates a competing set of meanings, organized around principles of sustainability, reciprocity, and mutuality. Its embodiment as a living organism implicitly rebukes tenets of colonial and development discourse, signifying a resistive counter-rhetoric where the land isn't an external "other" to be dominated, but a relative who imparts gifts on to those who are wise enough, and prudent enough, to accept them.

As with all spiritual entities, though, there's something of the unknown and unknowable in tribal corn. Impervious to theorization, it travels beyond reason, beyond language, into realms of the ineffable. "The resiliency of farmers, ranchers and Native families can not be put into words," writes Kleeb. "Perhaps that is why a seed of resistance corn speaks for us." Tribal corn materializes that which cannot be expressed through discourse or linguistic symbols, communicating on its own terms instead—through embodied presence, through root and soil. "Vivid entities," writes Bennett, are "not entirely reducible to the contexts in which (human) subjects set them, never quite exhausted by their semiotics" (5). Tribal corn seems quite vivid in this sense, always exceeding the frames in which it is planted, always drifting across the boundaries—whether material or discursive—that have been set to contain it.

Like the red pipestone that TallBear analyzes, the significance of tribal corn doesn't flow from some hidden source, tucked away inside the organism. It emerges relationally through interactions with people, places, events, and other life-forms. Growing and sustaining a plot of corn is an investment of time and energy that requires nurturance, care, and attention—from humans, yes, but also from other organisms. Recent research has demonstrated that belowground microbe communities are essential to increasing plant vigor and survivability rates in corn, as well as circulating nutrients that would otherwise be "locked up in undecomposed detritus" (Megali et al. 1512). In other words, tribal corn is connected with a network of human and more-than-human agencies that give shape to its myriad forms of expression. Part of its sacredness, then, is exercised through these complex relationships—and through the stories that emerge from them.

The leaves of Ponka corn grow long and gangly in the summer months, and sometimes volunteers sprout up in unexpected places—places they weren't intended to grow, but grow they do, tall and strong, as if planted there by a knowing hand. Such is the way assemblages form—through a mix of intentionality and sheer randomness. An intervener "makes the difference" not always through force of will but through improvisation—by "being in the right place at the right time" (Bennett 9).

"Every Seed You Plant Should Be a Prayer": The Seeds of Resistance Ceremony

Landscapes become meaningful in two ways, according to Tuan: through "the steady accretion of sentiment" over time, but also through "an intense feeling [to] illuminate a place for life" (qtd. in Knopp 155). The first is much more gradual, a steady drip, drip, drip—one experience adding and compiling onto another in a process that can take years, even centuries. But the second is explosive, occurring within an instant, prompted by some great joy or pain—like crashing a car or falling in love. In a moment, the place is different, radically transformed, seen with new eyes, felt with new emotions. Never to be the same.

•

The protest site sits smack in the middle of a cornfield—a portion of which had been recently tilled to expose long furls of silty brown soil. Arriving there in a flatbed trailer, we parked at the entrance gate, moving into the field on foot, passing a fencepost with bulging bags of blue corn seed slumped against it. A woman was there to meet the protestors as we filed by. Again and again, she plunged her arm into the bags, scooping out big cupfuls of seed and pouring them into open hands. "Take some," she said. The cup was so full that the seeds brimmed over the top, the excess spilling into weeds and slipping through people's fingers, landing in dusty little crevices between clumps of grass. The seeds looked nothing like the bright gold ones I grew up planting in the garden. They were deep blue, almost purple—the color of prairie sky at twilight. I studied the little pile of them in my palm, then slipped the seeds into a back pocket, joining the other protestors who had gathered in the newly tilled soil.

Mekasi Camp Horinek led the ceremony. Tall and broad, with raven-black hair and tattooed forearms, he has an outsized presence, communicating much even when he says nothing. As more protestors arrived, trailing into the field, he shepherded them into the circle, which grew wider and wider until there was a space large enough to accommodate a small playground in the center. The folks gathered at the edge (approximately sixty of us in total) were an eclectic bunch: farmers, ranchers, professors, retirees, a few high school students, and citizens of at least four Native American tribes—the Ponca Tribe of Nebraska, the Ponca Tribe of Oklahoma, the Cheyenne River Sioux Tribe, and the Winnebago Tribe. It was a mix of leather boots and bandanas, baseball caps and blue jeans. Many sported T-shirts emblazoned with anti-Keystone slogans like "Pipeline Fighter" and "Earth Rights." Some looked as if they'd come directly from the field—dirt on their hands, sweat under their arms, the kind of Midwest folks you'd see running a produce stand at a farmer's market or saddling up for a long trail ride.

The chatter died down almost instantly as Horinek stepped into the circle. He thanked the attendees and spoke a few words of acknowledgment, then produced a sage bundle, lit it, and passed it clockwise around the circle. A moment of silence passed as participants fanned themselves with the smoke, wafting in onto their clothes, their hair, their bodies. Horinek closed his eyes and commenced with a prayer to the four directions, speaking in the Siouan language of his ancestors. The ceremony had begun.

•

At the conclusion of the opening prayer, Horinek called up five or six teenagers, who, after much prodding, inched their way into the circle. As Horinek announced their recent graduation from a youth Indigenous leadership camp, they smiled sheepishly, kicking their shoes in the dust while the crowd looked on. Applause broke out as the graduates were honored with gifts. Horinek, meanwhile, walked over to his wife, who was holding their infant daughter in a bundle of blankets. He gathered the child in his arms. After each graduate had been recognized, he turned to the crowd, holding his daughter aloft: "This ceremony isn't just about the people here today. It's about her generation too. These kids," he said with a wide smile, "they are our future."

Horinek then turned to Jane Kleeb, who stepped into the circle wearing black, knee-high boots and an expression of solemnity. A change in atmosphere came over the crowd, as Kleeb paid tribute to pipeline opponents who were terminally ill with cancer, notably Frank LaMere, a Winnebago activist. Silence settled over the field, as families of these individuals were honored with ceremonial blankets. Some openly wept. Others pressed their eyes shut, mumbling prayers into the wind. It was time for the corn-planting.

At Horinek's urging, the gathering of volunteers transformed shape, changing from a circle to a long line. Positioned along the outer edge of the tilled soil, we extended our arms, brushing fingertips with neighbors, spacing ourselves every five to six feet. "Take a step!" shouted Horinek, and the whole line lurched forward, all sixty volunteers moving to the first crop row. I reached down, following the rhythms of those beside me, making three shallow divots in the upturned soil and dropping into each one a seed of blue Ponka corn. Smoothing over the holes with the flat of my palm and patting them into place, I rose just in time for the second command: "Take another step!" and the line lurched forward again, this time to the second crop row—our bodies moving synchronously over the field.

As we planted, Horinek walked among the volunteers, offering encouragement and guidance. "This isn't just a symbolic gesture that we're doing," he said. "It's actually a ceremony that you're participating in. Every seed that you plant should be a prayer" (Abourezk).

Reaching the final crop row, we planted the remaining seeds. Some people closed their eyes in a moment of reflection. Some laughed and joked with their neighbors. Some took a final opportunity to thank the seeds, holding them aloft and whispering their gratitudes. A gentle wind kicked up—the skies threatening rain. In less than an hour's time, we'd seeded roughly three and a half acres with blue Ponca corn. Returning to the head of the field, Kleeb addressed the crowd once more: "I can't wait to unveil the message to send a very clear signal to the president that we are still here, we are still standing, and this pipeline will never be built," she said.

The statement prompted a flurry of cheers, whoops, and fist pumps. Strangers hugged other strangers. Promises were made to return next year.

Photographs were taken. And as the crowd dispersed from the field, the first drops of a spring shower began darkening the soil.

Conclusion

Planting tribal corn in the path of a pipeline materializes a rhetoric of survivance, writing it into the soil, expressing it in a language that can be felt, touched, embodied. By setting up a visual-material comparison between corn and oil, the ceremony operates through oppositionality, undermining a key trope in colonial discourses where Indigenous practices are said to be "savage" and "backward" and those affiliated with white culture are labeled as "civil" and "modern." Juxtaposing the life-giving properties of corn against the life-taking properties of oil targets that invocation, folds it back upon itself, reverses the line of argument so that white society appears backward and savage, unable to control its own self-defeating addiction to fossil fuels. Tribal corn takes on a rhetorical cutting edge through its disassociation from oil, absorbing intimations of reciprocity and sustainability, and simultaneously expelling those of dominance and hierarchy, in a not-so-subtle rebuke to the Eurocentric philosophies that underpin projects like the Keystone XL.

But the ceremony is as much a celebration as it is critique—not a response to settler colonialism, but an invited opportunity to affirm Indigenous lifeways through the rhetorical practice of survivance. Converting a fallow field into a growing site of tribal corn, the Alliance traces over the symbolisms of the Tanderup farm, transforming it, materially and conceptually, into a growing site for Indigenous culture and traditions. The ceremony revises the story of the Tanderup farm through a creative act of place-making, intervening in its existing meanings, rewriting them in a style that reflects Indigenous values, epistemologies, and experiences. This practice of reinscription occurs year after year, as it is now customary for the Alliance to hold two annual ceremonies: one in the spring to plant the Ponka corn, and another in fall to harvest it. The rhythmic, seasonal nature of this practice reflects a story of continuance. For members of the Alliance, the planting of the corn isn't just a momentary disruption of settler colonial ideology—it's a long-term commitment to cultivating a greener, more just future.

I conceive of tribal corn not as a character in this story, but as a coauthor—a vital presence in decolonial survivance. As a case study, the Seeds of Resistance ceremony invites a different perspective of the protest assemblage, complicating theories that might implicitly privilege human embodiment and, as a result, overlook other corporeal entities. Rather than the settler colonial tradition of not seeing plant life, or imposing onto them frameworks of silence, I wish to join other scholars in this collection by centering their presence, particularly in the area of protest studies, bringing them out from the shady recess where they've been (mis)planted and into the light of day.

In so doing, I mean not to elevate plants above other material aspects of the protest assemblage, but to locate them on the same playing field. Tribal corn is most certainly a powerful entity, exhausting and exceeding its semiotic frames. But its vibrance—its "thing-power"—doesn't flow from a singular source; it emerges relationally from other material entities. Without hands to plant it, without a sky to water it, without soil to feed it, without a place to grow it—without all these agencies coalescing around it, tribal corn would wilt and cease to be. As a form of political protest, the ceremony immerses participants within these webbed relations, outsourcing much of the rhetorical work to "other" nonhuman agencies. The germination process is, after all, contingent upon the right temperature, the right oxygen levels, the appropriate moisture content, and the metabolic systems of the organism itself. At the ceremony, these forces commingle with human protestors to author new political and social realities.

Robin Wall Kimmerer writes that "ceremonies large and small have the power to focus attention to a way of living awake in the world" (36). Perhaps the power of the Seeds of Resistance ceremony stems not from its ability to enact counter-dominance by "defeating" and "triumphing over" the Keystone XL pipeline, but from an ability to further Indigenous lifeways by promoting more reciprocal, more sustainable ways of knowing and relating to the material world. As scholars, we can forward this "way of living awake in the world" by questioning animacy hierarchies, by seeing through nature/culture binaries, by acknowledging "the relatedness of all things" and the vitality of nonhuman beings, by expanding rhetoric's focus beyond the textual and the propositional, by lifting up Indigenous voices, and by decolonizing theories that (consciously or not) support strains of settler colonial thought. The project will be difficult and I offer no shortcuts, but perhaps we might begin by listening more carefully to what plants have to tell us.

Works Cited

Abourezk, Kevin. "'Seeds of Resistance': Ponca Corn Planted in Path of Keystone XL Pipeline." *Indianz: Media by and about Native Americans*, 10 June 2019, https://www.indianz.com/News/2019/06/10/seeds-of-resistance-ponca-corn-planted-1.asp. Accessed 10 June 2019.

Alexander, Johnathan, et al., editors. *Unruly Rhetorics: Protest, Persuasion, and Publics*. U of Pittsburgh P, 2018.

Andrei, Mary Anne. "Cowboy and Indian Alliance Plants Sacred Ponka Corn in the Path of Keystone XL." *Bold Nebraska*, http://boldnebraska.org/ponca2019/. Accessed 27 Feb. 2020.

Apple, Michael. "The Critical Divide: Knowledge about the Curriculum and the Concrete Problems of Curriculum Policy and Practice." *Nordic Journal of Studies in Educational Policy*, vol. 4, no. 2, 2018, pp. 63–66. https://doi.org/10.1080/20020317.2018.1492692. Accessed 27 Feb. 2020.

Barad, Karen. *Meeting the Universe Halfway: Quantum Physics and the Entanglement of Matter and Meaning*. Duke UP, 2007.

Bennett, Jane. *Vibrant Matter: A Political Ecology of Things*. Duke UP, 2010.

Cox, Robert, and Christina R. Foust. "Social Movement Rhetoric." *The SAGE Handbook of Rhetorical Studies*, edited by Andrea A. Lunsford et al., SAGE, 2011, pp. 605–27.

Deloria, Vine, Jr. "American Indian Metaphysics." *Power and Place: Indian Education in America*, edited by Vine Deloria Jr. and Daniel R. Wildcat, Fulcrum Publishing, 2001, pp. 1–6.

DeLuca, Kevin Michael. "Unruly Arguments: The Body Rhetoric of Earth First!, ACT UP, and Queer Nation." *Argumentation and Advocacy*, vol. 36, no. 1, 1999, pp. 9–21. https://doi.org/10.1080/00028533.1999.11951634. Accessed 27 Feb. 2020.

Dickinson, Greg, and Giorgia Aiello. "Urban Communication | Being through There Matters: Materiality, Bodies, and Movement in Urban Communication Research." *International Journal of Communication*, vol. 10, 2016, pp. 1294–308. https://ijoc.org/index.php/ijoc/article/view/4280. Accessed 27 Feb. 2020.

Eastman, Charles A. *The Soul of the Indian*. Houghton Mifflin, 1911.

Endres, Danielle, and Samantha Senda-Cook. "Location Matters: The Rhetoric of Place in Protest." *Quarterly Journal of Speech*, vol. 97, no. 3, 2011, pp. 257–82, https://doi.org/10.1080/00335630.2011.585167. Accessed 27 Feb. 2020.

Keller, Evelyn Fox. *A Feeling for the Organism: The Life and Work of Barbara McClintock*. Henry Holt & Company, 1984.

Kimmerer, Robin Wall. *Braiding Sweetgrass*. Milkweed Editions, 2013.

Gries, Laurie. "Agential Matters: Tumbleweed, Women-Pens, Citizens-Hope, and Rhetorical Actancy." *Ecology, Writing Theory, and New Media*, edited by Sidney I. Dorbin, Routledge, 2012, pp. 67–89.

Grinnell, George Bird. "Pawnee Mythology." *The Journal of American Folklore*, vol. 6, no. 21, 1893, pp. 113–30. https://www.jstor.org/stable/533298. Accessed 27 Feb. 2020.

Grossman, Zoltán. *Unlikely Alliances: Native Nations and White Communities Join to Defend Rural Lands*. Washington UP, 2017.

Hansen, Matthew. "Neligh Never Forgot: 140 Years after White Buffalo Girl's Death, Town Still Tends to Her Grave." *Omaha World Herald*, https://www.omaha.com/lifestyles/neligh-never-forgot-years-after-white-buffalo-girl-s-death/article_c2c1f8d8-a9e6057fe-8fe0-8742100d71e8.html. Accessed 27 Feb. 2020.

Haraway, Donna. *The Companion Species Manifesto: Dogs, People, and Significant Otherness*. Prickly Paradigm Press, 2003.

"Indigenous Leaders Sign Opposition to Keystone XL in Calgary." *CBC*, 17 May 2017, https://www.cbc.ca/news/canada/calgary/transcanada-keystone-calgary-indigenous-1.411 9301. Accessed 27 Feb. 2020.

Kleeb, Jane. "Sacred Ponca 'Resistance Corn' Again Planted in Path of Keystone XL." *Bold Nebraska*, http://boldnebraska.org/ponca2019/. Accessed 27 Feb. 2020.

Knopp, Lisa. *What the River Carries*. U of Missouri P, 2012.

Leizens, Tish. "The Ponca and Pawnee Nations' Drive to Preserve Ancestral Corn." *Indian Country Today,* July 2014, https://newsmaven.io/indiancountrytoday/archive/the-ponca-and-pawnee-nations-drive-to-preserve-ancestral-corn-6kL-N9ETOkmkL5ISyUai7A/. Accessed 9 Dec. 2018.

Megali, Lea, et al. "Soil Microbial Inoculation Increases Corn Yield and Insect Attack." *Agronomy for Sustainable Development,* vol. 35, 2015, pp. 1511–19. https://doi.org/10.1007/s13593-015-0323-0. Accessed 31 Mar. 2021.

Nahigyan, Pierce. "From Oil Sands to Farmland: Art Tanderup vs. the Keystone XL." *Planet Experts,* http://www.planetexperts.com/oil-sands-farmland-art-tanderup-vs-keystone-xl/. Accessed 27 Feb. 2020.

Native American Ethnobotany: A Database of Foods, Drugs, Dyes and Fibers of Native American Peoples, Derived from Plants. University of Michigan–Dearborn, 2003, http://naeb.brit.org/. Accessed 31 Mar. 2021.

"The Ponca Trail of Tears." *Nebraska Studies,* http://www.nebraskastudies.org/1875-1899/the-trial-of-standing-bear/the-ponca-trail-of-tears/. Accessed 27 Feb. 2020.

Powell, Malea. "Rhetorics of Survivance: How American Indians Use Writing." *College Composition and Communication,* vol. 53, no. 3, Feb. 2002, pp. 396–434.

Pratt, Mary Louise. "Arts of the Contact Zone." *Profession,* 1991, pp. 33–40.

Ratcliffe, Krista. "Rhetorical Listening: A Trope for Interpretive Invention and a 'Code of Cross-Cultural Conduct.'" *College Composition and Communication,* vol. 51, no. 2, 1999, pp. 195–224.

Ravenscroft, Alison. "Strange Weather: Indigenous Materialisms, New Materialism, and Colonialism." *Cambridge Journal of Postcolonial Literary Inquiry,* vol. 5, no. 3, 2018, pp. 353–70.

Soar, Katy, and Paul-François Tremlett. "Protest Objects: Bricolage, Performance and Counter-Archaeology." *World Archaeology,* vol. 49, no. 3, 2017, pp. 423–34.

Song, Lisa. "Nebraska Landowners Hold Keystone XL at Bay with Lawsuit." *Inside Climate News,* https://insideclimatenews.org/news/30092015/nebraska-homeowners-victorious-one-front-keystone-xl-transcanada. Accessed 27 Feb. 2020.

Sundberg, Juanita. "Decolonizing Posthumanist Geographies." *Cultural Geographies,* vol. 21, no. 1, 2014, pp. 33–47.

TallBear, Kim. "Beyond the Life/Not Life Binary: A Feminist-Indigenous Reading of Cryopreservation, Interspecies Thinking and the New Materialisms." *Cryopolitics: Frozen Life in a Melting World,* edited by Joanna Radin and Emma Kowal, MIT P, 2017, pp. 179–202.

———. "An Indigenous Reflection on Working beyond the Human/Not Human." *Theorizing Queer Inhumanisms,* edited by Mel Y. Chen and Dana Luciano, Duke UP, 2015, pp. 230–35.

Thrift, Nigel. *Non-Representational Theory: Space, Politics, Affect.* Routledge, 2007.

Tonino, Leath. "Two Ways of Knowing: Robin Wall Kimmerer on Scientific and Native American Views of the Natural World." *The Sun,* Apr. 2016, https://www.thesunmagazine.org/issues/484/two-ways-of-knowing. Accessed 27 Feb. 2020.

Tuan, Yi-Fu. *Space and Place.* U of Minnesota P, 1977.

Vizenor, Gerald. *Native Liberty: Natural Reason and Cultural Survivance.* U of Nebraska P, 2009.

Weisser, Christian R. "Subaltern Counterpublics and the Discourse of Protest." *JAC,* vol. 28, 2008, pp. 608–20.

Will, George Francis, and George E. Hyde. *Corn among the Indians of the Upper Missouri.* William Harvey Miner Company, 1917.

Wilson, Shawn. *Research Is Ceremony: Indigenous Research Methods.* Fernwood, 2008.

CHAPTER 7

Top Down, Bottom Up

Ecological Restoration, Rhetorical Resistance, and Decolonization

JUDY HOLIDAY AND ELIZABETH LOWRY

As a means of curbing a continuing sixth mass extinction, the "wanton degradation" of environmental ecosystems (Healy 330), and their subsequent collapse, many groups around the world have recently been fighting for the expansion of legal "personhood" to include nonhuman entities, from wild rice to rivers, in an existential struggle for a sustainable human and nonhuman future. The root of the struggle is epistemological, calling upon humans to rethink how socialities should be (re)organized to secure what Lorraine Code calls "ideal cohabitation" (24)—that is, a model of sustainable living and mutual flourishing wherein the voices of all beings within a particular ecosystem, both human and nonhuman, are heard. Ideally, personhood considers the subjectivity of all persons equally. However, the atomistic conception of personhood that animates contemporary legal systems and colonial-derived social systems, by its very nature, reifies hierarchical thinking by pitting one "person" against another and by usually privileging[1] those "persons" with greater legal access. Colonial constructions of personhood clearly demonstrate that any social imaginary predicated upon selfhood that omits the immediate and inextricable role of others cannot support a politics of ideal cohabitation.

1. *Privilege* in this chapter is used in its scholarly sense as conceived of by Peggy McIntosh: as an unearned advantage accrued to a group.

While feminist scholarship has for decades taken up the topic of participatory democracy, calling for "successor epistemologies" (Code 70) that counter the atomistic, exclusionary, and hierarchical precepts of Euro-American epistemology,[2] as white feminist scholars we remain conscious of one of the basic lessons of feminist history, aptly expressed by Karen Offen: "Amnesia, not lack of history, is feminism's worst enemy today" (15). The absence of public memory regarding feminism along with its misrepresentation have frequently resulted in a Butlerian "unintelligibility" (3) of feminism that requires a reinventing of the wheel, so to speak, from the ground up. As white feminist scholars, we[3] are oriented toward an understanding of feminism as a body of knowledge aimed at eradicating "hierarchy, elitism, racism, class bias, sexism, and ethnocentrism" (Hawkesworth 32), which situates feminism as a much-needed critique of the status quo, one that has fueled programs and ideas for bringing about the well-being of all persons. Despite that important work and the devotion of countless individuals to feminist programs, we argue that humans do not need to reinvent the wheel with respect to models of ideal cohabitation due to the fact that there is a long history of Indigenous wisdom based upon egalitarianism, respect, interconnectedness, and reciprocity (Simpson; Kimmerer; Watts).

Indigenous epistemologies based upon values of mutual flourishing and egalitarianism are not new, yet they are frequently presented outside the context of indigeneity and thereby appear progressive and new, an illusion prevalent in feminist and new materialist scholarship. We are invigorated to hear of recent revolutionary theoretical "discoveries" in the academy, such as the "ontological turn," which exposes the spurious assumption of what is known as "the social turn"—that representation is more accessible than what is represented. In such a worldview, it is impossible to "know" the "external" world. Furthermore, the ontological turn acknowledges the imbrication of the material and the social (i.e., nature via nurture) because the existence of the turn signals an important development in Euro-American thinking, which had not previously acknowledged the indispensable role of the nonhuman in the human world. Nevertheless, we recognize that this turn is not new, but actually very old.

2. Here, when we refer to Euro-American epistemology, we are referencing patriarchal systems of belief that insist on hierarchy, with humans as evolutionarily superior, and a consequent separation of the human and the nonhuman. However, because so many "non-Western" cultures are also patriarchal by this definition, we choose to use the term *colonial* instead of *Western* or *patriarchal*. Patriarchy is an organizing structure of colonial power.

3. As a matter of clarity, the authors use *we* only to refer to themselves.

We thus turn to "predecessor epistemologies" to draw upon the remarkable work of Indigenous scholars[4] who illustrate how many Indigenous epistemologies recognize the consciousness of all forms of life and thus already provide answers to the question of what socialities should and could look like when thought and matter are not perceived as discrete, that is, when the epistemological and ontological are merged to honor the ineluctable imbrication of the two. But before looking at the ideal, we look at what is and examine colonial thinking as a body of knowledge (i.e., atomistic) to demonstrate the harm it enacts and justifies. We compare two legal cases that sought the status of personhood for rivers, the Colorado River (US) and the Whanganui River (New Zealand), to illustrate the epistemological differences undergirding them and to show why colonial thinking is untenable as an epistemology for any commonwealth that purports to uphold human well-being and happiness. Comparison of the two cases demonstrates that the legal failure of the US case can be traced to atomistic conceptions of personhood, whereas the legal success of the New Zealand case emanated from an epistemological shift brought on by "nearly a half century of progressive integration of Indigenous Maori beliefs into New Zealand jurisprudence" (Healy 333). The New Zealand case arguably serves as an inspirational model of what can be achieved at the state level by Indigenous activist organizing by laying out an epistemology that facilitates understandings of what decolonized lifeways might look like. Such a model also shows the kind of practical and organizational knowledge required for transforming long-standing national institutions. However, we worry about enforcement of the agreement as well as the fifty-year time frame involved in recognizing the Whanganui River as a living entity. Considering the urgency of and suffering associated with climate disruption, not to mention the possibility of human extinction, we argue that it is imperative for people to recognize, as Melanie Yazzie (Diné) so eloquently explains (in a paraphrase of Vine Deloria, Jr., who was Sioux): Climate change is not the crisis. Falling out of right relation with the Earth is. Yazzie represents Indigenous activist scholars who have long identified and spoken about the real problem, and we remind readers that what is known of variously as difference (Lorde), subject position (Royster), standpoint (Harding), or epistemic privilege (Bar On) is a foundational asset-based premise for community organizing and global transformation. Given the urgency of climate disruption, it verges on the impossible for humanity to make the radical changes it needs unless

4. We do not mean to conflate the work of these scholars, or to elide the differences across Indigenous epistemologies; we aim simply to point out some key similarities.

Indigenous peoples with "knowledge of governance and science and technology" (Yazzie)—that is, those groups "on the frontlines of climate justice" who have stayed true to their value systems[5]—become recognized by imperial nation-states for their knowledge and granted the resources and power to guide top-down and bottom-up societal change.

Ecological Thinking and the Ontological Turn

As non-Indigenous thinkers who grew up immersed in colonial epistemologies and internalized them, we argue that to draw on Indigenous epistemology and scholarship in order to reimagine the colonial world, it is important for "settlers"[6] to think about what social imaginaries accomplish with respect to the making of worlds in order to understand what is wrong with the colonial social imaginary and why it will never deliver on its promises of social justice. Lorraine Code's *Ecological Thinking: The Politics of Epistemic Location* performs both of these functions—Code explains the limitations of colonial epistemologies, including the disadvantages of an atomistic worldview and rhetorics of self-reliance and mastery (8), and she attempts to lead readers into considering alternative social imaginaries. She draws upon the work of Cornelius Castoriadis to discuss two fundamental types of imaginary, those that are naturalized or "instituted" and those that provide alternatives, or "instituting" (32), as a means of advocating the latter. Code clearly decries the world's dominant social imaginaries without getting into the specifics of how colonial epistemologies have been naturalized, as evidenced, for instance, by profligate use of natural sources, immense economic stratification, and an obscene disregard for the value of each life (human and nonhuman).

As Code's work shows, it is clear that non-Indigenous scholars have arrived theoretically at an epistemological turn that upends colonial epistemology. For instance, Code critiques colonial epistemology for naturalizing a view of the world that places humans outside the natural world. In such a world-

5. As evidence of staying true to Indigenous value systems, Melanie Yazzie shares that Indigenous peoples comprise 5 percent of the population but maintain 80 percent of the Earth's biodiversity.

6. We endorse the use of *conquistador* over *settler*, a change in terms that Tiffany Lethabo King advocates. *Settler* works as a euphemism in "settler-colonialism," obscuring the "kinds of violence committed by settlers for their benefit or self-actualization" (57) (i.e., the genocide and fungibility). As King explains, "it is important to note that the defining and distinguishing aspect of the colonization of the Americas and other settler states is genocide, not settlement or settlers" (57).

view, humans learn a "spectator consciousness" (32) that assumes humans can "know the world well enough to be able to manipulate, predict, and control it to serve human needs" (32). Influenced by Enlightenment thought, this imaginary claims that humans can be objective and "indifferent" knowers of an "inert, indifferent world" (qtd. in Code 32), capable of becoming knowledgeable enough to achieve mastery over it. Given that instituted social imaginaries, according to Code, carry "the normative social meanings, customs, expectations, assumptions, values, prohibitions, and permissions—the habitus and ethos—into which human beings are nurtured from childhood" (30), subjects of such a system learn to perceive themselves in isolation not only from the world around them, but as abstractions "inhabiting" their own bodies, separate from the material world of which they are part.

While instituted imaginaries are normative and hegemonic, Code explains that they are "never seamless or static" (33), and she turns to "ecological thinking" (7) as a possible instituting imaginary, that is, one that offers epistemic alternatives. According to Code, ecology is a study of patterns and relationships, and she defines ecology as "a study of habitats both physical and social where people endeavor to live well together" and "ways of knowing that foster or thwart such living" (25). Ecological thinking is predicated upon two interrelated assumptions: one, that humans cannot be separated from the physical world, and two, because humans cannot be separated from the world, their lives are dependent upon the lives of others. The first assumption situates people as "self-consciously part of nature" (Code 32). By placing humans epistemologically within the world, ecological thinking decenters them; being no longer central to, outside, or above the rest of the natural world renders humans and any other part of the natural world always already in relation to each other. Code argues that because all life is interrelated and mutually interdependent in an ecological model, it naturally follows that humans would be less narcissistic, and in acknowledging their relationship with all of life, treat that life with gratitude and respect.

Code's ecological thinking is useful in terms of "adjudicating knowledge" (5–6) in that it directly challenges colonial constructions of empirical knowledge about the physical-material world. Ecological thinking collapses artificial boundaries between the human and nonhuman and moves discursivity beyond discourse to include, well, everything. As such, we honor Code's work and many other feminist contributions to the academy in appreciation of their spirit of calling for "revisionary ways to engage knowledgeably and wisely with the palpable material-social interactions of 'nature' and 'human nature'" (Code 97). Nevertheless, their discussions feel more intellectual than palpable and elide the question of what onto-epistemological socialities look and feel like.

There are exceptions, however. One area of feminist theorizing that we know has developed concrete practices and a prefigurative politics in support of ecological thinking surfaces in the context of human-to-human relationships: abolition politics (Kaba; Davis). Abolition politics exposes the relationship among racism, genocide, and capitalism and is inherent to any program of healing humanity's relationship to the Earth. Socialist projects that work toward abolition are vitally important, no doubt, for they envision viable alternatives for social organization. They challenge the founding precepts of capitalist democracies, fight corporate hegemony, and refuse to accept the logics of oppression (Kaba 4) inherent to colonial systems.[7] Abolition politics thus align with Indigenous values of the interconnectedness of life and the inestimable value of each human being by instituting new structures and institutions grounded in "cooperation instead of individualism, on mutual aid instead of self-preservation" (Kaba 17), wherein all people are safe and "remain in right relationship to each other and with the land, with the environment" (148).

However, many such projects focus only on the human and elide the larger context of humanity's relationship to the entire Earth, neglecting to credit epistemologies that move well beyond the theoretical or prefigurative (i.e., instituting imaginaries), epistemologies that actually have been instituted and naturalized, as in the case of Indigenous epistemologies. Such omissions understandably come off as colonial. Perhaps most indicative of Indigenous scholars' apt critique that they are overlooked and elided in the academy is the fact that even as feminist theorizing can take readers to an understanding that the ontological turn does not merely mean that scholars need to attend to "material factors in addition to discursive ones" but, "rather, the issue is the conjoined *material-discursive* nature of constraints, conditions, and practices (Barad 823; emphasis added), that understanding of the paradox of the hyphenated as a condition (e.g., material-discursive, onto-epistemological), remains largely an abstraction and is not discussed in terms of practices. What would human daily activities and economies look like in a world that recognized the paradox of the hyphenated? What additional ways of knowing and modalities of being would be cultivated? The onto-epistemological turn implies that both being and knowing are involved in agency, but for readers

7. As Kaba and many feminists before her point out, "the system isn't broken" (6). Kaba shares the story of Martin Shkreli to make the point. Shkreli became famous for price gauging, "raising the price of Daraprim from $13.50 to $750 per pill," yet he was not punished for "forcing AIDS patients to pay hundreds of thousands of dollars a year for a lifesaving medication," because, as Kaba explains, "rich people simply are not punished for practicing capitalism in the United States." Instead, Kaba continues, "Shkreli was punished for securities fraud," for breaking the economic rules of the rich, yet because he also harmed "everyday people," the case is held up as one where the system worked (22).

who have not been raised in cultures with some remaining access to what Anishinaabe and Haudenosaunee scholar Vanessa Watts calls the "precolonial mind" (22), how do they go about incorporating such revisionary "ways"?

Because so many scholarly discussions of societal transformation are more intellectualized than operationalized, they fail to capture the epistemic delinking of which David Grant speaks in "Writing *Wakan*: The Lakota Pipe as Rhetorical Object." Quoting Métis anthropologist and feminist Zoe Todd, who explains that "the danger with the ontological turn is that it's still coming from a Eurocentric perspective and doesn't acknowledge, not just ideas, but the laws that Indigenous people form that hold people accountable and that place the environment as a sentient thing" (62–63), Grant introduces Scott Lyons's discussion of "rhetorical sovereignty" and provides examples of it to help readers better understand what Todd means.

Rhetorical sovereignty, according to Grant, not only recognizes the rights of nonhuman persons to engage in decision making, but it also captures the sentience and sapience of the nonhuman. However, even the words *sentience* and *sapience* do not capture the powerful and rhetorical presence of nonhuman persons in Indigenous epistemology, which includes forces such as wind and objects such as stones. As Grant so eloquently explains, in much of Indigenous teaching, teaching is "*wakan*—great, mysterious and holy" (61). That is, Indigenous epistemologies teach the opposite of "spectator consciousness" discussed earlier, the flip side of which entails orienting humans toward the onto-epistemological whereby faculties of and knowledge about engaging with nonhuman entities would be fostered. As should be obvious, doing so requires a celebration of difference as a creative force (Lorde 112) and an inability to uniformly lump nonhuman groups together as having identical properties. One plant species is not the same as another. Unlike colonial religions and epistemologies that separate the material and the mind, Indigenous epistemologies do not separate the two, and thus honor and recognize the site-specific knowledge that is required to interact with others in any given place. That is, they acknowledge each subject position as intrinsically valuable and distinct. "Intrinsically valuable" invokes a right to life and well-being that ethically commands an approach to each life as invaluable, precious, and even sacred. "Distinct" evokes a sense that life is irreplaceable and further exacts an understanding that each subject position is different and cannot immediately be understood without intimate knowledge of that position, which is learned, on the ground, from the bottom up via immersion.

Grant illustrates rhetorical sovereignty with the example of the Inuit, who recognize polar bears as nonhuman persons who understand, assess, and respond to human intent.[8] Grant writes, "This is not just between individual hunter and individual bear; but also at the political level so that if one community behaves inappropriately, the polar bear community may retaliate" (64). Clearly, then, rhetorical sovereignty not only ascribes nonhumans with an intrinsic right to live and flourish but also acknowledges the social and political dimension of the nonhuman and the ability of specific animal and plant populations to organize communally and to respond to their circumstances. Grant notes, however, that colonial scholars dismiss such thinking as ludicrous, for "such ideas have long been dismissed by Western scholars as myth" (64), and he traces the inability of people to listen to their nonhuman relations to the lack of language and concepts in colonial epistemologies (what Grant calls "terms" [64], drawing from Walter Mignolo) that would convey this kind of nonanthropocentric ecological thinking.

The following comparison of two legal cases concerning the rights of rivers illustrates the importance of underlying epistemological terms in societal transformation and how the New Zealand case won because it hinged upon "terms," particularly the notion of rhetorical sovereignty.

Rivers as Legal Persons: The Colorado River versus the Whanganui

In 2017, the environmental group Deep Green Resistance filed a suit, *Colorado River Ecosystem / Deep Green Resistance v. the State of Colorado,* asking the court to confer personhood on the Colorado River ecosystem. According to Brent Gardner-Smith of the *Aspen Times,* the plaintiffs argued that as a person, the Colorado River should have "the right to exist, flourish, regenerate and naturally evolve," contending that the river's ecosystem is quickly being depleted. Deep Green Resistance petitioned to serve as "friends of the river" because US environmental law relies upon the notion of "next friends" (Healy 328). "Next friends," as Meredith Healy explains, are crucial legal constructs "because the judicial system affords no specific legal guardianship for natural resources" (328–29). That is, humans concerned about the well-being of liv-

8. Many non-Indigenous people who work with "conscious" nonhuman animal populations (see Low), including bonobos (de Waal), elephants, and dolphins (Herzing), are similarly transformed by the nonhuman populations with whom they work. Because animals in scientific studies have frequently shown themselves to adapt to and learn about human culture and language more rapidly than the researchers do with the animal populations they study, many researchers have remarked that they see humans as less capable of cross-special learning than the nonhuman groups with whom they work (see, for example, Herzing's *Dolphin Diaries*).

ing nonhuman entities must advocate for them as "next friends" and speak for their interests. Problematically, however, as Healy makes clear, "there is no way for these third parties to represent the interests of a river absent an injury to the third party," which limits claims to "economic injuries rather than direct environmental injuries to rivers" (329). The case was dismissed for several reasons, including the fact that because so many jurisdictions draw water from the Colorado River, any overuse that might result in future injury could not be directly attributed to the state of Colorado. Despite the fact that federal law grants personhood status to corporations, and also despite *Sierra Club v. Morton,* in which Supreme Court Justice Douglas "highlighted the irony of judicial protection of fictional entities at the expense of protection for actual, natural entities" (Healy 339), the state of Colorado opined that granting personhood to "*inanimate* objects, like the soil, water, and plants that, together with animals, create an ecosystem," "are matters reserved to Congress by the Constitution" (Gardner-Smith; emphasis added). Because it seems ludicrous to confer rights to nonliving legal fictions such as corporations while denying the intrinsic right to life of the natural world—not only to exist, but to flourish and naturally evolve—the "Counsel for the plaintiff, Jason Flores-Williams analogized legal standing for natural resources to legal standing for another non-person legal entity: corporations. He reasoned that it was unjust that non-person corporate entities that depend on nature have legal standing, but nature alone does not merit legal rights" (Healy 346). Flores-Williams was later forced to withdraw the lawsuit after he was threatened with sanctions by the state of Colorado over having made "frivolous arguments." In the end, the Colorado court rejected the Colorado River complaint on the grounds that "no environmental statute or other law authorizes the ecosystem to bring a suit on its own behalf." The state of Colorado additionally articulated how potentially threatening they perceived such legislation to be, claiming that conferring personhood to ecosystems "who could be defended in court by self-declared representatives" would have "the potential to alter the fabric of American domestic and foreign policy" (Gardner-Smith). Clearly, Indigenous understandings of rhetorical sovereignty are missing from US law.

The state of Colorado made quite clear the threat that rhetorical sovereignty poses: The conferral of rights to ecosystems would forever legally alter the fabric of corporate life in the US and abroad by not only institutionalizing the idea of a commonwealth and its reliance on a diversity of subjects as sovereign subjects, but also by criminalizing self-interest at the expense of communal well-being. Indeed, in the eyes of the court, an ecosystem is as inanimate as a corporation. Sadly, such an instrumentalist approach to the natural world is common to many professions and disciplines. Potawatomi scholar Robin

Wall Kimmerer laments that even among environmentalists, one sees mechanistic views of nature that conceive of the natural world as inanimate wherein "land is a machine and humans are the drivers" (331) For example, replanting large swathes of deforested land with a single crop may prevent soil erosion, but it does not restore functional integrity to a place. Kimmerer explains that "restoring land without restoring relationship is an empty exercise" (338). An "ecosystem," she writes, "is not a machine, but a community of sovereign beings, subjects rather than objects" (331).

In contradistinction to the US judiciary, in March of 2017 New Zealand media reported that the New Zealand Crown Parliament legally conferred personhood to the Whanganui River, the third longest and the longest navigable river in New Zealand. In actuality, according to Healy, New Zealand did more than grant personhood: They "created a new legal entity, *Te Awa Tupua,*" and thereby bypassed the need to prove injury to third parties to protect the interests of the Whanganui River. Because Te Awa Tupua cannot speak for itself, the Crown "compared Whanganui's personhood to a charitable trust or incorporated society which would have have trustees legally obliged to act in the river's best interest" (Healy 334), and the Crown assigned one guardian from the Whanganui iwi (Maori) and one from the Crown to represent the river (New Zealand Parliament). The Whanganui iwi thus circumvented the need to argue that the river's rights were greater than those of industry (the riverbed had been mined for gravel for years by the state) by demonstrating that the Crown had violated the Treaty of Waitangi since its signing in 1840. The treaty promises the "Tribes of New Zealand . . . the full exclusive and undisturbed possession of their Lands and Estates Forests Fisheries and other properties which they may collectively or individually possess so long as it is their wish and desire to retain the same in their possession." However, the English version of the treaty inaccurately translates the Maori word for *sovereignty* and uses "kawanatanga" (governance) in lieu of "tino rangatiratanga" (full authority) (Healy 333). The use of "possess" and "possession" in the English version show that the ideological presumptions of 1840 have remained much the same to this day in colonial thought: Humans are agential and divisible from their surroundings, which are under their domain. However, the work of the Maori in New Zealand reflects a tremendously different orientation, one that recognizes a people inextricably and reverently connected with the place they live: the Whanganui iwi. Healy cites Pawnee scholar Walter Echo-hawk, who writes that "tribal religions cannot be considered in a vacuum, but must be understood within the context of the primal world, for tribes in their aboriginal places are embedded in their Indigenous habitats so solidly that the line between nature and the tribe is not easy to establish" (351).

In comparing these two cases, it becomes evident that legal entity-ship is a fundamentally important move that acknowledges the rhetorical sovereignty of all living beings. For one, there is no need to demonstrate injury to humans when making a legal claim. Additionally, appointing long-term guardianship of an ecosystem acknowledges Indigenous communities and their sovereign right to their ways of thought. Perhaps most importantly, however, these examples demonstrate the transformative power that lies in structural stewardship by those with the epistemic understanding and long-standing commitment needed for humanity to successfully deal with climate change.

Reconceptualizing Epistemological Ground

Many countries (and tribes) have begun to legally codify an ecological understanding of rhetorical sovereignty and the interconnectedness of life. For instance, the Ecuadorian Constitution "codified the rights of nature" in 2008 (Healy 330), and Bolivia did the same in 2009–10. Ecuador has used those rights successfully since then against corporate environmental malpractice. The four environmental articles added to the Ecuadorian Constitution recognize "Nature, or Pachamama," as having a right to "integral respect for its existence and for the maintenance and regeneration of its life cycles . . . and evolutionary processes" (Healy 331). Furthermore, "Nature has a right to be restored" where depleted and exploited. Article 73 provides the state the right to prevent any activities that "might lead to the extinction of species, the destruction of ecosystems, and the permanent alteration of natural cycles," including the right to prohibit the introduction of organic and nonorganic materials that "might definitively alter the nation's genetic assets" (Healy 331). Article 74 articulates the right of everyone to "benefit from the environment and the natural wealth enabling them to enjoy the good way of living" (Healy 331). "Everyone" includes "persons, communities, peoples, and nations" (Healy 331). While we think "everyone" refers to nonhuman beings, whether it does or does not doesn't really matter because the Ecuadorian Constitution effectively makes clear that the communal and individual health of *any* being cannot be separated from planetary health—the ability to enjoy a healthful existence derives from the health and well-being of all life. Twelve years have passed since Ecuador changed its constitution, and the Ecuadorian economy is still heavily reliant on the petrochemical industry. Despite decolonial moves such as granting bodies of water and other nonhuman relations personhood, countries such as Ecuador, Bolivia, New Zealand, and the US continue to operate economically, politically and socially according to colonial models. Or, as Medina-Lopez and Sharp-Hoskins (this volume) put it, "Demands for political, juridical, and economic recognition come in the context of the historical and ongoing violence that subtends misrecognition—that is, when the lives, bodies, experiences, and knowledges of Indigenous peoples are elided, discounted, or appropriated in service to ongoing colonization" (52). Therefore, even as attempts are made to decolonize, colonization is continually reinscribed and reified. Colonization is not static, it is not something that happened in the past and is over and done with it—it is, as Medina-Lopez and Sharp-Hoskins argue, an ongoing project. For instance, while Bolivia made radical constitutional and legislative changes that grant Mother Earth (Pachamama), as a living deity, eleven rights, including the right "to not be affected by mega-infrastructure and development projects that affect the balance of ecosystems and the local inhabitant communities" (Vidal), it is uncertain if those rights will stand. Since the writing of the first draft of this chapter, Evo Morales, the Indigenous and Indigenous-backed Bolivian president whose administration, the Movement Towards Socialism, helped realize and codify Pachamama's rights into law, was overthrown. Furthermore, according to Elise Swain of *The Intercept,* the "anti-colonial and anti-imperialist movements" that brought Morales to power had already been "co-opted by the state."

We thus submit to readers that given humanity's reliance on the rest of life on this planet, the task of contending with climate change requires an immense cultural revolution, one that could be surprisingly joyful to participate in and bring about, one that could bring "a good way of living" or "*buen vivir*" for everyone (Ecuadorian Constitution). The notion of *buen vivir* (see also Lestón, this volume) is significant because it suggests not just living well, but living correctly—or specifically, "in *buen vivir* humans are only stewards of the earth and its resources and individual rights subjugated to that of communities and nature" (Balch). Scholar Eduardo Gudynas states that the concept of *buen vivir* is not equivalent to the "western notion" of well-being or welfare: "With *buen vivir,* the subject of wellbeing is not [about the] individual, but the individual in the social context of their community and in a unique environmental situation" (Gudynas, qtd. in Balch).

However, despite the fact that *buen vivir* is flagged as Indigenous epistemology with no Euro-American equivalent, there are—in some colonized communities—efforts being made to change the script. As Watts writes, "historical Indigenous events . . . are increasingly becoming not only accepted by Western frameworks of understanding, but sought after in terms of non-oppressive and provocative or interesting interfaces of accessing the real. This traces Indigenous peoples not only as epistemologically distinct but also as a gateway for non-Indigenous thinkers to re-imagine their world" (26). Differences between Indigenous and colonial imaginaries convincingly demonstrate that contemporary instituted imaginaries have gotten it all wrong and are, in essence, problematic in their binarizing: from male to female, from atomistic to ecological, from universal and abstracted to situated and material, respectively. Binaries tend to favor one entity at the expense of another. What if we did away with binaries altogether and focused on a way of living that privileges ecological thinking and that encourages both sovereignty and site-specific literacy?

However, if decolonization did happen on a broad scale across multiple communities, it would still be necessary to look beyond those individual communities and to think on a global scale. On a planet in which all life is interconnected, widespread ecological revitalization cannot be successful when it occurs in isolated communal pockets. The notion that conferring personhood on ecosystems would result in "the potential to alter the fabric of American domestic and foreign policy" (Gardner-Smith) is no exaggeration—it recognizes that Americans (and indeed other colonial cultures) would need to undergo a profound shift in how humans relate to the nonhuman. An entirely different kind of sociopolitical leadership would be necessary, one including collaboration with Indigenous communities. As such, there has always been, and continues to be, a strong need for attention to Indigenous and other noncolonial systems of thought—and for leadership from Indigenous communities. As Megan Schoen writes, "scholars of non-Western rhetorics discuss the necessity of using terms and conceptual systems that are endemic to the cultures being studied rather than simply importing existing Western concepts and applying them. Without a situated, grounded framework, the work of cultural rhetorics becomes problematic" (19). This framework, then, must be one that recognizes the importance of the land in the absence of territorialism, and that also privileges noncolonial epistemologies.

Survivance, Resurgence, and Internationalism

In *As We Have Always Done,* Leanne Betasamosake Simpson (Michi Saagiig Nishinaabeg) beautifully and compellingly describes Nishinaabeg communities and the knowledge systems that structure them. All of the systems, educational, economic, and political, she writes, "were designed to generate life—not just human life but the life of all living things" (3). To achieve such a system in which "stable governing structures emerged when necessary and dissolved when no longer needed" (Simpson 3), Simpson makes clear that *all* governance structures, from family to government, fostered self-determination and self-actualization:

> There was a high degree of individual self-determination in Michi Saagiig Nishnaabeg[9] society. Children were full citizens with the same rights and responsibilities as adults. They were raised in a nest of freedom and self-determination. Authoritarian power—aggressive power that comes from coercion and hierarchy—wasn't a part of the fabric of Michi Saagiig Nishnaabeg philosophy or governance, and so it wasn't a part of our families. People were expected to figure out their gifts and their responsibilities through ceremony and reflection and self-actualization, and that process was really the most important governing process on an individual level—more important than the gender you were born into. In the context of gender fluidity and sexualities and relationship orientations outside of colonial conceptualizations . . . this idea of freedom . . . permeated the fabric of precolonial Nishnaabeg society. (3–4)

It may be difficult for many readers to imagine organized societies in which coercion and hierarchical thinking do not exist, but it is important to point out that relationality, one's relationship with self and with others, provides the very foundation of decolonial systems. In other words, "freedom" is not a synonym for "liberty" (i.e., liberty *from* thinking about others) but is in fact the opposite, an ethical obligation to think about one's relationship to every other sovereign being.

To that end—that of developing both cultural and individual ethical ecological orientations that recognize the intrinsic value and sacrosanctity of each life—as a botanist and Indigenous scholar, Kimmerer speaks about foundational Indigenous principles shared across tribes in *Braiding Sweetgrass*. For instance, Kimmerer describes the principles of the Honorable Harvest, the collective "Indigenous canon of principles and practices that govern the exchange of life for life" (180) because of "the need to resolve the inescapable tension between honoring life around us and taking it in order to live [as] part of being human" (177). Kimmerer depicts the Honorable Harvest as "rules of sorts that govern our taking, shape our relationship with the natural world, and rein in our tendency to consume—that the world might be as rich for the seventh generation as it is for our own" (180). Said rules include "knowing the ways of the ones who take care of you," "ask[ing] permission before taking,"

9. Nishnaabeg is a variant of Anishinaabeg.

"abid[ing] by the answer," "never tak[ing] the first" (or last), "taking only what you need," "never tak[ing] more than half," "never wast[ing] what you have taken," "giv[ing] thanks," and "reciprocat[ing]" (183). As reading Kimmerer's work drives home, a culture based upon honoring life necessitates a noncolonial orientation to consumption because "killing a *who* demands something different than killing an *it*" (183).

Many Indigenous cultures thus based their cultures on generosity and reciprocity. Kimmerer calls such cultures gift (rather than commodity) cultures. She explains that Indigenous cultures would never use fossil fuels, for "the earth gives away for free the power of wind and sun and water," and she laments, "Had we taken only that which is given to us, had we reciprocated the gift, we would not have to fear our own atmosphere today" (383). When speaking about the ideological differences between gift economies and wage economies (i.e., commodity or property), Kimmerer explains that "a gift creates ongoing relationships" and "establishes a feeling-bond between two people" (26). In contrast, however, "from the viewpoint of a private property economy, the 'gift' is deemed to be 'free' because we obtain it free of charge, at no cost" (28). Gift economies, however, operate in reverse, wherein "gifts are not free" but instead "create a set of relationships" (28) and thus, responsibilities. Kimmerer adds, "The currency of a gift economy is, at its root, reciprocity" (28). She writes, "In Western thinking, private land is understood to be a 'bundle of rights,' whereas in a gift economy property has a 'bundle of responsibilities' attached" (28). What does such a bundle of responsibilities look and feel like? In a commodity exchange, responsibilities are at best transactional and at worst, bankrupting. Moreover, in commodity exchanges where prices are low, there's a propensity for overbuying, whereas in a gift exchange, one doesn't want to overtake.

In short, we'd argue that the cultural transformation needed for a sustainable future requires an epistemological shift from inanimacy to animacy. That shift can be seen in a comparative analysis of Indigenous and non-Indigenous languages. For instance, Anishinaabe languages render the world alive, not dead, according to Kimmerer, "full of unseen energies that animate everything" (49). Interestingly, words in Potawatomi are not inflected by gender. Rather, Potawatomi words are marked by animation, by the force of life, which provides a clear sign of cultural salience. Seventy percent of words in Potawatomi are verbs. Kimmerer notes that every part of speech "provide[s] different ways to speak of the living world and the lifeless one" and that morphemes, from assigning plurals to using verbs, depend upon whether what is spoken of is alive (53). The idea that everything in the natural world is alive could be a revolutionary act—yet it would also simply be a return to something very familiar, encoded in our genetic memory. For instance, Kimmerer describes how toddlers naturally assign personhood "to plants and animals as if they were people, extending to them self and intention and compassion—until we teach them not to. We quickly retrain them and make them forget" (57). Other evidence also supports the idea that humans need to be intimately connected with their nonhuman relations. For instance, working outside in the earth produces oxytocin in human brains, the same chemical produced by intimate sexual pleasure.

Although it may be difficult for adults to fully reorient themselves to decolonial knowledge systems, there is much to encourage humans with respect to making such profound and radical changes in their social organizations. For one, there is a pressing need to do so. Humanity is facing a sixth mass extinction, and while Indigenous sovereignty is profoundly important, pockets of sustainable communities will not save the world. Second, there is the ontological, the willingness of the nonhuman to interact with the human—and humanity's biological disposition to do the same. While social construction has certainly demonstrated that humans can implement toxic ideas, why not choose constructions that work in tandem with our biological dispositions and that foster ideal cohabitation? Third, predecessor epistemologies exist that contain the terms (the language, stories, and concepts) that humanity needs. Kimmerer encourages her readers to recognize that humanity can choose. She writes that "in many Indigenous ways of knowing, time is not a river, but a lake in which the past, the present, and the future exist. Creation, then, is an ongoing process and the story is not history alone—it is also prophecy" (342). According to Kimmerer, time may be a lake, rather than a river, but both are nonhuman relations that need to be recognized on their own terms. In this analogy, if a lake symbolizes synchronic time and a river symbolizes diachronic time, it is clear that with the depletion of riparian ecosystems, we are quickly running out of time. Although we see across the globe a change in consciousness with respect to climate change, and while we understand that historically, social movements progress gradually over time, we are reminded that time is running out—or has run out—depending upon the population of "everyones" being asked.

Yet Kimmerer also makes it clear that even as "Indigenous stories are rich in wisdom," she does not "advocate their wholesale appropriation" (344). She advises instead that "as the world changes, an immigrant culture must write its own new stories, stories of relationship to place," that contain their own spirit but that are "tempered by the wisdom of those who were old on this land long before we came" (344). We hope that readers will recognize that adapting to onto-epistemological dispositioning will play out differently according to place and culture, as Black feminist abolitionists, such as Davis and Kaba, have demonstrated.

That is, we suggest that stories can be used as Kimmerer contends: as "user manuals" (343). Imagine if the colonial world adapted to the concept of *buen vivir* as it faces climate change. The concept of rhetorical sovereignty in itself provides just such a transformative function, even for those who already consider themselves to be "nature lovers." As Kimmerer notes, "Knowing that you love the earth changes you, activates you to defend and protect and celebrate. But when you feel that the earth loves you in return, that feeling transforms the relationship from a one-way street into a sacred bond" (125).

Works Cited

Balch, Oliver. "Buen Vivir: The Social Philosophy Inspiring Movements in South America." *The Guardian*, 4 Feb. 2013, https://www.theguardian.com/sustainable-business/blog/buen-vivir-philosophy-south-america-eduardo-gudynas.

Bar On, Bat-Ami. "Marginality and Epistemic Privilege." *Feminist Epistemologies*, edited by Linda Alcoff and Elizabeth Potter, Routledge, 1993, pp. 83–100.

Barad, Karen. "Posthumanist Performativity: Toward an Understanding of How Matter Comes to Matter." *Signs*, vol. 28, no. 3, Spring 2003, pp. 801–31.

Butler, Judith. *Bodies That Matter: On the Discursive Limits of "Sex."* Routledge, 1993.

Code, Lorraine. *Ecological Thinking: The Politics of Epistemic Location*. Oxford UP, 2006.

Davis, Angela Y. *Freedom Is a Constant Struggle: Ferguson, Palestine, and the Foundations of a Movement*. Haymarket Press, 2016.

de Waal, Frans. *The Bonobo and the Atheist: In Search of Humanism among the Primates*. W. W. Norton & Co., 2013.

Gardner-Smith, Brent. "Colorado AG Moves to Dismiss Request Seeking 'Person' Status for Colorado River." *Aspen Times*, 20 Oct. 2017, https://www.aspentimes.com/news/colorado-ag-moves-to-dismiss-request-seeking-person-status-for-colorado-river/.

Grant, David M. "Writing *Wakan*: The Lakota Pipe as Rhetorical Object." *College Composition and Communication*, vol. 69, no. 1, Sept. 2017, pp. 61–86.

Harding, Sandra. "Feminist Standpoints." *Handbook of Feminist Research: Theory and Praxis*, edited by Sharlene Nagy Hesee-Biber, Sage, 2007, pp. 45–70.

Hawkesworth, Mary E. *Globalization & Feminist Activism*. Rowman & Littlefield, 2006.

Healy, Meredith N. "Fluid Standing: Incorporating the Indigenous Rights of Nature Concept into Collaborative Management of the Colorado River Ecosystem." *Colorado Natural Resources, Energy & Environmental Law Review*, vol. 30, no. 2, 2011, pp. 327–60.

Herzing, Denise L. *Dolphin Diaries: My 25 Years with Spotted Dolphins in the Bahamas*. St. Martin's Griffin, 2011.

Kaba, Mariame. *We Do This 'Til We Free Us: Abolitionist Organizing and Transforming Justice*. Haymarket Books, 2021.

Kimmerer, Robin Wall. *Braiding Sweetgrass: Indigenous Wisdom, Scientific Knowledge, and the Teachings of Plants*. Milkweed Editions, 2013.

King, Tiffany Lethabo. *The Black Shoals: Offshore Formations of Black and Native Studies*. Duke UP, 2019.

Lorde, Audre. "The Master's Tools Will Never Dismantle the Master's House." *Sister Outsider: Essays and Speeches*. Crossing Press, 2007, pp. 110–14. https://collectiveliberation.org/wpcontent/uploads/2013/01/Lorde_The_Masters_Tools.pdf.

Low, Philip. "The Cambridge Declaration of Consciousness." Edited by Jaak Panksepp et al. Francis Crick Memorial Conference on Consciousness in Human and Non-Human Animals, 7 July 2012, Churchill College, University of Cambridge. https://fcmconference.org/img/CambridgeDeclarationOnConsciousness.pdf.

New Zealand Parliament. "Innovative Bill Protects Whanganui River with Legal Personhood." 28 Mar. 2017, https://www.parliament.nz/en/get-involved/features/innovative-bill-protects-whanganui-river-with-legal-personhood/.

Offen, Karen M. "Feminism and Feminist Scholarship Today." *Journal of Feminist Scholarship*, vol. 1, 2018, pp. 14–15. https://digitalcommons.uri.edu/jfs/vol1/iss1/11.

Royster, Jacqueline Jones. "When the First Voice You Hear Is Not Your Own." *College Composition and Communication*, vol. 47, no. 1, 1996, pp. 29–40.

Schoen, Megan. "Toward a Rhetoric of Kagiso: Rhetoric and Democracy in Botswana." *Constellations: A Cultural Rhetorics Publishing Space*, vol. 1, 15 Nov. 2018, pp. 1–28. http://constell8cr.com/issue-1/toward-a-rhetoric-of-kagiso-rhetoric-and-democracy-in-botswana/.

Simpson, Leanne Betasamosake. *As We Have Always Done: Indigenous Freedom through Radical Resistance*. U of Minnesota P, 2017.

Swain, Elise. "The Coup That Ousted Bolivia's Evo Morales Is Another Setback for Latin American Socialism." *The Intercept*, 15 Nov. 2019, https://theintercept.com/2019/11/15/bolivia-evo-morales-coup-brazil-intercepted/.

Vidal, John. "Bolivia Enshrines Natural World's Rights with Equal Status for Mother Earth." *The Guardian*, 10 Apr. 2011, https://www.theguardian.com/environment/2011/apr/10/bolivia-enshrines-natural-worlds-rights.

Watts, Vanessa. "Indigenous Place-Thought & Agency amongst Humans and Non-Humans (First Woman and Sky Woman Go on a European World Tour!)." *Decolonization: Indigeneity, Education & Society*, vol. 2, no. 1, 2013, pp. 20–34.

Yazzie, Melanie. "Decolonization or Extinction: Indigenous Red Deal Lays Out Plan to Save Earth." Interview by Amy Goodman. *DemocracyNow!*, 22 Apr. 2021, https://www.democracynow.org/2021/4/22/the_red_deal_book.

CHAPTER 8

Becoming Relations

Braiding an Indigenous Manifesto

ANDREA RILEY MUKAVETZ AND MALEA POWELL

ANDREA: *We come to you with a good heart.*
MALEA: *This is a story.*

Dear readers, these stories braid a living vision of an Indigenous relational framework in order to build common ground upon which Indigenous and settler scholars can stand together to imagine more equitable approaches to our collective work. We enact an Indigenous intellectual approach to our story to show the rich, complex, and ancient qualities of these epistemologies and ontologies *as well as* the common sense of connection, community, and relationality that have made them the primary theoretical forces present across Turtle Island for millennia. While we won't shy away from some brief critiques and engagements with Euro-American[1] object-focused[2] rhetorics, our main

1. We use the word *Euro-American* throughout to designate practices that are rooted both in traditional Western and European colonizing traditions.

2. For the sake of space and efficiency, we will refer to a cluster of practices that include object-oriented ontology (OOO), object-oriented rhetoric (OOR), new materialism, and posthumanism as object-focused throughout this story. Yes, we understand they are different and there are nuances to how specific scholars are engaged with these primarily Euro-American theoretical movements; however, our critique of them is centered in what they share, not in their particular difference.

goal will be to offer stories that demonstrate[3] interventions into the colonizing force of those ontologies. We offer these stories as an invitation to engage with us and become relations to our Indigenous intellectual practices.

As you enter our story space, we'd like to situate ourselves so you can see us. We are—Andrea and Malea—sitting at Malea's kitchen table in her 1901 Queen Anne home. This is something we've done a hundred times. The local newspaper is spread around, covered with the sweetgrass[4] we've harvested from the bed in Malea's backyard. We are each drinking coffee and there are snacks arranged on small fiestaware plates. Bishi, Malea's gray tiger cat, is getting into trouble. The sun streams through the dining room window—through a large aloe plant, making spiky shadows on the old oak table, a survivance from Malea's great-aunt Bonnie.[5] We're sitting here and visiting and braiding sweetgrass. Andrea is overly focused and task-oriented on getting it just so and panics when her braid doesn't come out even. Traditionally, each strand of a braid of sweetgrass is made up of seven individual leaves of grass, but not all leaves are the same size and thickness, so sometimes the braid isn't even. Malea is telling her to listen to sweetgrass and to the grandmother who is trying to speak to her as she braids. Can you see us? We can see you.

This story space of braiding sweetgrass isn't just a metaphorical orientation for us, though it may be useful for non-native readers to use it that way to engage and navigate our stories. Instead, this scene is anchored in Robin Wall Kimmerer's reminder that, in Indigenous traditions, humans are

> often referred to as "the younger brothers of Creation." We say that humans have the least experience with how to live and thus the most to learn—we must look to our teachings among the other species for guidance. Their wisdom is apparent in the way that they live. They teach us by example. They've been on the earth far longer than we have been, and have had time to figure things out. (9)

---

3. Pay attention to the word *demonstrate* throughout, please. Indigenous pedagogies are demonstrative in that they *show* teachings instead of tell about them. So, there is no list here of how you can enter into relation with us, there are only practices, demonstrations of our relationality with others, with one another, and with you. We hope you are willing to take these teachings in the loving way they are being offered.

4. The scientific name for sweetgrass is *hierochloe odorata*, fragrant holy grass.

5. In the OED sense of the word, *survivance* is an inheritance; in the well-known Vizenorian sense, it refers to the survival, resistance, and ancestral inheritance of contemporary Indigenous peoples. Our use here invokes both senses of the word since Great-Aunt Boni was an Indigenous woman who ran a "comfort house" in Huntington, Indiana, during the middle part of the twentieth century—the table came from that house.

So we have turned to sweetgrass for guidance. Sweetgrass "was the very first [plant] to grow on earth, its fragrance a sweet memory of Skywoman's[6] hand," and is "one of the four sacred plants" for Great Lakes people (Kimmerer 5). Our teachings tell us that breathing in the fragrance of sweetgrass will help you start "to remember things you didn't know you'd forgotten (5), and smudging with it will bring peace to you and to those you hold in your prayers. Sweetgrass is a rhizome, and is best planted by "putting roots directly in the ground," thus it is "passed from hand to earth to hand across years and generations" (1). Sweetgrass requires a community of relations. It is "both medicine and a relative" (5). Most importantly for our purposes today, sweetgrass invokes two things. First, an embodied collaborative practice—while one person *can* braid sweetgrass, it's a task done best with two people (one to hold the tied bundle of grass to maintain proper tension, the other to do the braiding, trading tasks back and forth while their skin absorbs the fragrance of "grandmother's hair"). Second, its own life practices—sweetgrass "thrives along disturbed edges," places and spaces where water meets land, or where fields meet forest (1).

Let's go back to Malea's for a bit. There's an untidy pile of newspapers on the floor. Michael (Malea's partner) sorted through in that grumbling "the world is awful" kind of way before he cleared our plates, started another pot of coffee for us, and headed outside to work in the yard (once the sweetgrass is picked, the bed needs to be cleared and prepared for winter). The table is covered by layers of newspapers protecting the table from the damp and dirt (and bugs) of the piles of sweetgrass. The newspapers are, for us here, a physical manifestation of Western alphabetic literacy. They remind us of how Indigenous scholars have always had to accommodate ourselves and our knowledges to the same cultural structures used to oppress and diminish our ancestors' way of life. We think about our connections to that long chain of ancestors and how the seeming necessity of those accommodations continues even in the context of the story, and the braid, we are weaving right here and now. The context for this collection—Western-centric object-focused scholarship—is an uneasy space for us. On the one hand, we have many things to say about canonical object-focused scholarship, and have done so in other venues, easily falling into the acceptable patterns of critique and proving ourselves worthy to critique that Euro-Western academia demands we demonstrate. On

6. For a relevant telling of the Skywoman story, see Kimmerer's "Skywoman Falling" chapter in *Braiding Sweetgrass,* where she reminds of how this creation story "is a constant star in the constellation of teachings we call Original Instructions, . . . [which] provide an orientation but not a map. The work of living is creating that map for yourself" alongside your relations (7).

the other hand, we'd much rather braid this pile of sweetgrass. So, for once, as Indigenous scholars who are always pressed to accommodate ourselves to the academy, we are going to ignore that pressure and begin the work of braiding, together.

Together: Gathering for the First Strand of the Braid

As Anishinaabe and Miami women who live in Michigan, we were mindful to gather this first strand by being deliberate about who we cite and acknowledge. These scholars are our (intellectual) relations, many of whom are not in rhetoric studies. We did so to show you how Indigenous theory takes place in other spaces, beyond traditional modes of academic writing, and beyond academia in general. We return to these teachings, these stories, to create a path for our scholarly practices. This section is not intended to be inclusive or exclusive but is a reflection and demonstration of our orientation. There is so much more out there for us to learn. As we've been taught, knowledge comes to us when we are ready. It is not to be discovered or claimed as mere convenience for our use.

We are drawn to Indigenous thinking that is attentive to how knowledge (and the production of it) is constellated, relational, and nonhierarchical. These discussions occur in sites like Indigenous research methodologies and paradigms (see Wilson; Smith; Absolon), land-based practices (see Kimmerer; Brooks; Simpson; Erdrich), and practices outside and beyond academia. Both of us have written extensively on relationality, knowledge production, and Indigenous research paradigms (see Riley Mukavetz, "Towards"; Powell; Davis; Powell et al.). We believe that Malea's contributions on offering a Native rhetorics orientation to knowledge-making is a significant starting point in this discussion. In an interview with Andréa Davis, Malea describes her own work and Indigenous rhetorics as engaging in a triad of body, space/place, and culture (Davis). Through the triad, we are able to trace a particular orientation to materials and traditions in which Indigenous knowledge is circulated and constellated. What this triad allows us to know and share with you all is through Indigenous worldviews: Objects are not objects at all. They are relatives and ancestors who already have names and practices and relationships.

We began explaining that we are making a sweetgrass braid and inviting you to watch us work together in the making. We want to return to *Braiding Sweetgrass* and the sweetgrass teaching to further explain an Indigenous relational framework useful for ontological and cosmological theories. Kimmerer explains that to braid sweetgrass is an act of reciprocity.

> Will you hold the end of the bundle while I braid? Hands joined by grass, can we bend our heads together and make a braid to honor the earth? And then, I'll hold it for you, while you braid it too? I could hand you a braid of sweetgrass, as thick and shining as the plait that hung down my grandmother's back. But it is not mine to give, nor yours to take. *Wiingashk* belongs to herself. (x)

Reciprocity begins with a request for help and collaboration on an agreed-upon task. Working together, the braiders and the material create something together. No one owns the product or the materials. They exist to make knowledge and we exist to listen to and learn from those knowledges. As we said before, it is possible to braid by oneself—either holding the ends with your teeth or tying the tail to a chair. Yet, as Kimmerer explains, "the sweetest way is to have someone else hold the end so that you pull gently against each other, all the while leaning in, head to head, chatting and laughing . . ." (ix). Here, a subtle critique lives within this teaching of reciprocity. We can work on our own or with an inanimate object like a chair, but the knowledge that is made is not relational or accountable to anyone but ourselves. What can we learn from a chair? It tells a story, but it is still a story where human agents are at the center because the knowledge is produced by and for people. We could use the practice of sweetgrass harvesting and braiding to tell a series of stories about two Indigenous women in academia collaborating and mentoring each other through and beyond academia to form right relations. We love a good story. But that story could be read or understood as a metaphor for:

- A symbol for navigating multiple spaces and worldviews—that is what NDNs[7] have always had to endure
- An artifact that links coauthors to a particular source material
- An object, still at Andrea's desk, that she looks at when she needs to reflect on her role as Anishinaabekwe in academia.

Additionally, that kind of story centers us—as humans—and that the benefit of the sweetgrass braid is for our benefit and need.

Through an Indigenous perspective, the sweetness of braiding sweetgrass is a teaching to understand that the plant produces knowledge whether or not humans notice it. As Kimmerer and many others remind us, again and again, the plants are talking whether we choose to listen. We don't always know

7. NDN is a common endonym of self-reference for many indigenous North Americans. Because it is self-referential, its relational aspect must not be abused or appropriated by others.

what they are saying, and we shouldn't expect that knowledge. Knowledge is a gift—the sharing of knowledge is a complicated and relational process. If we seek to listen to plants, then we need to develop a reciprocal relationship that shifts one's orientation to learn to listen. And yet, this is something Indigenous people have believed and practiced since time immemorial. Colonialism and imperialism destroyed, deterred, remade these practices.[8] The academic industrial complex, whether it's the humanities or the sciences, contributed to that and profit off of it. As Andrea once said, it's like when someone shares a new NPR article on Facebook where white scientists realized that trees can speak or have a heartbeat and all the NDNs are like "DUH." It is through tending to the land that we receive and store our knowledges.

In *Kaandossiwin: How We Come to Know*, Kathleen Absolon offers an Anishinaabekwe orientation to Indigenous research. There are many commonalities within Absolon's paradigm and the work of Shawn Wilson, author of *Research Is Ceremony*: It's rooted in the land and community relations and is committed to axiology, cosmology, epistemology, and methodology as interconnected and relational. As Absolon observes:

> Thus, in my search for principles of Indigenous Methodologies, I begin with my own knowledge of searching in the bush. I was taught to *attune* to the land and what the animals were doing. *Announcing my intentions* to the land or warning the creatures of my presence was a central philosophy that *respected* the animals and our *relationship* to Creation. (26)

Through this particular land-based approach, Absolon has always been a part of the natural world and cosmologies. Through the teachings received from her relations (humans, nonhumans, and the ecosystem), she has developed a relational approach to knowledge. We are particularly drawn to the practice of "announcing one's intentions" as an already in-operation technique to research. It is rooted in the land and the cosmologies. It addresses power,

8. There is a wealth of anti-colonial, postcolonial, decolonial, and critical race literature that grapples with the impacts of colonialism and imperialism, whether it's addressing how coloniality of power impacts one's relationship with space and time (see Mignolo) or seeking to understand how anti-colonial ideologies are deeply embedded in colonized communities (see, for example, Sefa Dei; Thiong'o; Césaire; and so many others). What's important to take away from these discussions and our own thinking about the relationship between colonialism and imperialism on knowledge-making practices is that we are all impacted by and complicit in the colonial project. That, for us, to talk freely and openly about our relationship with plants can be touching. And also, it is reflective of our ongoing work to enact our Indigenous belief systems in a paracolonial space.

human impact, respect, and care. For Absolon, her knowledge begins, is contextualized by, and is for the ongoing relationship she has with the land.

Malea: Gathering for the Second Strand of the Braid

This is a making story.

I am sitting at a table during the National Center for Great Lakes Native American Cultures spring education workshops with a small group of learners. On the table in front of us there are bins full of quills dyed many different colors, spools of Nymo thread, small bowls of water, scissors, small beading needles, and a large brain-tanned hide. We are in a two-day workshop to learn how to sew quills, taught by Bonita Bent, a well-known member of the northern Indiana Native community and a master quillworker. Everyone is anxious to choose a pattern and begin sewing quills. But Boni has other plans. She begins telling us stories about porcupines—how porky got her quills, their place in their set of animal relations, how to respect and honor them before gathering their quills, how to properly gather quills from a dead animal, and how dangerous quills can be if you don't handle them properly. She goes on to talk about cleaning and processing the quills—bleaching them, dyeing them, clipping them, storing them. At this point, some people start to get restless. They will never harvest quills from a dead porcupine, nor process them, nor dye them—they just want to learn how to sew quills and, if they're good at it, they'll just buy them online. One of the students says, "When can we learn to sew quills?" Boni pauses and looks at me meaningfully. I've been a learner at the table of many Native makers in my life, and I've been the teacher at many tables as well. One of the many values that Boni and I share is that you never share our traditional ways of making without also offering the teachings—the stories that form our web of relations, our histories and responsibilities. I say, "You're learning it right now." Boni says, "That's right." And she moves on to the history of quillwork in the Americas, how one becomes a quillworker (as opposed to just someone who knows how to sew quills), and then outlines what we'll be doing for the rest of the day.

My own turn toward "thing theory," material culture, and the neo-Marxist materialist work at the turn of the twentieth century was prompted by my experiences in Native women's circles of making. Having spent a great deal of time looking for ways to talk about what I saw happening around making and things, I was disappointed to find ways I *did not* want to represent Native making in my interactions with that work. I was ecstatic when I stumbled over the *Writing without Words: Alternative Literacies in Mesoamerican and the Andes* collection. What I found there was a set of scholars who were also struggling for language to talk about making and things in Indigenous/decolonial communities. And though both Boone and Mignolo seem to struggle with ways to talk about nonalphabetic "writing" in that collection, their struggle helped me think deeply about *why* we all seemed to be having so much trouble. To make a long story short, they were trying to textualize nonalphabetic meaning production in order to understand it *as writing*. What I've come to understand, though,

> is that textualizing "things" makes them institutionally recognizable and useful to "us" academics but this process of transformation frequently allows us to miss the point of how these things are used, how they mean, elsewhere. I am interested in that elsewhere—*in the systemic order and ritual practices of our everyday lives. In the rhetoricity of things*, you might say. Further, to say that a thing is not a text does not mean it doesn't "mean," that it can't be "discerned," that it doesn't "signify." There is a space *between* textualization and discernability/signification, a place where story and thingness meet. We don't have to turn this wampum strand into a text in order for it to have meaning—its presence invokes meaning, *it's part of an entire structure of meaning.* (Powell; emphasis added)

And that structure is decidedly not one currently operating in Euro-Western academic culture.

My desire to make Native making "discernable" inside Euro-Western theoretical scholars was, in fact, consistently making it "other" as a rhetorical practice. And I realized that I'd been making this mistake for a long time. Since the very beginnings of my career as a scholar, I'd been trying to explain Indigenous rhetorical practices to the Euro-Western academy in terms it could understand (a practice I'd observed in nineteenth-century Native intellectuals as a survivance tactic). This got Native people included in the story that rhet/comp as a discipline tells itself, but only as a marginal, alternative, other set of practices set off to the side of colonial and settler practices (aka the "real" ones). My complicity with upholding settler colonial knowledge systems made me both angry and curious. What would happen, I thought, if I just quit explaining and instead started centering Indigenous knowledges—theories, epistemologies, ontologies, methodologies—and quit paying homage to those of the Euro-Western academy? What if I quit the struggle to find appropriate language, theory, and methodology to talk about the Indigenous rhetoricity of things within the traditions of Euro-American scholarship? And that's when I went back and relistened to those Indigenous aunties, those makers, and built an Indigenous scholarly orientation from the practices and teachings of the makers I was engaged with. To look back on it, it seems like a giant "duh," but in the moments of extricating myself from the boundaries set for me by traditional, colonizing academic pressures and practices, I really couldn't see that the simplest way to find a theory was to use the ones already in existence for millennia on Turtle Island. I'd been taught, you see, that Native people don't make theory, don't have theory, and that I needed to borrow theory from white people in order to show that Native people were "really" intellectuals. It took me twenty years of consistently trying to unbelieve this lie to finally get there. So, what does an Indigenous scholarly orientation that centers Indigenous practices as the foundations of our own intellectual and rhetorical traditions look like?

In *Research Is Ceremony: Indigenous Research Methods,* Shawn Wilson offers some principles for understanding such a practice, and those principles require some major conceptual shifts for those who've been inculcated into Western colonial scholarly practices. First, we have to learn to understand that knowledge = relationships (Wilson 55–56), and that these relationships structure our reality. The goal of an Indigenous scholarly practice, then, is not scholarly fame, nor is it to add Natives to the traditional Western canon; it is, instead, to do things in a good way with a good heart, to be accountable to *all* of our relations.

ANDREA: This reminds me of Indigenous intellectuals like Christi Belcourt and Isaac Murdoch and Erin Konsom. They are highly respected artists who have devoted their everyday lives to using bush knowledge for knowledge production that promotes sovereignty, self-determination, and cultural continuance. In 2014, the Onaman Collective was created and sustained by these three artists. As they say on their website:

> We are Indigenous artists and environmentalists who love the land and believe in the spirits of the land. We believe in the resilience and beauty of our people. We believe in our Elders and our young people. With everything we do, the underlying theme is always respect for the land and reclamation of the ways of our ancestors.

They are funded through donations, self-designed auctions, and Indigenous grassroots movements instead of government and corporate funding. We share this because it reflects how they understand sovereignty and self-determination. The site for this knowledge-making is the camp Nimkii Aazhibikong, "an Ojibway language revitalization camp for youth that is working towards producing the next generation of fluent speakers on the land. Guided by elders, it is also a camp for cultural resurgence of sustainable Indigenous practices and restoration of traditional Indigenous land and resource protection and management." What the Onaman Collective makes visible is that knowledge production is always for present and future generations. It is intentional to call Nimkii Aazhibikong a camp as it is an effort to replicate how our ancestors lived with each other and on the land before settler colonialism. We dwell with the purposes and teachings of the Onaman Collective because we, as Indigenous rhetoricians—as Indigenous women in academia—look to our communities and their knowledge-making practices to guide us as we create our theoretical and methodological frameworks. We've always understood our communities outside of academia as the source of why, how, and what we research.

MALEA: Yes! Our communities are a central source of knowledge and they sustain us as we make our way in academia. One of the very best things about the many years I've been immersed in the project with this community of Native makers is that I'm frequently engaged in the practice of making alongside them. We sit together and talk. Stories come out of the beads and the quills and the rivercane, and they want to be told, so we tell them. But I want to make one thing clear: It isn't that we tell stories *about* a beadwork making. Or that a quillwork making *tells* a story. It's that the basket itself—the thing itself—is *made* of story. It *is* story. It is the story of who we are in relation to one another, instructions about our responsibilities to each other, and to the land. These "makings" create for their practitioners—and for their users—a series of habitable stories that connect the land to the body to the people across artificial temporal distinctions like "past," "present," "future." These connections reveal a rhetorical relationship in which a material discourse spins out from the bodies of makers who are situated at the intersection of the spiritual and the everyday in the overlap between ancient originary events to the present moment in which they live. Lee Maracle puts it another way: "There is a story in every line of theory. The difference between us and European scholars is that we admit this, and present theory through story" (7). *In every line of theory, there's a story.* The beadwork or quillwork making becomes an intersection of history and creation, a constellation of epistemology and existence. The making, and its maker, both carry culture. Culture is, after all, a storied practice. And the practice of culture is rhetorical. Further, each making is a map—connected to a specific landbase, a specific history, a specific set of relations among humans, animals, plants, the elements, the ancestors. And each map is a point of contact in a constellative set of relations that is almost always shifting and changing.

This immersive, embodied, Indigenous-centered set of knowledges has taken me, in truth, a lifetime to learn. And when I spoke about the aliveness of things/objects to many of my Euro-American colleagues, they often expressed skepticism: "You really think that trees can think? that they communicate with one another?" followed by eye rolls or shrugs or laughs of disbelief. Imagine, then, my surprise when, suddenly, a whole slew of rhetoric scholars began to pay attention to things and began using words like *maker space,* and began to propose ontological rhetorical investigations (spurred on, no doubt, by post-classical theorists' critique of the modern and the absolute fascination with the agency of locks). Even more, imagine how utterly surprised I was to go to their papers at conferences and hear them talk about these "object-oriented" ideas as "posthuman" when I know objects and their stories and their makings and their relationships to the land, to animals, to one another, and to humans to be integrally connected in a vitally substantial way. And, yes, I understand the use of the word *posthuman* as indicating a desire to decenter a certain modernist definition and orientation of humans in the world, but it seems completely unnecessary to invent such a term when Indigenous cultures all over the world already have a way of talking about the relationality of all things . . . but I digress.

One of the memories I still hold in my body is of slipping into a seat at a national conference to hear a paper given by a brilliant mid-career Indigenous scholar who was trying to center Indigenous knowledges in her arguments about Native making. While I listened to her talk, I thought about how I had struggled with the same kind of balance she was trying to attain between explaining these Indigenous practices to a mostly Euro-Western academic audience using their own language while also emphasizing her desire for them to hear her argument from the Indigenous center she was trying to enact. During the Q&A, I watched several Euro-American members of the audience offer questions that (1) suggested she could fit those Indigenous practices into the OOR frameworks they had already written and presented about, (2) questioned her in a way that marked her as naive for using basic Indigenous concepts about the potential aliveness of things like rocks, and (3) outright laughed at her as she kept twisting herself up to answer their questions in a way that would please them. While such insistences on these kinds of accommodation aren't anything new to me, my initial reaction was my stomach began to ache, and then I got overwhelmingly tired. "Really," I thought, "we're still doing this same old thing?" But as I watched her answer, watched the folks in the room respond, my body went back to those moments of my own struggles to justify my work in the language of the colonizer. *This* is how they do it, I thought. Everything in how we are trained in academia sets up this scenario, which is how they maintain the supremacy of Euro-American traditions at all costs. The sick feeling I had in my stomach that day has become a kind of persistent anger that I haven't been able to shake. It's an anger that demands I be less than polite when confronted with the sheer audacity of colonial academic practices—deliberate or offhand. It's that same anger that has me in this text, on this page, today.

I want to take a moment here and make a theoretical point that I thought I'd made often enough for it to be common knowledge. The Indigenous invocation "all our relations" isn't a metaphor, it's an ontological and epistemological entry point for all of creation. All of creation. Humans, animals, plants, elements, earth, insects, planets. All our relations. A web woven of interdependencies that even Western science can no longer deny (trees talk to each other, crows communicate, etc.). One of the problems with a Euro-American, object-focused view isn't that it decenters human exceptionalism, it's that it *re-centers* it under the guise of the disconnected observer position it gives to the scholar. Additionally, it allows scholars to disconnect themselves from the material realities of oppression in order to fall into a world where all objects are equal; none can be implicated in history because that would be imposing human agency onto them. The scholar can just look away and shed the rough scales of their own imbrication in actions of injustice and hatred, and turn instead to the view of objects interacting with other objects in order to understand the objections of those objects that cause what we might perceive as actions. Further, it's not just that object-focused scholars often ask us to look away from the humans as relations; they also often shame us for our desires to attend to those relations. This brings back echoes of those tech scholars who call human bodies "meat suits," diminishing the existence and subjectivity of all animals in the process, and who designated the embodied world as a "meat space,"[9] thus emphasizing the product-oriented consumption view of the relational world. This also elides the current overculture's determination to differentiate bodies in a way that makes some more expendable than others. For me, this is a tendency that we have to say "no" to, no matter how many times we're shamed for "romantic notions" of humanity.

I want to offer one small example about how that re-centering works in Euro-American scholarly practices. In recent years, many object-focused and digital humanities scholars have turned toward understanding the object-

9. I'm using this in the way that cyberpunks and other usenet users began using it in the 1990s. This use is documented in many news stories from the time as well as popular and scholarly articles and books thereafter. It was supposed to designate the physical world as distinct from the cyberworld.

ness of digital objects through creating and celebrating maker spaces as part of a general "maker movement"—what John J. Burke calls "a surge of interest in creating physical items with digital tools and internet-shared plans" distinguished from previous versions of people simply making things by its "impact on community-building and on the collaboration of people working to make things within a single space" (1, 27). Got it. At any rate, most folks who are writing about the maker movement link it to the MIT FabLab projects focused on digital tools and makings plus the advent of *Make* magazine in 2005. Missing in all of these discussions, however, is reference to the long traditions of collective "making" all over the Americas, as well as reference to already-existing Indigenous rhetorical scholarship focused on the constellated relationship between makers and things. Making is not new. Spaces in which collective making happens are not new, nor are they unique to digital culture or digital tools. But there is no reference in Euro-American scholarship to those ancient practices as anything but "simple" or "human essentialist." So I guess all those weekends I've spent with Native women doing beadwork and feasting and sitting in ceremony around a fire were "simple" and these "maker spaces" are much more complex.

Let me demonstrate one small decolonial intervention around the language we use. *Maker,* according to the dictionary, is "a noun that indicates an individual." *Maker,* then, is "a person or thing that makes or produces something" and is also used to refer to God as a Creator. *Making,* on the other hand, is "a verb that indicates activity, individual or collective, and a noun that indicates the results of that activity"; as a gerund, it refers to (1) the process of making or producing something; (2) the product of making or producing something ("Making"). (All definitions come from the online dictionary *Lexico,* easily accessible to anyone.) So, *maker* designates the individual, puts the focus on the individual locus of creation, and remains embroiled in the Euro-American focus on the individual as the purest expression of the self. *Making,* conversely, shifts the focus from who to how and what—from the individual to the process of making, to the thing made. A maker space, then, is a place where the centrality of the individual is practiced in relation to production of a thing. A *making* space, orthogonally then, is a place where all kinds of makings are practiced in relation to the production of things. This might seem like a fine distinction, and in some ways it is. One small shift in language, in naming, can reorient a set of activities to be more relational and collaborative, less individualistic and competitive. It seems like such a small thing, but inside its logic lives an entire history of colonialism. At any rate, the gaps, elisions, insults, and persistent absences in my search for language to talk about the relational making of Indigenous women got me closer to a way to tell a story about the rhetoricity of things. But that story will have to wait a little while.

Andrea: Gathering for the Third Strand of the Braid

Like Malea, I've had a particular disciplinary training in English studies focusing on narrative theory, cultural studies, new historicism, structuralism, and material cultures. This training has been extremely helpful as I've argued for the necessity of interdisciplinary scholarship that draws from multiple methodological and theoretical frameworks outside of rhetoric studies—not just rhetoric scholars' interpretations and applications of these frameworks. This training has provided me with a critical awareness of the various ways objects have been theorized to be or not to be with culture, history, or intelligence. It's provided me with a long view of how the academic industrial complex has promoted settler belief systems. It's within the interconnectedness of the academic industrial complex, settler belief systems, and how both are reflected in OOO/OOR where I want to dwell. I want to dwell a bit on the actual impact of white supremacy and settler colonialism on the bodies and intelligence of Indigenous people. As Eve Tuck and K. Wayne Yang have acknowledged,

> Settler colonialism is different from other forms of colonialism in that settlers come with the intention of making a new home on the land, a homemaking that insists on settler sovereignty over all things in their new domain. Within settler colonialism . . . land is what is most valuable, contested, required. This is both because settlers make Indigenous land their new home and source of capital, and also because the disruption of Indigenous relationships to land represents a profound epistemic, ontological, cosmological violence. (5)

As settlers have narrated our lands and bodies as savage and in need of control—this is also the case with our paradigms. To be very clear, Malea and I are not being metaphorical here. Settler belief systems exist, are promoted, and are replicated in the academic industrial complex. These belief systems are rooted within settler innocence—the belief that land and the natural world are objects to be claimed, owned, and used for the benefits of humans and that one is able to claim "first-ness" over knowledge.[10] This insistence of claiming knowledge and ownership over ideas is why I consistently reframe indigeneity as not just the "first" peoples but the peoples who will always be here due to our deep connection with aki, the land (Riley Mukavetz, "Baskets"). Many Indigenous scholars, outside of rhetoric studies, have made this argument. I turn to one scholar who also experienced fallout from critiquing OOO.

---

10. When I teach about settler colonialism and constructing the white race, I situate these concepts with the nativist movement of the nineteenth century. This movement exemplifies settler innocence because settlers justified xenophobia by claiming they were the original inheritors or natives of the United States.

In "An Indigenous Feminist's Take on the Ontological Turn: 'Ontology' Is Just Another Word for Colonialism," Zoe Todd makes a connection between the harm created by anthropologists and object-oriented ontology. Like us, her critique is not about one theorist or scholar but how settler harm and violence on Indigenous bodies are being replicated. She writes,

> My concern here is not really with Latour himself, but with how a Euro-Western audience consumes Latour's argument (and the argument of others writing and thinking about the climate, ontologies, our shared engagements with the world) without being aware of competing or similar discourses happening outside of the rock-star arenas of Euro-Western thought. (8)

This concern for how Euro-Western audiences consume the ontological turn reflects an awareness of how methodologies, research approaches, and paradigms can create harm without intention or awareness of impact. I see a connection between Todd's critique and my own critique regarding Bogost's theory of flat ontology.[11] For example, Bogost theorizes flat ontology as a process of classification that is very reflective of early anthropological research that classified and measured the remains and bodies of Indigenous people. This approach to listing and classification is used as an approach to decentering humans from the analysis, but it actually doesn't decenter humans—it removes the agency, self-determination, and intelligence of "objects" that we would call subjects. These kinds of frameworks increase and continue harm on Indigenous people engaging in decolonization due to the erasure of our worldviews and the appropriation of our language and systems, and as Scott Sundvall argues, leads to the commodification/fetishization of objects in service of abstract imperialism/colonialism (233).

As Malea and I physically write the story drafts that will become this chapter, both of us are preoccupied with the Wet'suwet'en matriarchs[12] fighting to hold the line on their ancestral land and to ensure that pipelines are not built. Daily, I check in with my relatives in First Nations territory, including my brother studying in Ontario, miles away from our ancestral land. They are

11. "Dear White Guys w/Your 3-D Printers: Please Stop Manspreading over Indigenous Epistemologies," 2016 Cultural Rhetorics Conference presentation.

12. The Wet'suwet'en people are First Nations people who live in British Columbia. They are currently protecting their ancestral land against a gas pipeline. The hereditary chiefs (leaders who inherit a position) approved an initial plan that would not cause ecological damage or be run through their sovereign, unceded land. Yet, TC Energy choose to not listen to the hereditary chiefs and is attempting to build the pipeline anyway. The Nation has been actively protecting the territory from pipeline companies since 2010, and this act of solidarity/ceremony has gained recent international attention due to the 2020 nationwide blockade of Canada's railways (Design Action Coalition).

posting and sharing images, including one that says "Reconciliation is Dead #Shut_down_Kanada. This is Indian Land." As Tuck and Yang have argued, decolonization is not a metaphor for social justice (and we would add, or a replacement for critical race theory) and instead is about the actual repatriation of Indigenous land and life. For us, we interpret the repatriation of land and life to valuing our paradigms, engaging in revitalization efforts, and holding the systems that harm us accountable. I dwell on these systematic and historical atrocities because as an academic who teaches at a historically white institution and the only "out" Native academic faculty member on her campus, I spend most of my day persisting from the impact of settler belief systems, teaching settlers how to save themselves from themselves, and empowering Nish students to speak their truth. In other words, my everyday academic existence is entrenched within the discourses of truth and reconciliation.

To be direct, truth and reconciliation is about settler forgiveness and Indigenous/settler relationships, whereas decolonization has no concern about the well-being of settlers. In "Top Down, Bottom Up: Ecological Restoration, Rhetorical Resistance, and Decolonization," Holiday and Lowry (this volume) demonstrate settler harm reduction through an awareness of Indigenous worldviews and ontologies that we hope more white settlers would enact in their research when writing about OOO/OOR. They write,

> We argue that humans do not need to reinvent the wheel with respect to models of ideal cohabitation due to the fact that there is a long history of Indigenous wisdom based upon egalitarianism, respect, interconnectedness, and reciprocity (Simpson; Kimmerer; Watts). (175)

By turning to and making space for what they call the "predecessor epistemologies" of Indigenous peoples, they disrupt and reframe their scholarship to be in relation *with* Indigenous paradigms. In further effort to join this relation, we consider our essay, in this collection, to join Holiday and Lowry in using cultural performances like braiding sweetgrass to enact epistemic disobedience. What we want to underscore is that for Indigenous intellect, our socialities are already and have always been merged. This is what we hope settler scholars attempt to further understand. As we braid, we hold the theories of settler belief systems, settler harm reduction, and my own investment in decolonization. Like the Wet'suwet'en matriarchs, we want to emphasize that we have the right to exist. We have the right for our knowledge/bodies/communities/ancestors to be recognized. We have the right for our knowledge/bodies/communities not to be appropriated and misused to continue to feed the black snake of settler colonialism and the academic industrial complex.

MALEA: When Andrea and I visit together at my house, we almost always walk in the yard. There are black raspberries, tiger lilies, common plantain, and other medicines growing there. This time, we find a cache of grape leaves in a hidden corner along the fence line that prompts Andrea to another kind of settler colonial story.

ANDREA: This is an offering.

Home is always where the grape leaf vine grows. A grape leaf vine lives on a shared metal fence of my childhood home in Metro Detroit. This vine fed my family for over two decades. It has fed the natural world for far longer. For those who do not know, a wild grape leaf is used as the wrapper to stuff something delicious. For my Chaldean and Lebanese relatives, it's often ground meat like lamb or beef, rice, tomato paste or clarified butter, and spices. For us, a pot of dolmas, cooked for hours on the stove and served with warm bread and pickled turnips, is an act of love, reciprocity, respect, and sustaining relations. It stories and assists in the story of the immigration and survival of Middle Eastern people. If you are lucky enough to be invited into a home where dolmas are made or they are brought to a potluck event, please know, you are considered a relative. When I was pursuing my PhD, my neighbor cut down the grape leaf vine living on our shared fence. He cut it down because he simply didn't like the look of it after twenty years, even though he witnessed us picking leaves from June to August, witnessed aunties and Grandma coming over and sitting outside with chai while instructing the younger generations what to do, experienced a plate of dolmas that my mother would bring over for him and his sons after his pretty awful divorce. I'm not really sure why he cut the vine down except that he was just sick of looking at it—for him, it was a thing that was wild, unkempt, and growing too much on his side of the property. When I am feeling particularly mean, I sometimes frame this story through settler innocence.

It took a few years, but the vine grew back. The grape leaf vine grows where it wants to. I've only heard of a few people who've been able to dig up the roots and put it in their backyards. This is what it means to live in relation to the natural world as equally meaningful subjects: I do not force it to be. Instead, I make decisions based on the kind of relationship I want to it.

I've spent my entire life foraging, harvesting, and cooking grape leaves. My grandma Najiba and Aunty Ibtisam used to keep plastic Farmer Jack bags in their car. I have many memories of my aunt pulling over on a busy street if they saw a new grape leaf vine. We would pile out and pick—always leaving enough for next time. From an early age, I've been taught how to care for and tend to the vine in a relational and constellative way. All of us—the bugs, birds, other plants, and humans—benefited from the sweet ripeness of the vine. As my aunties have helped me understand, we pick during June to August since that's when the leaves are at their softest and sweetest. After that, we leave the rest for the bugs and birds. There is always enough to share. Then, the vine turns yellow and withers. It's time for it to rest, tell stories, and do what it needs to in those cold Michigan months. Don't worry, though, it'll come back bigger the following year.

Like sweetgrass, the wild grape leaf vine thrives "along the disturbed edges"—where land and water meet, where forest and roadways come together. I always like to think that the wild grape leaf vine prefers to spy on humans: peeking out from roadways, wooded areas, and behind fences. "Can you see us? We can see you." I have so many grape leaf stories. The grape leaves also have stories. I know some of them based on the relationship we have with each other. But I don't know all of them, and that's okay. The grape leaf vine is storying. It stories. I can listen for some. I can feel some of them, but I can't always translate them into words. That is also okay.

We have finished this braid. We offer it to you.

Earlier, we promised that we would demonstrate interventions into the colonizing force of Euro-American object-focused ontologies and would offer those interventions as an opening for you to make congenial relations with Indigenous intellectual practices. As we offer you this braid of sweetgrass, we hope that you have taken the teachings from our stories as well as the stories of always-already-in-operation techniques of Indigenous knowledge-making. Those teachings, those stories, this braid *is* our decolonial option.

For the next generation of Indigenous scholars, makers, writers, and activists: As the aunties telling this story, we want to say to you that your worldviews, stories, experiences, and relationships to the land and our communities are valuable and intellectual regardless of whether settlers acknowledge or praise your existence and beliefs. We write for you. We story for you. We gather and braid for you—the next seven generations. This braid of story is about more than a clash of cultures or a disagreement about scholarly paradigms. This braid is a reassertion of our sovereignty and self-determination over our traditions and knowledge-making practices, and over our bodies as Indigenous women in an overculture where both our knowledge and our bodies are often seen as disposable.

For the settlers and non-natives who read this piece and seek a decolonial option: We encourage you to enter into relation with us and practice settler harm reduction[13] in your research, writing, teaching, and other everyday prac-

13. Tuck and Yang reference settler harm reduction as acknowledging Indigenous worldviews and practices. Settlers can and should responsibly echo, affirm, and practice Indigenous ways of knowing.

tices of living and being. We encourage you to expand and shift the historical, theoretical, methodological, ontological, and epistemological frameworks you work within. We hope these stories prove useful and meaningful to you. We hope that as you pass a waterway or field, you linger just a bit to watch as the red-tailed hawk hunts, the squirrel hops to gather for the upcoming winter, or the trees story while the wind shakes their leaves, passing nutrients and seeds. The question for you, though: What gift will you give in reciprocity for the stories and teachings you've received?

And we end with an invocation. All our relations.

Works Cited

Absolon, Kathleen E. (Minogiizhigokwe). *Kaandossiwin: How We Come to Know.* Fernwood, 2011.

Bogost, Ian. *Alien Phenomenology, or What It's Like to Be a Thing.* U of Minnesota P, 2012.

Brooks, Lisa. *The Common Pot: The Recovery of Native Space in the Northeast.* U of Minnesota P, 2008.

Burke, John. *Makerspaces: A Practical Guide for Librarians.* 2nd ed., revised by Elyssa Kroski, Rowman & Littlefield, 2018.

Césaire, Aimé. *Discourses on Colonialism.* Translated by Joan Pinkham, Monthly Review Press, 1972.

Davis, Andréa D. "Growing Our Discipline: An Interview with Malea Powell." *Composition Forum,* vol. 23, Spring 2011, https://compositionforum.com/issue/23/.

Design Action Collection. *Unist'ot'en Heal the People, Heal the Land.* 2017, https://unistoten.camp/. Accessed 11 May 2021.

Erdrich, Louise. *Books and Islands in Ojibwe Country: Traveling in the Land of My Ancestors.* National Geographic, 2003.

Kimmerer, Robin Wall. *Braiding Sweetgrass: Indigenous Wisdom, Scientific Knowledge, and the Teachings of Plants.* Milkweed Press, 2013.

"Making." *Lexico,* https://www.lexico.com/en/definition/making. Accessed 11 May 2021.

Maracle, Lee. *On Oratory: Coming to Theory.* Gallerie, 1990.

Mignolo, Walter. *The Darker Side of Western Modernity: Global Futures, Decolonial Options.* Duke UP, 2011.

Onaman Collective. http://onamancollective.com/. Accessed 28 Feb. 2020.

Powell, Malea. "Rhetorical Powwows: What American Indian *Making* Can Teach Us about Histories of Rhetoric." Hutton Lecture, Purdue University, 11 Nov. 2010. *You Tube,* http://www.youtube.com/watch?v=uchRArrkBwQ.

Powell, Malea, et al. "Our Story Begins Here: Constellating Cultural Rhetorics." *enculturation: A Journal of Rhetoric, Writing, and Culture,* vol. 18, 2014.

Riley Mukavetz, Andrea. "Baskets, Birchbark Scrolls, and Maps of Land: Indigenous Making Practices as Oral Historiography." *The Arts of Indigenous Health and Well-Being,* edited by Nancy Van Styvendale et al., U of Manitoba P, 2021, pp. 40–59.

———. "Dear White Guys W/Your 3-D Printers: Please Stop Manspreading over Indigenous Epistemologies." The Cultural Rhetorics Conference, 1 Oct. 2016, Kellogg Center, East Lansing, Michigan.

———. "Towards a Cultural Rhetorics Methodology: Making Research Matter with Multigenerational Women from the Little Traverse Bay Band." *Rhetoric, Professional Communication and Globalization,* vol. 5, no. 1, 2014, pp. 108–25.

Sefa Dei, George. "Indigenous Anti-Colonial Knowledge as 'Heritage Knowledge' for Promoting Black/African Education in Diasporic Contexts." *Decolonization: Indigeneity, Education & Society,* vol. 1, no. 1, 2012, pp. 102–19.

Simpson, Leanne Betasamosake. "Land as Pedagogy: Nishnaabeg Intelligence and Rebellious Transformation." *Decolonization: Indigeneity, Education & Society,* vol. 3, no. 3, 2014, pp. 1–25.

Smith, Linda Tuhiwai. *Decolonizing Methodologies: Research and Indigenous Peoples.* Zed Books, 1999.

Sundvall, Scott. "Without a World: The Rhetorical Potential and 'Dark Politics' of Object-Oriented Thought." *Philosophy and Rhetoric,* vol. 51, no. 3, 2018, pp. 217–44.

Thiong'o, Ngũgĩ wa. *Decolonising the Mind: The Politics of Language in African Literature.* East African Educational Publishers, 1986.

Todd, Zoe. "An Indigenous Feminist's Take on the Ontological Turn: 'Ontology' Is Just Another Word for Colonialism." *Journal of Historical Sociology,* vol. 29, no. 1, Mar. 2016, pp. 4–22.

Tuck, Eve, and K. Wayne Yang. "Decolonization Is Not a Metaphor." *Decolonization: Indigeneity, Education & Society,* vol. 1, no. 1, 2012, pp. 1–40.

Wilson, Shawn. *Research Is Ceremony: Indigenous Research Methods.* Fernwood Press, 2011.

CONTRIBUTORS

A professor of English at Bridgewater State University, JOYCE RAIN ANDERSON traces her heritage to Algonquin, Wampanoag, English, and Irish ancestors. She is a founding member of the CCCC American Indian Caucus. At Bridgewater, she coordinates ethnic and Indigenous studies and is the faculty associate for the Pine Ridge Partnership. She is coeditor of the award-winning collection *Survivance, Sovereignty, and Story: Teaching American Indian Rhetorics* (2015) and author of "Walking with Relatives: Indigenous Bodies of Protest" in *Unruly Rhetorics* (2018). Her current research is on 1887 Bridgewater student Walter Battice (Sauk and Fox).

CHRISTINA V. CEDILLO is an assistant professor at the University of Houston–Clear Lake. Her research examines embodied rhetorics of race and disability. Her work appears in *Feminist Studies in Religion, Argumentation and Advocacy, Present Tense,* and *Composition Forum*. She is lead editor of the *Journal of Multimodal Rhetorics.*

JENNIFER CLARY-LEMON is an associate professor of English at the University of Waterloo. She is the author of *Planting the Anthropocene: Rhetorics of Natureculture, Cross Border Networks in Writing Studies* (with Mueller, Williams, and Phelps), and co-editor of *Relations, Locations, Positions: Composition Theory for Writing Teachers* (with Vandenberg and Hum). Her research interests include rhetorics of the environment, theories of affect, writing and location, material rhetorics, critical discourse studies, and research methodologies. Her work has been published in *Rhetoric Review, Discourse and Society, The American Review of Canadian Studies, Composition Forum, Oral History Forum d'histoire orale, enculturation,* and *College Composition and Communication.*

DAVID M. GRANT is an associate professor at the University of Northern Iowa, where he teaches introductory courses in writing studies and in the Professional Writing program. He has published scholarship in *College Composition and Communication, Rhetoric Review, enculturation,* and *Pre/Text,* among other venues both print and digital. His research currently explores the thermodynamics of information to understand pluriversal occasions for rhetorical consideration. He has worked alongside indigenous teachers in many places: Diné students in Arizona, Lakota informants in South Dakota, and Meskwaki artisans in Iowa. While he lives within an urban part of Cedar Falls, Iowa, he and his family are trying to re-indigenize what they can.

JUDY HOLIDAY is an associate professor of rhetoric and writing at the University of La Verne. Her research interests focus primarily on issues related to postmodern difference. She has published scholarship in *Rhetoric Review* and *Composition Forum* and has coedited and contributed book chapters to *Reinventing (with) Theory in Rhetoric and Writing Studies: Essays in Honor of Sharon Crowley* and *What We Wish We'd Known: Negotiating Graduate School.* Additionally, she has contributed chapters to *Serendipity in Rhetoric, Writing and Literacy Research,* and *The WPA Outcomes Statement—a Decade Later.* She is currently working on a single-authored book about violence as a socially constructed cross-cultural episteme.

SHANNON KELLY is a PhD student at Michigan State University, where she teaches courses in rhetoric, writing, and document design. Her work has appeared in *Soundwriting Pedagogies* and is forthcoming in *The Journal of Multimodal Rhetorics.* She is currently excited by creative critical making and scholarship.

ROBERT LESTÓN is an associate professor and chair of the English Department at the New York City College of Technology, CUNY. He is working on a book that investigates the relationship between decolonial rhetorics, autonomous communities, and social movements in the Global South.

ELIZABETH LOWRY received her PhD in rhetoric and composition from Arizona State University, where she now holds a lecturer position in the same. Her research interests include religious rhetorics, Indigenous rhetorics, and gender studies. She is the author of *Invisible Hosts: Performing the Nineteenth Century Spirit Medium's Autobiography* (SUNY 2017); *The Seybert Report: Rhetoric, Rationale, and the Problem of Psi Research* (Palgrave Pivot, 2017); and *Indigenous Rhetoric and Survival in the Nineteenth Century: A Yurok Woman Speaks Out* (Palgrave Pivot, 2018).

KELLY MEDINA-LÓPEZ is an assistant professor of composition studies at California State University, Monterey Bay. She specializes in critical Chicanx/Latinx rhetorics and writing studies. Her work appears in *Constellations, Querencia: Essays on the New Mexico Homeland,* and *Latinx Writing and Rhetoric Studies.*

EHREN HELMUT PFLUGFELDER is an associate professor at Oregon State University, where he teaches courses in rhetoric, technical and science writing, and writing pedagogy. His research has appeared in various rhetoric and technical communication journals, and he is the author of *Communicating Mobility and Technology: A Material Rhetoric for Transportation* (Routledge). For the most part, he knows how to prune fruit trees.

MALEA POWELL is a professor of arts and letters at Michigan State University, where she is a faculty member in American Indian and Indigenous studies. She is editor of *College Composition and Communication,* lead organizer of the Cultural Rhetorics conference, director of the Cultural Rhetorics Consortium, founding editor of *constellations: A Journal of Cultural Rhetorics,* past chair of the CCCC, and editor emerita of *SAIL: Studies in American Indian Literatures.* A widely published scholar and poet, her current book project, *This Is a Story,* examines the continuum of Indigenous rhetorical production in North America, from beadwork to alphabetic writing. Powell is a mixed-blood of Indiana Miami, Eastern Shawnee, and Euro-American ancestry. In her spare time, she hangs out with her granddaughters and with other Native aunties, artists, and poets, does beadwork, and writes romance novels.

A. I. RAMÍREZ is a proud parent to Dominick and Xavier, a doctoral candidate at the University of Arizona, and an award-winning artist. Her work has been published in *El Mundo Zurdo 6* edited collection, and in *Understanding and Dismantling Privilege* and *Constellations* journals. Ramírez has forthcoming work in *Nuestra America* and in *Amplified Voices Intersecting Identities* edited collections.

ANDREA RILEY MUKAVETZ is an associate professor of integrative, religious, and intercultural studies at Grand Valley State University. She is cochair of the American Indian Caucus, past chair of the Cultural Rhetorics conference, board member of the Cultural Rhetorics Consortium, and past managing editor of *constellations: A Journal of Cultural Rhetorics.* Her scholarship has appeared in *Studies in American Indian Literature*; *enculturation*; *Rhetoric, Professional Communication, and Globalization*; and *Composition Studies.* She is a citizen of the Chippewa of the Thames First Nation (Deshkan Ziibiing Anishinaabek) and of Chaldean and Lebanese heritage. In her spare time, Mukavetz enjoys gardening, spending time at Lake Michigan, learning to sew, and caring for her two daughters.

KELLIE SHARP-HOSKINS is an associate professor of English at New Mexico State University, where she specializes in critical rhetorics and writing studies. Her work appears in *enculturation, JAC, Peitho,* and *Rhetoric Review*; she coedited *Kenneth Burke + The Posthuman* (Penn State, 2017).

MATT WHITAKER is a lecturer in the English Department at Utah State University, where he teaches courses in rhetoric, writing, and composition. His work explores the intersections of language and the environment, with a special focus on rhetorics of animality.

INDEX

NEW DIRECTIONS IN RHETORIC AND MATERIALITY

WENDY S. HESFORD, CHRISTA TESTON, AND SHUI-YIN SHARON YAM, SERIES EDITORS

Current conversations about rhetoric signal ongoing attentiveness to and critical appraisal of material-discursive phenomena. New Directions in Rhetoric and Materiality provides a forum for responding to and extending such conversations, but also asks that books published in the series attend to social events of consequence unfolding around the world—such as violence based on misinformation, continued police brutality, immigration legislation and migration crises, and more. The series therefore seeks to amplify books that examine rhetoric's relationship to materiality while also confronting material-rhetorical forces of oppression, power imbalances, and differential vulnerabilities.

Decolonial Conversations in Posthuman and New Material Rhetorics
EDITED BY JENNIFER CLARY-LEMON AND DAVID M. GRANT

Untimely Women: Radically Recasting Feminist Rhetorical History
JASON BARRETT-FOX

Violent Exceptions: Children's Human Rights and Humanitarian Rhetorics
WENDY S. HESFORD

Zoetropes and the Politics of Humanhood
ALLISON L. ROWLAND

Ecologies of Harm: Rhetorics of Violence in the United States
MEGAN EATMAN

Raveling the Brain: Toward a Transdisciplinary Neurorhetoric
JORDYNN JACK

Post-Digital Rhetoric and the New Aesthetic
JUSTIN HODGSON

Not One More! Feminicidio on the Border
NINA MARIA LOZANO

Visualizing Posthuman Conservation in the Age of the Anthropocene
AMY D. PROPEN

Precarious Rhetorics
EDITED BY WENDY S. HESFORD, ADELA C. LICONA, AND CHRISTA TESTON